BY MICHELLE OBAMA

American Grown

Becoming

The Light We Carry

THE LIGHT WE CARRY

THE
LIGHT
WE
CARRY

OVERCOMING IN UNCERTAIN TIMES

MICHELLE
OBAMA

VIKING
an imprint of
PENGUIN BOOKS

VIKING

UK | USA | Canada | Ireland | Australia
India | New Zealand | South Africa

Viking is part of the Penguin Random House group of companies
whose addresses can be found at global.penguinrandomhouse.com.

Penguin
Random House
UK

First published in the United States by Crown, an imprint of Random House,
a division of Penguin Random House LLC, New York 2022
First published in Great Britain by Viking 2022
001

Photograph credits appear on page 317.

Book design by Elizabeth Rendfleisch

Printed and bound in Great Britain by Clays Ltd, Elcograf S.p.A.

The authorized representative in the EEA is Penguin Random House Ireland,
Morrison Chambers, 32 Nassau Street, Dublin D02 YH68

A CIP catalogue record for this book is available from the British Library

ISBN: 978–0–241–62124–0

www.greenpenguin.co.uk

MIX
Paper from
responsible sources
FSC
www.fsc.org   FSC® C018179

Penguin Random House is committed to a
sustainable future for our business, our readers
and our planet. This book is made from Forest
Stewardship Council® certified paper.

To all those who use their light to
make sure that others feel seen

This book is dedicated to my mom and dad,
Marian and Fraser, who instilled in me the values
I've long used to navigate the world. Their commonsense
wisdom made our home a space where I felt seen and heard,
where I could practice making my own decisions,
where I could become the kind of person I wanted to be.
They were consistently there for me, and their unconditional
love taught me that I had a voice very early on in my life.
I am so grateful to them for igniting my light.

If someone in your family tree was trouble,
A hundred were not:

The bad do not win—not finally,
No matter how loud they are.

We simply would not be here
If that were so.

You are made, fundamentally, from the good.
With this knowledge, you never march alone.

You are the breaking news of the century.
You are the good who has come forward

Through it all, even if so many days
Feel otherwise.

—ALBERTO RÍOS,
FROM "A HOUSE CALLED TOMORROW"

CONTENTS

CONTENTS

THE LIGHT WE CARRY

Here's my dad helping me cool off during a hot South Side summer.

INTRODUCTION

A T SOME POINT when I was a child, my father started using a cane to keep himself balanced when he walked. I don't remember exactly when it showed up in our home on the South Side of Chicago—I was maybe four or five years old at the time—but suddenly it was there, slim and sturdy and made of a smooth dark wood. The cane was an early concession to multiple sclerosis, the disease that had given my father a severe left-legged limp. Slowly and silently and probably long before he received a formal diagnosis, MS was undermining his body, eating away at his central nervous system and weakening his legs as he went about his everyday business: working at the city's water filtration plant, running a household with my mom, trying to raise good kids.

The cane helped my dad get himself up the stairs to our apartment or down a city block. In the evenings, he would set it against the arm of his recliner and seemingly forget about it as he watched sports on TV, or listened to jazz on the stereo, or pulled me onto his lap to ask about my day at school. I was fascinated by the cane's curved handle, the black rubber tip at its end, the hollow clatter it made when it fell to the floor. Sometimes I'd try to use it, imitating my father's motions as I hobbled around our living room, hoping to feel what it was like to walk in his shoes. But I was too small and the cane was too big, and so instead I would incorporate it as a stage prop in my games of pretending.

As we saw it in my family, that cane symbolized nothing. It was just a tool, the same way my mother's spatula was a tool in the kitchen, or my grandfather's hammer got used any time he came over to fix a broken shelf or curtain rod. It was utilitarian, protective, something to lean on when needed.

What we didn't really want to acknowledge was the fact that my father's condition was gradually growing worse, his body quietly turning on itself. Dad knew it. Mom knew it. My older brother, Craig, and I were just kids at the time, but kids are no dummies, and so even as our father still played catch with us in the backyard and showed up at our piano recitals and Little League games, we knew it, too. We were starting to understand that Dad's illness left us more vulnerable as a family, less protected. In an emergency, it'd be harder for him to leap into action and save us from a fire or an intruder. We were learning that life was not in our control.

Every so often, too, the cane would fail our father. He would misjudge a step, or his foot would catch a lump in the rug, and suddenly he'd stumble and fall. And in that single freeze-frame instant, with his body in midair, we would catch sight of everything we were hoping not to see—his vulnerability, our helplessness, the uncertainty and harder times ahead.

The sound of a full-grown man hitting the floor is thunderous—a thing you never forget. It shook our tiny apartment like an earthquake, sending us rushing to his aid.

"Fraser, be careful!" my mom would say, as if her words could undo what had happened. Craig and I would leverage our young bodies to help our dad back to his feet, scrambling to retrieve his cane and eyeglasses from wherever they'd flown, as if our speed in getting him upright might erase the image of his fall. As if any one of us could fix anything. These moments left me feeling worried and afraid, realizing what we stood to lose and how easily it could happen.

Usually, my father would just laugh the whole thing off, downplaying the fall, signaling that it was okay to smile or crack a joke. There seemed to be an unspoken pact between us: We needed to let these moments go. In our home, laughter was yet another well-worked tool.

Now that I'm an adult, what I understand about multiple sclerosis is this: The disease impacts millions of people worldwide. MS trips up the immune system in such a way that it starts attacking from within, mistaking friend for foe, self for other. It disrupts the central nervous system, stripping away the protective casing from neural fibers called axons, leaving their delicate strands exposed.

If MS caused my father pain, he didn't talk about it. If the indignities of his disability dimmed his spirit, he rarely showed it. I don't know if he ever took falls when we weren't around—at the water-filtration plant, or walking in or out of the barbershop—though it stands to reason he did, at least occasionally. Nonetheless, years passed. My dad went to work, came home, kept smiling. Maybe this was a form of denial.

Maybe it was simply the code he chose to live by. *You fall, you get up, you carry on.*

I realize now that my father's disability gave me an early and important lesson about what it feels like to be different, to move through this world marked by something you can't much control. Even if we weren't dwelling on it, that differentness was always there. My family carried it. We worried about things that other families didn't seem to worry about. We were watchful in ways it seemed others didn't need to be. Going out, we quietly sized up the obstacles, calculating the energy it would take for my father to cross a parking lot or navigate his way through the bleachers at Craig's basketball games. We measured distance and elevation differently. We viewed sets of stairs, icy sidewalks, and high curbs differently. We assessed parks and museums for how many benches they had, places where a tired body could rest. Everywhere we went, we weighed the risks and looked for small efficiencies for my dad. We counted every step.

And when one tool stopped working for him, its utility dwarfed by the strength of his disease, we'd go out and find another—the cane replaced by a pair of forearm crutches, the crutches replaced eventually by a motorized cart and a specially equipped van that was packed with levers and hydraulics to help make up for what his body could no longer do.

Did my father love any of these things, or think they solved all his problems? Not at all. But did he need them? Yes, absolutely. That's what tools are for. They help keep us upright and balanced, better able to coexist with uncertainty. They help us deal with flux, to manage when life feels out of control. And they help us continue onward, even while in discomfort, even as we live with our strands exposed.

I have been thinking a lot about these things—about what we carry, what keeps us upright in the face of uncertainty, and how we locate and lean on our tools, especially during times of chaos. I've been thinking, too, about what it means to be different. I'm struck by how so many of us wrestle with feeling different, and by how central our perceptions of differentness continue to be in our broader conversations about what sort of world we want to live in, who we trust, who we elevate, and who we leave behind.

These are complicated questions, of course, with complicated answers. And "being different" can be defined in many ways. But it's worth saying on behalf of those who feel it: There's nothing easy about finding your way through a world loaded with obstacles that others can't or don't see. When you are different, you can feel as if you're operating with a different map, a different set of navigational challenges, than those around you. Sometimes, you feel like you have no map at all. Your differentness will often precede you into a room; people see *it* before they see *you*. Which leaves you with the task of overcoming. And overcoming is, almost by definition, draining.

As a result—as a matter of survival, really—you learn, as my family did, to be watchful. You figure out how to guard your energy, to count every step. And at the heart of this lies a head-spinning paradox: Being different conditions you toward cautiousness, even as it demands that you be bold.

I AM BEGINNING work on this new book from exactly that place, feeling both cautious and bold. When I published *Becoming* in 2018, I was surprised—floored, honestly—by the response. I'd poured myself into it, as a means of processing not just my time as First Lady of the United States, but my life more generally. I shared not just the joyful and glamorous parts, but also the harder stuff I'd been through—my father's death when I was twenty-seven, the loss of my best friend from college, the struggles Barack and I had in getting pregnant. I revisited certain undermining experiences I'd had as a young person of color. I spoke candidly about the pain I felt when leaving the White House—a home we'd come to love—and the legacy of my husband's hard work as president in the hands of a reckless and uncaring successor.

Giving voice to all this felt a bit risky, but it was also relieving. For eight years as First Lady, I'd been vigilant and cautious, deeply aware that Barack and I and our two daughters had the eyes of the nation upon us, and that as Black people in a historically white house, we could not afford a single screwup. I had to make sure I was using my platform to make a meaningful difference, that the issues I worked on were well-executed and also complemented the president's agenda. I had to protect our kids and help them live with a small level of normalcy, and support Barack as he carried what sometimes felt like the weight of the world. I made each decision with extreme care, considering every risk, evaluating every obstacle, doing everything I could to optimize my family's chances at growing as people and not merely as symbols of what others either loved or hated about our country. The tension was real and pressing, but it was not unfamiliar. Once again, I was counting the steps.

Writing *Becoming* felt like an exhale. It marked the start of my next phase of life, even as I had no idea how any of it would go. This was also the first project that was mine alone—not tied to Barack or his administration or the lives of our kids or to some part of my previous career. I loved the independence, but I also felt myself far out on a new limb, vulnerable in ways I'd never been before. One night, just before the book was released, I lay awake in bed in our post–White House home in Washington, imagining this most honest version of my story landing on shelves in bookstores and libraries, translated into dozens of different languages, scrutinized by critics around the world. I was scheduled to fly the next morning to Chicago to launch an international arena tour that would take me to thirty-one different cities over the course of the next year or so, putting myself in front of audiences of up to twenty thousand people at a time. I stared hard at the bedroom ceiling, feeling the anxiety rise like a tide in my chest, the doubts looping through my head. *Have I said too much? Can I pull this off? Will I blow it? What then?*

Beneath this lay something deeper, more primal, more fixed, and fully terrorizing—the bedrock question upon which all other doubts rest—four words that reliably plague even the most accomplished and powerful people I know, four words that have followed me since I was a young girl on the South Side of Chicago: *Am I good enough?*

In that moment, I had no answer except for *I don't know.*

IT WAS BARACK who finally set me straight. Sleepless and still stewing, I had wandered upstairs and found him working by lamplight in his study. He listened patiently as I unloaded every last doubt in my head, detailing all the ways things could go wrong. Like me, Barack was still processing the journey that had led our family to and through the White House. Like me, he nursed his own private doubts and worries, his own feelings—however occasional, however irrational—of being possibly not good enough. He understood me better than anyone else.

After I'd spilled all my fears, he simply reassured me that the book was great and so was I. He helped me remember that anxiety was a natural part of doing something new and big. He then wrapped his arms around me and touched his forehead lightly to mine. It was all I needed.

I got up the next morning and took *Becoming* on the road. And this kicked off what became one of the happiest and most affirming periods of my life so far. The book received excellent reviews and, to my surprise, set sales records around the globe. I put aside time on the book tour to visit with small groups of readers, meeting in places like community centers, libraries, and churches. Hearing all the various points of connection between their stories and mine was one of the most fulfilling parts of the experience. In the evenings, more people piled into arenas—tens of thousands of them at a time. The energy in each venue was electric: music blasting, folks dancing in the aisles, snapping selfies and hugging one another as they waited for me to take the stage. And each time, sitting down with a moderator for a ninety-minute conversation, I told my truth full-blown. I held nothing back, feeling okay with the story I was offering, feeling accepted for the experiences that made me

The *Becoming* book tour was one of the most meaningful experiences of my life.

who I was, hoping that it might help others to feel more accepted themselves.

It was fun. It was joyful. But it was also more than that.

When I looked out into those audiences, I saw something that confirmed what I knew to be true about my country and about the world more generally. I saw a colorful crowd, full of differences, and better for it. These were spaces where diversity was recognized and celebrated as a strength. I saw different ages, races, genders, ethnicities, identities, outfits, you name it—people laughing, clapping, crying, sharing. I sincerely believe that many of those people had turned up for reasons that stretched well past me or my book. My feeling was they'd shown up at least in part to feel less alone in the world, to locate some lost sense of belonging. Their presence—the energy, warmth, and diversity of those spaces—helped tell a certain story. People were there, I believe, because it felt good—it felt *great,* actually—to mix our differentness with togetherness.

I DOUBT THAT anybody at the time could have guessed the magnitude of what was about to happen. Who would have forecast that the very type of togetherness we were reveling in at those events was, in fact, on the verge of sudden extinction? Who knew a global pandemic would force us to abruptly give up things like casual hugs, unmasked smiles, and easy interactions with strangers, and, far worse, trigger an extended period of pain, loss, and uncertainty that would touch every corner of the world? If we'd known, would we have done anything differently? I have no idea.

What I do know is that these times have left us wobbly and unsettled. They have caused more of us to feel cautious, watchful, less connected. Many people are for the first time feeling something that millions upon millions of others have had to feel every day of their lives, which is what it's like to feel off-balance, out of control, and deeply anxious about the future. Over the past couple of years, we have endured unprecedented stretches of isolation, unfathomable amounts of grief, and a generalized sense of uncertainty that's truly hard to live with.

While the pandemic may have jarringly reset the rhythms of everyday life, it has also left older, more entrenched forms of sickness untouched. We've seen unarmed Black folks continue to get killed by police—while leaving a convenience store, while walking to the barber, and during routine traffic stops. We've seen vile hate crimes carried out against Asian Americans and members of the LGBTQ+ community. We've seen intolerance and bigotry growing more acceptable rather than less, and power-hungry autocrats tightening their hold on nations around the world. In the United States, we watched a sitting president stand by as police officers unleashed tear gas on thousands of people who'd gathered peacefully in front of the White House, asking only for less hate and more fairness. And after Americans turned up in droves to fairly and decisively vote that president out of office, we witnessed a mob of angry rioters tearing violently through the most sacred halls of our government, believing they were somehow making our country great by kicking down doors and pissing on Nancy Pelosi's carpet.

Have I felt angry? Yes, I have.

Have I felt despondent in moments? Yes, that too.

Am I shaken any time I see rage and bigotry masquerading as a populist political slogan about greatness? You bet.

But am I alone in this? Thankfully, no. I hear almost every day from people, near and far, who are trying to find their way over these obstacles, who are measuring their energy, holding tight to their loved ones, and doing what they can to stay bold in this world. I speak often with those who struggle with a sense of differentness, who feel undervalued or invisible, drained by their efforts to overcome, feeling that their light has been dimmed. I have met young people from all over the world who are trying to find their voice and create space for their most authentic selves inside their relationships and their work-places. They are full of questions: How do I create meaningful connections? When and how do I speak up to address a prob-lem? What does it mean to "go high" when you find yourself in a low place?

Many of the people I hear from are trying to locate their power inside of institutions, traditions, and structures that weren't built for them, attempting to scan for land mines and map boundaries, many of them ill-defined and hard to see. The penalties for failing to avoid these obstacles can be devastating. It can be mightily confusing and dangerous, this stuff.

I'm frequently asked for answers and solutions. Since my last book was published, I've heard many stories and fielded many questions, conversing with a wide range of people about how and why we navigate unfairness and uncertainty. I've been asked if I might have, in some pocket somewhere, a formula for dealing with these things, something to help cut through the confusion, something to make the overcoming easier. Trust me, I understand how useful that would be. I'd love to produce a clear, bullet-pointed set of steps to help you conquer every uncertainty and hasten the climb to whatever heights you hope to reach. I wish it were that simple. If I had a formula, I'd hand it right over. But keep in mind that I, too, lie in bed at night sometimes, wondering whether I'm good enough. Please know that, like everyone else, I find myself needing to overcome. Also, those heights so many of us are striving toward? I've reached a fair number of them at this point, and for what it's worth, I can tell you that doubt, uncertainty, and unfairness live in those places, too—in fact, they flourish.

The point is, there is no formula. There's no wizard behind the curtain. I don't believe there are tidy solutions or pithy answers to life's big problems. By nature, the human experience defies it. Our hearts are too complicated, our histories too muddled.

WHAT I CAN offer is a glimpse inside my personal toolbox. This book is meant to show you what I keep there and why, what I use professionally and personally to help me stay balanced and confident, what keeps me moving forward even during times of high anxiety and stress. Some of my tools are habits and practices; some are actual physical objects; and the rest are attitudes and beliefs born out of my personal history and set of experiences, my own ongoing process of "becoming." I don't intend this to be a how-to manual. Rather, what you'll find in these pages is a series of honest reflections on what my life has taught me so far, the levers and hydraulics of how I get myself through. I'll introduce you to some of the people who keep me upright and share lessons I've learned from certain amazing women about facing unfairness and uncertainty. You'll hear about the things that occasionally still knock me down, and what I lean on in order to get back up. I'll tell you, too, about certain attitudes I've let go of over time, having come to understand that tools are different from and entirely more useful than defenses.

It should go without saying that not every tool helps in every situation, or uniformly for every person. What's sturdy and effective for you may not be what's sturdy and effective in the hands of your boss, or your mother, or your life partner. A spatula won't help you change a flat tire; a tire iron won't help you fry an egg. (Though by all means, feel free to prove me wrong.) Tools evolve over time, based on our circumstances and growth. What works in one phase of life may not work in another. But I do believe that there's value in learning to identify the habits that keep us centered and grounded versus those that trigger anxiety or feed our insecurities. My hope is that you'll find things here to draw from—selecting what's useful, discarding what's not—as you identify, collect, and refine your own essential set of tools.

Lastly, I'd like to dissect some notions about power and success, reframing them so that you might better see all that's within your reach and feel more encouraged to grow your own strengths. I believe that each of us carries a bit of inner brightness, something entirely unique and individual, a flame that's worth protecting. When we are able to recognize our own light, we become empowered to use it. When we learn to foster what's unique in the people around us, we become better able to build compassionate communities and make meaningful change. In the first part of this book, I'll look at the process of finding strength and light within yourself. The second part considers our relationships with others and our notions of home, while the third is meant to open a discussion on how we may better own, protect, and strengthen our light, especially during challenging times.

Throughout these pages, we'll talk about finding personal power, communal power, and the power to override feelings of doubt and helplessness. I'm not suggesting that any of these things are simple, or that there aren't dozens of obstacles that get in the way. Keep in mind, too, that everything I know, all the various tools I lean on, have come to me only through trial and error, over years of constant practice and reevaluation. I spent decades learning on my feet, making mistakes, adjustments, and course corrections as I went. I've progressed only slowly to where I am today.

If you are a younger person reading this, please remember to be patient with yourself. You are at the beginning of a long and interesting journey, one that will not always be comfortable. You'll spend years gathering data about who you are and how you operate, and only slowly will you find your way toward more certainty and a stronger sense of self. Only gradually will you begin to discover and use your light.

I've learned it's okay to recognize that self-worth comes wrapped in vulnerability, and that what we share as humans on this earth is the impulse to strive for better, always and no matter what. We become bolder in brightness. If you know your light, you know yourself. You know your own story in an honest way. In my experience, this type of self-knowledge builds confidence, which in turn breeds calmness and an ability to maintain perspective, which leads, finally, to being able to connect meaningfully with others—and this to me is the bedrock of all things. One light feeds another. One strong family lends strength to more. One engaged community can ignite those around it. This is the power of the light we carry.

I ORIGINALLY CONCEIVED of this book as something that would offer a form of companionship to readers going through periods of flux—useful and steadying, I hoped, for anyone entering a new phase of life, whether that phase is marked by a graduation or a divorce, a career change or a medical diagnosis, the birth of a child or the death of someone close. My idea was that I'd be looking at flux primarily from the outside, examining the challenges of fear and uncertainty from a survivor's remove, speaking as someone who—approaching the age of sixty—had managed to safely pass through it.

I should have known better, of course.

The past several years have thrown all of us into deep flux and kept us there largely without relief. It's unlike anything many of us have ever experienced, since most people my age and younger haven't lived through a global pandemic, or bombs falling in Europe, or a time when women didn't have the fundamental right to make informed decisions about their own bodies. We've been relatively sheltered. And now we are less so. Uncertainty continues to soak itself into nearly every corner of life, manifesting in ways that are as broad as the threat of nuclear war and as intimate as the sound of your own child beginning to cough. Our institutions have been shaken, our systems have faltered; people who work in healthcare and education have been stressed beyond measure. Young adults are reporting unprecedented rates of loneliness, anxiety, and depression.

We are struggling to know who and what to trust, where to put our faith. And the hurt will surely stay with us. Researchers estimate that more than 7.9 million children around the globe have lost a mother, father, or custodial grandparent to COVID-19. In the United States, more than a quarter million children—most of them from communities of color—have experienced the death of a primary or secondary caregiver due to the virus. It feels impossible to imagine the impact of any of this—all those pillars of support now gone.

It may be a while before we find our footing again. The losses will reverberate for years to come. We will get shaken and shaken again. The world will remain both beautiful and broken. The uncertainties aren't going away.

But when equilibrium isn't possible, we are challenged to evolve. In my last book, I described how my own journey has taught me that in life there are few fixed points—that the traditional markers we think of as beginnings and endings are really no more than that, markers on a much longer path. We ourselves are always in motion, in progress. We are perpetually in flux. We keep learning even when we're tired of learning, changing even when we're exhausted by change. There are few guaranteed outcomes. Each day we are tasked with becoming some newer version of ourselves.

As we continue to navigate pandemic challenges, reckon with issues of injustice and instability, and worry over an uncertain future, I wonder if it's time to stop asking "When will this end?" and to instead start considering a different, more practical set of questions about staying upright inside of challenge and change: How do we adapt? How do we get more comfortable, less paralyzed, inside of uncertainty? What tools do we have to sustain ourselves? Where do we find extra pillars of support? How can we create safety and stability for others? And if we work as one, what might we manage to overcome together?

As I've said, I don't have all the answers, but I would like to have the conversation. There's value in looking at this together. I'd like to hold open the space for a larger, broader dialogue. I believe it's how we grow steadier on our feet.

PART ONE

Nothing can dim the light that shines from within.

—MAYA ANGELOU

Knitting has helped show me how to settle an anxious mind.

CHAPTER ONE

THE POWER OF SMALL

SOMETIMES YOU RECOGNIZE a tool only after it starts working for you. And sometimes, it turns out, the smallest of tools can help us to sort through the largest of feelings. I learned this a couple of years ago when I mail-ordered myself some knitting needles without quite realizing what I needed them for.

This was during the first fraught weeks of the pandemic, and I was in our house in Washington, D.C. I'd been online-shopping in a scattershot way, laying in things like board games and art supplies on top of food and toilet paper, unsure of how anything would go, fully and sheepishly aware that impulse shopping is a classic American response to uncertainty. I was still trying to wrap my head around the fact that in what felt like an instant we'd gone from "normal life" to a full-scale global emergency. I was still trying to wrap my head around the fact that hundreds of millions of people were suddenly and seriously in harm's way. And that the safest, most helpful thing the rest of us could do at the time was to sit quietly at home.

Day after day, I stared at the news, struck by the acute unfairness of our world. It was embedded in the headlines, in the job losses, in the death counts, and in the neighborhoods where ambulances screamed loudest. I read articles about hospital workers who were scared to go home after their shifts, afraid that they might infect their own families. I saw images of morgue trucks parked on city streets, concert venues being converted into field hospitals.

We knew so little and feared so much. Everything felt big. Everything felt consequential.

Everything *was* big. Everything *was* consequential.

It was hard not to feel overwhelmed.

I spent the first few days checking in by phone with friends and making sure that my mother, now in her eighties and living alone in Chicago, had a safe way to get groceries. Our daughters arrived home from college, both of them shaken by what was happening and a little reluctant to leave their friends. I hugged them both tight and assured them this was all temporary, that before long they'd be back to going to loud parties, fretting about a sociology exam, and eating ramen in dorm rooms. I said it in order to help myself believe it. I said it because I know that's part of the job of being a parent—to project an extra smidge of certainty even as your own knees are buckling a little bit beneath you, even as you are privately anxious about far bigger things than returning your kids to their friends. Even when worried, you say your best hopes out loud.

As time went by, our family settled into a quiet routine, anchored by longer-than-usual dinners in the evenings. We'd process the news, comparing notes on what we'd heard or read—the day's somber statistics or the unnervingly erratic messaging coming out of the White House, our former home. We tried out the board games I'd bought, did a few puzzles, and watched movies on the couch. Any time we found something to laugh about, we laughed. Because otherwise, it all felt too scary.

Sasha and Malia continued their schoolwork online. Barack was busy writing his presidential memoirs and increasingly focused on the fact that American voters would soon be deciding whether Donald Trump should stay or go. I, meanwhile, put my energy toward an initiative I'd helped start in 2018 called When We All Vote, meant to empower voters and increase turnout at the polls. At the request of our mayor, I took part in a public-service campaign pointedly named Stay Home D.C., urging city residents to shelter in place and get tested if they felt ill. I recorded encouraging messages to be passed on to exhausted emergency room workers. And in an effort to ease some tiny part of the burden I knew many parents were carrying, I launched a weekly video series in which I read storybooks out loud for kids.

It hardly felt like enough.

It surely wasn't enough.

This was a reality I think many of us were sitting with at the time: Nothing felt even remotely like enough. There were just too many holes to fill. Next to the enormity of the pandemic, every effort felt small.

Trust me, I have no illusions about my own relative luck and privilege in this situation. I understand that being forced to sit largely on the sidelines of a devastating worldwide emergency is no sort of hardship, especially compared to what so many others went through during this time. My family did exactly what lots of us had been instructed to do in the name of safety for all—we battened down inside a wrecking storm.

AS I KNOW it was for many others, for me, this period of stillness and isolation was seriously challenging. It was like a trapdoor opening into a stew of worries I couldn't make sense of or begin to control.

I'd spent a lifetime at that point staying busy—*keeping busy*—in part, I think, as a means of trying to feel some sense of control. At work and at home, I'd always lived by lists, agendas, and strategic plans. I used them as my road map, a means of knowing where I was going, all in service of getting there as efficiently as possible. I could also be a little obsessive about making and measuring progress. It's possible I was born with this impulse preinstalled. Maybe it had been given to me by my parents, who maintained a rock-solid faith that Craig and I had the capacity for greatness, but who also rather pointedly weren't going to do the work for us, believing we were better off unburying it ourselves. It's likely, too, that some of that industriousness came from my circumstances, the fact that in our working-class neighborhood, opportunity seldom dropped itself on anyone's doorstep. You had to go looking for it. Sometimes, in fact, you had to doggedly hunt it down.

And I had no problem being dogged. I spent years throwing myself into getting results. Each new space I entered became a proving ground. I wore my busyness like a badge. I tracked my progress through stats—my GPA, my class rank—and was rewarded for it. Working in a corporate law firm on the forty-seventh floor of a Chicago skyscraper, I learned how to squeeze the maximum number of billable hours out of each day, week, and month. My life became a carefully counted stack of them, even as my happiness started to wane.

I was never one for hobbies. Occasionally, I'd catch sight of people—usually women—knitting in airports and university lecture halls, or while riding a city bus to work. But I never gave much thought to them, or to knitting, sewing, crocheting, or anything like it. I was too busy clocking my hours and tracking my stats.

Knitting was there, though, buried in my DNA. It turns out that I am the descendant of many seamstresses. According to my mother, every woman on her side of the family learned how to work a needle and thread, to sew, crochet, and knit. This was less about passion and more about practicality; sewing was a simple hedge against falling into poverty. If you could make or fix clothes, you'd always have a way to earn money. When little else was reliable in life, you could rely on your own two hands.

My great-grandmother Annie Lawson—known to me as "Mamaw"—lost her husband at an early age but managed to support herself and two little kids in Birmingham, Alabama, in part by taking in other people's mending. It kept food on the table. For similar reasons, the men in my mother's family learned skills like carpentry and shoe repair. The extended family shared resources, income, homes. As a result, my mother grew up in a household with two parents, six siblings, and also, for some years, Mamaw, who had moved from Birmingham to Chicago and continued to sew, mostly doing alterations for wealthy white folks. "We didn't have an overabundance of anything," my mother says, "but we always knew we were going to eat."

During the summer months, Mamaw would pack up her Singer sewing machine and travel with it by bus, heading hours north of the city to where one of the families she worked for had a lakefront summer home. She would stay there for a few days at a time. Nobody in our family could quite imagine the destination—a place where sailboats bobbed in the water, children wore linen, and vacations lasted for months—but what they did know was that the weather was hot, the Singer was heavy, and at this point Mamaw was anything but young.

The whole burdensome endeavor would cause her son—my grandfather Purnell Shields, whom we later called "Southside"—to shake his head and wonder out loud why it was that people who could afford a vacation home couldn't also manage to buy their own sewing machine for that home, sparing Mamaw the hassle of carrying that weight. But, of course, there was no way to politely pose the question to the people in charge. And anyway, the answer was already clear: It wasn't that they couldn't. It was just that they *didn't*. It's likely they never even gave it a thought. And so off Mamaw would go, lugging the Singer back and forth over the course of a summer to look after other people's clothes.

This story has stayed with my mother all these years. She tells it without moralizing, but what's beneath it is a quiet, passed-down reminder of the weight that's been carried over time by our family, our people—all that they needed to fix, serve, mend, and lug in order to get by.

I wasn't consciously thinking about these things when I was young, but I instinctively felt some part of that weight. It was there, baked into my relentless striving, a responsibility I felt on behalf of others, to get further, do more, and compromise less. And I think my mother felt it, too. When my father at one point declared that Craig and I should learn to mend the holes in our socks, my mother quickly shot him down, saying, "I want them focused on school, not socks, Fraser. That way, they'll be able to buy all the socks they need someday."

I guess you could say that I grew up focused exactly that way, aimed toward a life of sock buying rather than sock mending. I pushed hard at achievement, switching careers not once but a few times. I moved myself out of the cult of billable hours and into jobs that kept me closer to my community, though they were no less busy. I became a parent, which was incalculably joyful while also introducing a whole new set of variables into the obstacle course I felt like I was running each day. As a lot of mothers do, I planned, organized, decluttered, and economized. I memorized the aisle layouts at Target and Babies R Us for maximum efficiency. I carefully built processes and systems that worked—for our family, for my job, for my own health and sanity—revisiting and revamping them continually as the kids grew, as Barack's political career became all-consuming, and I pressed forward, trying to notch my own accomplishments.

If I had a stray thought, an unresolved hurt, or an uncategorizable feeling, I'd usually just tuck it on a distant mental shelf, figuring I'd come back to it later, during a less busy time.

There are tangible benefits to staying busy. Spending eight years in the White House confirmed this, as the onslaught of responsibility—to act, respond, represent, comment, console—rarely let up. As First Lady, I grew accustomed to operating in the realm of big—big issues, big events, big crowds, big results. And big, of course, went hand in hand with busy. The dizzying pace left me and Barack, not to mention those working alongside us, little opportunity to dwell on the negatives. We were a streamlined operation, unable to afford any drag. In a sense, this became clarifying. It helped us keep our view big and broad and generally optimistic. Being busy is a kind of tool this way. It's like giving yourself a suit of armor to wear: If someone's shooting arrows in your direction, you're less likely to register any hits. There simply isn't time.

THE FIRST MONTHS of the pandemic, however, bulldozed all this. It ripped away the structure of my days. The lists, schedules, and strategic plans I'd always relied on were suddenly full of cancellations, postponements, and giant maybes. When friends called, it was often to talk about what was making them anxious. Every future plan now came with an asterisk attached. The future *itself* seemed to have an asterisk attached. It was reminiscent of how I'd felt as a child, catching sight of my father's vulnerability any time he fell to the floor, those split seconds when we were shown the precariousness of everything.

Some of those old feelings had now reemerged. Just as I thought I'd figured things out, here I was again—feeling disoriented and out of control. It was as if I were in a city where the street signs and landmarks had been removed. Do I make a right turn or a left? Which way is downtown? I'd lost my bearings. And with it, I'd lost some of my armor, too.

I can see now that this is exactly what big storms do: They breach our boundaries and burst our pipes. They tear down structures and flood our normal routes and pathways. They strip away the signposts and leave us in a changed landscape, changed ourselves, with no choice but to find a new way forward.

I recognize this now, but for a time there, all I could see was the storm.

The worry and isolation had driven me inward, backward. I rediscovered all the unresolved questions I'd stashed on the shelves of my mind, all the doubts I'd previously tucked away. And once I'd pulled them out, I couldn't readily tuck them back in. Nothing seemed to fit. Nothing seemed finished. The tidiness I'd always relished was replaced by a cluttered sense of unease. Some of my questions were specific—*Had law school been worth the loans I'd taken out to pay for it? Had I been wrong to distance myself from a complicated friendship?*— while others were broader and heavier. I couldn't help but return to the choice our country had made to replace Barack Obama with Donald Trump. *What were we to take from that?*

Barack and I had always tried to operate on the principles of hope and hard work, choosing to overlook the bad in favor of the good, believing that most of us shared common goals, and that progress could be made and measured, however incrementally, over time. Sure, maybe that's an earnest, hopeful story, but we invested in it. We gave our lives over to it. And it carried our earnest and hopeful Black family all the way to the White House. Along the way, too, we encountered literally millions of Americans who seemed to feel similarly. For eight years, we'd tried to live those principles out loud, recognizing that we'd made it as far as we had despite—and maybe even in defiance of—the bigotry and bias so deeply embedded in American life. We understood that our presence as Black people in the White House said something about what was possible, and so we'd doubled down on the hope and hard work, trying to fully inhabit that possibility.

Whether or not the 2016 election was a direct rebuke of all that, it did hurt. It *still* hurts. It shook me profoundly to hear the man who'd replaced my husband as president openly and unapologetically using ethnic slurs, making selfishness and hate somehow acceptable, refusing to condemn white supremacists or to support people demonstrating for racial justice. It shocked me to hear him speaking about differentness as if it were a threat. It felt like something more, something much uglier, than a simple political defeat.

Running behind all this was a demoralizing string of thoughts: *It had not been enough. We ourselves were not enough. The problems were too big. The holes were too giant, impossible to fill.*

I know that pundits and historians will continue to offer their takes on the outcome of that election, distributing both blame and credit, analyzing the personalities, the economics, the fractured media, the trolls and bots, the racism, the misogyny, the misinformation, the disillusionment, the disparities, the swinging pendulum of history—all the ways, small and large, we landed in that spot. They will try to paint some broader logic over what happened and why, and my guess is it'll keep people busy for a long time to come. But stuck in my house over the frightening early months of 2020, I saw no logic to any of it. What I saw was a president whose lack of integrity was reflected in an escalating national death count. And whose poll numbers were still decent.

I kept on with the work I'd been doing—speaking at virtual voter registration drives, supporting good causes, acknowledging people's pain—but privately I was finding it harder to access my own hope or to feel like I could make an actual difference. I'd been approached by Democratic leadership to deliver a speech at the party's national convention being held in mid-August, but I hadn't yet committed. Any time I thought about it, I felt stalled out, caught up in my frustration and grief for what, as a country, we'd already lost. I couldn't imagine what I would ever say. I felt a blanket of despondency settling over me, my mind sliding toward a dull place. I'd never contended with anything like depression before, but this felt like a low-grade form of it. I was less able to muster optimism or think reasonably about the future. Worse, I felt myself skirting the edges of cynicism—tempted to conclude that I was helpless, to give in to some notion that when it came to the epic problems and massive worries of the day, nothing could be done. That was the thought I most had to fight against: Nothing seemed fixable or capable of being finished. *So why bother to try?*

I WAS IN a low place when I finally got around to picking up the two beginner-sized knitting needles I'd ordered online. I was wrestling with a sense of hopelessness—of not-enoughness—when I unrolled a small bit of the thick gray yarn I'd bought and looped it over a needle for the first time, securing it with a tiny slipknot before beginning a second loop.

I had also bought a couple of how-to books on knitting, but when I looked at them, I had a hard time translating the diagrams on the page to the motion of my hands. And so I moved myself over to YouTube, finding (as one does) a veritable ocean of tutorials and a worldwide community of passionate knitters offering hours of patient instruction and clever tips. Alone on my couch at home, my brain still stuffed with anxiety, I watched other people knit. I began to imitate. My hands followed their hands. We knit and purled, purled and knit. And after a time, something interesting started to happen. My focus narrowed; my mind felt a little splash of ease.

In all my decades of staying busy, I had always presumed that my head was fully in charge of everything, including telling my hands what to do. It hadn't really ever occurred to me to let things flow the opposite way. But that's what knitting did. It reversed the flow. It buckled my churning brain into the back seat and allowed my hands to drive the car for a while. It detoured me away from my anxiety, just enough to provide some relief. Any time I picked up those needles, I'd feel the rearrangement, my fingers doing the work, my mind trailing behind.

I'd given myself over to something that was smaller than my fear, smaller than my worries and my anger, smaller than the crushing sense of helplessness I felt. Something in that tiny and precise motion on repeat, the gentle rhythm of those clicking needles, moved my brain in a new direction. It put me on a certain road, one leading out of the wrecked city and up a quiet hillside to a place where I could see with more clarity, where I could spot some of the landmarks again. There was my beautiful country. There was the kindness and grace of people helping out their neighbors, recognizing the sacrifices of essential workers, tending to their kids. There were the crowds marching in the streets, determined not to let another Black person's death go unnoticed. There was the chance for new leadership, if enough people voted. And there was my hope, brought back into view.

It was from this quiet vantage point that I was able to see past my grief and frustration and locate my lost conviction—my faith that we had it in us to adapt, make change, and get through. My thoughts turned to my father, to Southside, to Mamaw, and to our ancestors before them. I considered all they'd had to mend, fix, and carry over time, and how their own faith had come from believing life would be better for their children and children's children. How could we do anything but honor their struggle, their sacrifices? How could we do anything but keep chipping away at the injustices that lay at the heart of American life?

AFTER STALLING ON coming up with a convention speech, I finally knew what I wanted to say. I put my thoughts into words, revised them a few times, and one day early in August, I sat down and recorded the speech in a small rented space with just a few other people around. I stared into the dark lens of a video camera and said what I most wanted to say to my country. I spoke with sadness and passion about what we'd lost and what we could still get back. I said as plainly as I could that Donald Trump was not someone capable of meeting the challenges coming at our country and our world. I spoke of the importance of having empathy for others, of pushing back against hate and intolerance, and I urged everyone to vote.

In some respects, it was a simple message. And at the same time, it felt like the most intense speech I'd ever made.

It was also my first experience giving a major address without a live audience, which meant there was no stage, no roar of applause, no confetti falling from the rafters, no hugs to exchange with anyone afterward. Like so much about 2020, the whole thing felt odd and a little lonely. And yet, I went to bed that night knowing I'd managed to come out of a dark place and make something of the moment I was in. Maybe more than I ever had, I'd experienced the kind of volcanic clarity that comes when you speak from the absolute center of your being.

WHAT'S PERHAPS STRANGE to say is that I'm not sure I would have gotten there without the period of enforced stillness and the steadiness I found inside of knitting. I'd had to go small in order to think big again. Shaken by the enormity of everything that was happening, I'd needed my hands to reintroduce me to what was good, simple, and accomplishable. And that turned out to be a lot.

I now knit while talking to my mom on the phone, during Zoom meetings with my team from the office, and on summer afternoons when friends come to sit on our back patio. Knitting has made watching the evening news a little less stressful. It has made certain hours of the day less lonely, and it's helped me think more reasonably about the future.

I'm not here to tell you that knitting is a cure for anything. It won't end racism or demolish a virus or vanquish depression. It won't create a just world or slow climate change or heal anything big that's broken. It's too small for that.

It's so small that it hardly seems to matter.

And this is part of my point.

I've come to understand that sometimes the big stuff becomes easier to handle when you deliberately put something small alongside it. When everything starts to feel big and therefore scary and insurmountable, when I hit a point of feeling or thinking or seeing too much, I've learned to make the choice to go toward the small. On days when my brain apprehends nothing but monolithic catastrophe and doom, when I feel paralyzed by *not-enoughness* and my agitation begins to stir, I pick up the knitting needles and give my hands a chance to take over, to quietly click us out of that hard place.

In knitting, when you create the first stitch of a new project, you *cast on*. When an item is finished, you *bind off*. Both of these actions, I've found, are incredibly satisfying—the bookends of something manageable and finite. They give me a sense of completion in a world that will always and forever feel chaotic and incomplete.

Any time your circumstances start to feel all-consuming, I suggest you try going in the other direction—toward the small. Look for something that'll help rearrange your thoughts, a pocket of contentedness where you can live for a while. And by this I don't mean sitting passively in front of your television or scrolling through your phone. Find something that's active, something that asks for your mind but uses your body as well. Immerse yourself in a process. And forgive yourself for temporarily ducking out of the storm.

Maybe, like me, you are hard on yourself. Maybe you see every problem as urgent. Maybe you want to do big things with your life, to drive yourself forward with a bold agenda, not wasting a single second of time. That's all good, and you are not wrong to want to go for big things. But once in a while, you'll want to allow yourself the pleasure of a small feat. You're going to need to step back and rest your brain from all the hard problems and wearying thoughts. Because the hard problems and wearying thoughts will always be there, largely unfinished and mostly unfixed. The holes will always be big, the answers slow to come.

So, in the meantime, claim a small victory. Understand that it's okay to be productive in a small way, to invest in endeavors that are adjacent to your big goals and larger dreams. Find one thing you can actively complete and give yourself over to it, even if it is of no immediate benefit to anybody but yourself. Maybe you spend an afternoon wallpapering your bathroom, or baking bread, or doing nail art, or making jewelry. It could be two hours spent meticulously producing your mom's fried chicken recipe, or ten hours building a miniature replica of Notre Dame Cathedral in your basement. Allow yourself the gift of absorption.

ONE OF THE things I did soon after leaving the White House was to help found a nonprofit program called the Girls Opportunity Alliance, which supports adolescent girls and grassroots leaders who are working to advance girls' education around the world. Late in 2021, through that program, I spent time with a group of young women, all of them high school students from the South and West sides of Chicago, a few as young as fourteen. About a dozen of us sat in a circle and traded stories one Thursday after school. I saw myself in these girls—I'd grown up on the same streets, in the same public school system, around the same issues—and I was hopeful that they'd be able to see themselves in me.

Like many students around the world, they'd lost more than a year of in-person schooling to the pandemic, and they were still unsettled by it. Some spoke of relatives who had died from COVID. One young woman described a sense of brokenness she felt among her peers at school. Another had recently lost her brother to gun violence and struggled to hold back sobs, just trying to say those words out loud. Many mentioned that they were feeling stress, trying to make up for lost time, lost momentum—everything that the months of sadness and stillness had cost not only them but their families and communities as well. The losses were real; the challenges felt big.

"I'm really upset because half of my sophomore year and all of my junior year was taken away," said one young woman.

"It was just so isolating," said another.

"It got draining really fast," added a third.

The first young woman spoke again. Her name was Deonna. She had thick braids and round cheeks and had already brightly announced to the group that she loved both to cook and to talk. The hardest part about being limited by the pandemic, she said, was how it had curbed her ability to see much of anything beyond her immediate surroundings, the block where she lived. "We don't really get that many opportunities to go out and explore and look at different things," she said. "And most of what we see is shooting, drugs, dice, gangs. So what are we really supposed to learn?"

She added that she was spending her time caring for her grandmother, working a part-time job, avoiding the troublemakers on her block, and finishing high school so that she could attend college to study culinary arts. And she was *tired*.

"It's just all pounding down," Deonna said, though with a quick shrug, she seemed to reverse herself back toward brightness. "But I know I can do it, so it ain't really *that* stressful . . ." She looked around at the group—the nodding heads of the other girls—and then tacked on one last acknowledgment: "But it is."

At which point everyone smiled, bobbing their heads even more.

I recognized what Deonna was saying, this idea we were all nodding at: the internal back-and-forth on how tough or not we've got it. A day can feel hard and not-hard; a challenge can seem giant, and then maybe conquerable, and then two hours later, it's overwhelming all over again. It depends not just on your circumstances but also on your mood, your attitude, your stance—all of which can change in an instant. We get pumped up and knocked down by the smallest of factors—whether the sun is shining, how our hair looks, how we slept, how we ate or didn't eat, whether someone bothers to look kindly in our direction or not. We may or may not acknowledge out loud all the other forces that knock so many of us down, the social conditions shaped by generations of systemic oppression. But of course they are there.

When it comes to sharing pain or dwelling on losses, a lot of us are careful about what we say, aware of how it might be mistaken for self-pity, which for a young Black woman intent on jumping over historically laid obstacles and getting herself to new places can seem like a bad look, a waste of precious time. We feel guilty for complaining because we know so many have it worse off than we do. So what do we do? We angle our strength outward for the world to see, often packing the rest— our vulnerabilities, our worries—away and out of sight. Privately, inwardly, though, we are riding a seesaw, bumping back and forth between feelings of *I got this* and *It's all too much*.

As Deonna might say: It ain't stressful, but it is.

A number of the students I met in Chicago that day expressed worries about larger issues. They said they were feeling guilty that they couldn't do more—for their families, for their neighborhoods, for all the broken pieces of our country and the ailing parts of our planet, for every last thing that remained unfixed. They were aware of the big stuff, feeling helpless and a little paralyzed. And beyond that, they felt ashamed for feeling paralyzed. We are lucky, of course, to have fifteen- and sixteen-year-olds in the world who are this mature, compassionate, and concerned, but let's stop and think about what a huge and heavy load that is to carry to and from school each day. How can that not seem like too much?

I get emails and letters all the time from people who are writing with a kind of urgency, expressing big dreams and big feelings. A remarkable number of them make one or sometimes both of the following declarations:

I want to make a difference.
I want to change the world.

These messages are brimming with exuberance and good intentions and often come from young people who express a kind of agony about all they see and want to fix, all they intend to accomplish. There's also a pervading sense that everything needs to happen fast, which of course is a hallmark of both youth and passion. A week or so after George Floyd was murdered in 2020, I heard from a young woman named Iman. "I want to change the whole system *now*," she wrote, "I just have an urge to fix everything." She went on to add that she was only fifteen years old.

A teen named Tiffany recently wrote in from Florida, outlining her dreams: "I want to take over the world with music, dance, and drama," she said. "I want to take over like Beyoncé, *but bigger*." She felt driven to fulfill her destiny in life, wanting to make her parents, grandparents, and ancestors proud. "I want to do it all," she declared, and then added, "But sometimes my mental health just gets in the way."

And here's what I'll say not just to Tiffany but to anyone, young or otherwise, who is trying to find their purpose inside of all that's big and fierce and urgent in the world: *Yes, that's exactly right. When you want to make a difference, when you want to change the world, your mental health will sometimes get in the way.*

And that's because it's *supposed* to. Health is built on balance. Balance is built on health. We need to tend carefully and sometimes vigilantly to our mental health.

Your mind is constantly and imperfectly working the levers, trying to keep you steady as you figure out what to do with your passion, ambition, and big dreams, as well as your hurts, limitations, and fears. It may tap the brakes and try to slow you down a little sometimes. It may throw up distress signals when it senses a problem—if you're trying to move too fast or working in a way that's unsustainable, or if you're getting caught up in disordered thinking or harmful patterns of behavior. Pay attention to how you're feeling. Notice what's being signaled by both your body and your mind. And don't be afraid to reach out for help if you or someone you know is struggling. There are a number of resources and tools out there to assist you (and I've listed some at the end of this book). Many of us seek out professional support to maintain our mental health, talking to therapists or school counselors, accessing helplines or consulting our healthcare providers. Please know that you are never alone.

It's okay to pace yourself, get a little rest, and speak of your struggles out loud. It's okay to prioritize your wellness, to make a habit of rest and repair. When it comes to wanting to make a difference in the world, I find that it can also be useful to break down those gigantic, all-or-nothing goals into their component parts. This way, you are less likely to get overwhelmed or exhausted, or crash into feelings of futility.

None of this is defeat. What becomes defeating is when great becomes the enemy of good—when we get so caught up in the hugeness of everything that we stall out before we've even started, when the problems appear so big that we give up on taking the smaller steps, managing what is actually in our control. Don't forget to prioritize the things you *can* do, even just to sustain your energy and broaden your possibilities. Maybe it's focusing on finishing high school. Maybe it's being extra-disciplined about your finances so that you have more options for your future. Maybe it's working to build sustaining relationships with others so that you have more support over time. Remember that solving big problems or achieving greatness often takes years. I suspect what Tiffany was trying to tell me is that there are times when she just can't summon the energy and fire needed to take over the world and get bigger than Beyoncé. I would also guess that Iman's burning drive to *change the whole system now* has been challenging to maintain over time.

Which is why we need to remember to keep laying the small alongside the big. One is a good companion for the other. Small endeavors help to guard our happiness, to keep it from getting consumed by all that's big. And when we feel good, it turns out we become less paralyzed. Research has shown that those who are happier in life are actually more likely to take action on large social issues than their less-happy peers, which reinforces the idea that it's okay to tend to your well-being with the same vigor you bring to your fiercest convictions. When we allow ourselves to celebrate tiny victories as important and meaningful, we start to understand the incremental nature of change—how one vote can help change our democracy; how raising a child who is whole and loved can help change a nation; how educating one girl can change a whole village for the better.

In springtime when I lived at the White House, we used to

plant what's called a "three sisters" vegetable patch in our garden on the South Lawn, mixing a crop of corn, beans, and squash together in one place. This is a traditional Native American method for growing food in a resourceful way, one that's been used for many hundreds of years and is based on the idea that each type of plant has something vital to offer the others: The corn grows tall and creates a natural pole for the bean plants to climb. The beans provide nitrogen, a nutrient that helps the other plants grow more efficiently, and the squash stays low to the ground, its large, spreading leaves helping to block weeds and keep the soil moist. The plants grow at different rates; the vegetables harvest at different times. But the mix provides a system of mutual protection and benefit—the tall and the small continually working together. It's not just the corn, and not just the beans, but rather the corn and the beans and the squash combined that yield a healthy crop. The balance comes from the combination.

I've started to think about both my life and our wider human community in these terms. We are here to share benefits and protection. Our balance rests upon this ideal, the richness of these combinations. If I begin to feel out of sync, if I'm feeling unsupported or overwhelmed, I try to take stock of what my garden holds, what I've planted and what I still need to mix in: What's feeding my soil? What's helping to block the weeds? Am I cultivating both the small and the tall?

This, for me, has become a valuable practice, another type of tool I rely on: I've learned to recognize and appreciate balance when I feel it—to enjoy and make note of the moments when I feel the steadiest, most focused, most clear—and to think analytically about what's helped me get to that place. I've found that when you're able to read yourself this way, you are better able to recognize when you're out of balance and to seek the help you need. You start to learn your own internal red flags and address them before things get out of hand. Did I just snap at someone I love? Am I worried about something I can't control? Is my fear starting to rev up?

Once I've identified the imbalance, I first sort through my arsenal of fixes, trying different approaches to get myself back on track. A lot of them are small. Sometimes what I most need is just to take a walk outdoors, or to sweat my way through a workout, or to get a full night of sleep. Or to pull myself together and do something as simple as making my bed. Or literally just taking a shower and putting on some decent clothes. Other times, it's having a long talk with a friend, or it's spending time alone and writing down my thoughts. In some cases, I realize I just need to stop avoiding something—a project or a certain interaction—I've been putting off. Sometimes I find that I'm helped by helping—by doing even one small thing to make somebody else's day easier or brighter. Often, I just need to reset my mood with a good laugh.

Sitting with the young women in Chicago that day, I asked what they'd done to counteract the loss and stillness and stresses of the pandemic, what little things had given them relief. In a sense, I was trying to help them begin to name their imbalances and identify the tools they had to soothe and steady themselves. And with this, we moved away from the talk of big worries, all the anxieties we'd already put on the table. The mood lifted. The answers came easily. People started to laugh more. A couple of the students talked about how dancing and music had helped get them through. Others said the same thing about playing sports. A girl named Logan proudly reported that she'd memorized every single line to every single song in *Hamilton,* just because.

It's these small rearrangements that help us untangle the bigger knots. It's the "just because" practices that feed our soil. Small victories, I've found, can also accumulate. One little boost often begets another, one act of balance creates more. We can steer ourselves by degrees toward greater action and impact, sometimes just by trying one new thing, completing one seemingly insignificant task.

I saw this in a fourteen-year-old named Addison, who told us that during the first hard months of the pandemic, she'd started making videos to share with loved ones who couldn't visit, which ultimately inspired her to write a business plan and launch her own filmmaking company. And Madison, who when overcome by the tumult and grief following George Floyd's death, started showing up to volunteer at local food drives and community cleanups and found that the work helped her feel more grateful and grounded. And there was Kourtney, who reported that she spent months lying around her house before realizing that "I needed to get out of my box and do something." So she took a chance, ran for student council (virtually), and lost. "But I did it!" she announced to the group, triumphant for having tried. Her failed political run, it turned out, gave her an unexpected rush of new confidence, which then motivated her to start a youth group that works on volunteer projects in her neighborhood.

This is the power of small, where the intermediate steps

matter, where it can be relieving to engage in what's immediately in front of you, and where a start can more readily lead to a finish.

This is how we move from *It's all too much* back in the direction of *I've got this.*

It's how we continue to grow.

WHEN YOU'RE BEGINNING something new, you can't always see where you're headed with it. You have to be okay with not knowing exactly how things will turn out. In knitting, you cast on your first stitch and follow a chart—a series of letters and numbers that to a non-knitter might appear cryptic and unreadable. The chart tells you which stitches to lay down in what order, but it takes a while before you can see anything adding up—before the pattern itself becomes visible in the yarn. Until then, you just move your hands and follow the steps. In this way, it's kind of an act of faith.

Which reminds me that it's actually not so trifling after all. We practice our faith in the smallest of ways. And in practicing it, we remember what's possible. With it, we are saying *I can.* We are saying *I care.* We are not giving up.

In knitting, as with so much else in life, I've learned that the only way to get to your larger answer is by laying down one little stitch at a time. You stitch and stitch and stitch again, until you've finished a row. You stitch your second row above your first, and your third row above your second, and your fourth row above your third. And eventually, with effort and patience, you begin to glimpse the form itself. You see some kind of answer—that thing you'd hoped for—a new arrangement taking shape in your hands.

Maybe it's an itty-bitty green hat you bring to a baby shower for a friend. Maybe it's a soft crewneck sweater you give to your Hawaiian-born husband who gets chilled easily in winter. Maybe you've turned out an alpaca halter top with pretty coiled straps that looks perfect against the beautiful brown skin of your nineteen-year-old daughter as she smiles, grabs the car keys, and rockets past you, out the door and off into this chaotic and never-complete world.

And for just a minute or two, you can see that it matters—that what you've made is exactly enough.

Maybe that counts as progress.

I like to think so, anyway.

So now let's cast on.

ABOVE: Chewbacca the Wookiee, the furry *Star Wars* character pictured here next to Barack, scared Sasha so badly that she retreated to her bedroom until we assured her he'd left the Halloween party. BELOW: Our family dressed up for the White House Halloween party the following year—Chewbacca was not invited back.

CHAPTER TWO

DECODING FEAR

A S A KID, my brother, Craig, loved scary things. He did not seem shaken by them at all. He'd lie in bed at night in the room we shared on Euclid Avenue, listening to some AM radio show dedicated to ghost stories as a means of falling asleep. Through the thin partition that divided the room into his space and mine, I'd hear a baritone-voiced radio host narrating tales of graveyards and zombies, dark attics and dead sea captains, punctuating his stories with jarring sound effects—creaking doors, cackles, and shrieks of horror.

"Turn it off!" I'd yell from my bed. "I can't take it."

But he wouldn't. Half the time, he was already asleep.

Craig was also devoted to a TV show called *Creature Features,* which played reruns of cult monster movies on Saturday nights. Sometimes, against my better judgment, I'd join him, the two of us wrapped in a blanket on the couch, absorbing old classics like *The Wolf Man* and *Dracula* and *The Bride of Frankenstein.* Or, rather, *I* absorbed these movies and Craig really did not. I would feel them in the marrow of my bones. I'd sit with my heart thudding wildly as coffins creaked open and bodies were snatched. I'd weep in horror as mummies came to life.

My brother, meanwhile, grinned through it all, pleasantly enthralled but also bizarrely lulled. By the time the credits rolled, he was often passed out cold.

Craig and I were watching the same movies, shoulder to shoulder on the same couch, but clearly having different experiences. This had everything to do with how we filtered what we were seeing. At the time, I had no filter whatsoever: I was seeing only the monsters, feeling only fear. Craig, who had the benefit of being a couple of years older, was able to see it all through a wider lens, with more context. This allowed him to enjoy the monsters, to give himself the thrill without ever getting hijacked by terror. He could decode what was before him: Those were actors in monster costumes. They were on the TV screen, and his panicky little sister notwithstanding, he was safely on the couch.

For him it was nothing; for me it was pretty hellish.

And yet, I kept going back. Every few weeks or so, I'd plop myself down next to Craig on the couch and settle in for another round of *Creature Features*—drawn partially by my wish to be around my big brother at every opportunity, but beyond that, I think, by some thought that I, too, might learn how to look at zombies and monsters and feel more comfortably afraid.

I NEVER DID come to love scary movies the way my brother did. To this day, I find myself completely uninterested in that sort of thrill. But I have, over time, realized the value of taking on fear and anxiety in direct ways, working to find my footing inside situations that scare me.

I was fortunate to grow up in a reasonably safe and stable environment, among people I could trust, and I'm aware that it's afforded me a certain baseline for understanding what safety and stability feel like—an advantage not everyone is so lucky to have. There's plenty I don't see and plenty I don't know about the experiences of others when it comes to being afraid. I've not had to survive abuse, for example. I have not known war up close. My physical safety has been threatened from time to time, but thankfully never compromised. And yet, I'm a Black person in America. I am a female person in a patriarchal world. And I'm a public figure, which has exposed me to the critique and judgment of others, in some instances making me a target for rage and hate. I wrestle sometimes with my nerves. I feel a sense of jeopardy that I wish wasn't there. Like a lot of people, I sometimes have to talk myself into bravery when I step out in public, or express my opinions, or take on something new.

Most of what I'm describing here is abstract fear—fear of embarrassment or fear of rejection, worries that things will go wrong or someone will get hurt. What I've come to realize, too, is that jeopardy is woven into the experience of being human, regardless of who you are, what you look like, or where you live. We may encounter it in different ways and with different stakes, but not one of us is immune. Consider that the *Oxford*

English Dictionary defines "jeopardy" as *danger of loss, harm, or failure.* Who among us isn't walking around fully attuned to those dangers? Who doesn't worry about loss, or harm, or failure? We are all constantly processing our fears, attempting to sort out actual emergencies from manufactured ones. This can be especially challenging in a media environment where fear is often leveraged as a sales tool. In January 2022, for example, in response to rising rates of violent crime, Fox News was running chyrons that read APOCALYPTIC HELLSCAPES TAKE OVER AMERICAN CITIES and THIS IS CIVILIZATION COLLAPSING IN REAL TIME, essentially creating its own monster-movie version of the United States. If any of this were actually true, it would feel impossible to know how to even respond. It would be astounding to think that any of us would ever leave the house, or that we might possibly make it to 2023.

But we do, we are, and we will.

Yes, these are challenging times. And yes, even legitimate news coverage can be deeply alarming. But when fear becomes paralyzing, when it robs us of our hope or our personal agency, that's when we slide into true disaster. Which is why I think we need to pay careful attention to how we evaluate our worries and learn to process fear. The choices we make when feeling afraid, I believe, often determine the larger outcomes in our lives.

The goal is not to shed fear altogether. I've met a lot of courageous people in my life, from everyday heroes to giants like Maya Angelou and Nelson Mandela—people who, from a distance, might appear impervious to fear. I've sat with (and also lived with) world leaders who make regular, high-pressure decisions that both imperil and save the lives of others. I know performers who are able to lay their souls bare before stadium-sized crowds, activists who've risked their freedom and safety to protect the rights of other people, and artists whose creativity is fueled by a profound boldness. Not a single one of them, I would say, would call themselves fearless. Instead, what I think they share is an ability to coexist with jeopardy, to stay balanced and think clearly in its presence. They've learned how to be comfortably afraid.

What does it mean to be comfortably afraid? For me, the idea is simple. It's about learning to deal wisely with fear, finding a way to let your nerves guide you rather than stop you. It's settling yourself in the presence of life's inevitable zombies and monsters so that you may contend with them more rationally, and trusting your own assessment of what's harmful and what's not. When you live this way, you are neither fully comfortable nor fully afraid. You accept that there's a middle zone and learn to operate inside of it, awake and aware, but not held back.

One of my earliest childhood memories is of being picked to perform in a holiday play that my great-aunt Robbie was putting on at her church when I was about four years old. I remember being thrilled by the prospect of it, because it meant I'd get to wear a pretty red velvet dress and patent leather shoes, and my only responsibility would be to twirl myself merrily in front of a Christmas tree onstage.

And yet when I showed up for the rehearsal, I encountered something I hadn't anticipated. Robbie and her team of diligent church ladies had decked out the performance area with holiday glitter and props, surrounding the Christmas tree with wrapped gifts and a handful of oversized plush animals that looked to be almost as tall as I was. Most notably, right next to the spot where I was supposed to stand, there was a creepy-looking green turtle with an oddly tilted head and enormous eyes made of black felt. The sight of that turtle set alarm bells ringing in my head. I don't know why, but I was petrified by it. Shaking my head and fighting tears, I refused to get on the stage.

Our childhood fears can appear a bit silly in retrospect, and mine are no different. They also often spring up as an instinctive reaction to the unknown, to what we are not yet able to understand: *What is that crackling and booming in the sky? What might live in that dark space beneath my bed? Who is this new person who looks different from the people I see every day?* Beneath these questions lies another set of questions, also instinctive, guiding a young mind's response: *Will this new thing hurt me? Why should I trust it? Would it be better to scream and run away?*

Sasha still shudders at the memory of our first Halloween party at the White House, when we threw open our doors to military families and hundreds of others and celebrated with snacks, costumes, and performers. Given that the bulk of our guests—including our own two children—were under the age of ten, the event was specifically designed to be not-scary, nothing more than a bit of lighthearted fun. Except that I'd made the ruinous and it turns out *barely* forgivable decision to invite a handful of *Star Wars* characters to the party.

Judging from how loudly and how long little Sasha sobbed after laying eyes on Chewbacca the Wookiee, you'd have thought I'd invited Satan himself. It meant nothing to her that the man in the brown furry suit was quiet and gentle, or that no other child at the party seemed even remotely rattled by his presence. My normally bold little girl flat-out panicked. She fled the party and spent the next couple of hours hiding in her bedroom upstairs, unwilling to come out until we'd assured her a dozen times over that Chewbacca had left the building.

Her Wookiee was my turtle. They were like intruders in our still-developing sense of how things ought to be.

IF YOU THINK about it, fear often arises this way, as an innate response to disorder and differentness, to the intrusion of something new or intimidating into our awareness. It can be fully rational in some instances and totally irrational in others. Which is why how we learn to filter it really does matter.

When it came to my participation in the holiday show, I remember being faced with a stark choice, laid out for me by the no-nonsense Aunt Robbie, who was pressed for time, managing a whole group of performers, and coddling nobody: I could either acquaint myself with the stuffed animals next to the Christmas tree onstage and have my star turn twirling in my red dress in front of a big audience, or I could sit on my mother's lap and watch the show go on without me. As I recall it, Robbie delivered this message with a shrug—her point being that it was up to me. The consequences were mine to bear. I could perform or not perform. It was really all the same to her. She wasn't going to accommodate my fear by taking that turtle off the stage.

I suppose it's a sign of how much I loved that red velvet dress and how badly I wanted to show it off that I eventually (after more tears and some sulking) sucked it up, got myself onstage, and, with a pounding heart, approached the tree. I can see now how much I was helped by Robbie's clear position on the matter. She had given me an opportunity to weigh my options and sort through the rationality of my fear. Whether she understood what she was doing or was just too busy to bother, she allowed me to do the decoding, knowing of course that the turtle posed no harm. She left me to make the discovery myself.

By the time I'd edged myself over to the designated spot next to the tree, I was surprised to find that the turtle wasn't as big as I'd thought it was. Its eyes didn't look nearly so mean once you got up close. I could see it for exactly what it was: something soft, inert, and unthreatening—and maybe even a little cute. There was no danger, only the newness. In my young mind, I was processing the fear I felt around stepping onto a stage I did not know. It was admittedly an uncomfortable feeling, but one that diminished with each passing second as familiarity set in. Once I was past it, I felt light on my feet, free to twirl my heart out.

And that's exactly what I did. On the day of the performance, I apparently went at it so hard onstage—my skirt flying, my face lifted in ecstasy—that my parents shed tears of laughter through the whole show. For me, that one little church rehearsal turned out to be a rehearsal for all sorts of life moments ahead. It was my first bit of practice in trying to layer my thoughts over my nerves.

MANY OF US, I think, spend decades crossing and recrossing this same psychological terrain, staring at one equivalent of a turtle or another, hesitant to step onto one stage or the next. Fear is physiologically potent. It hits like a wave of electricity, calling the body to alertness. It often jolts us in new situations, as we encounter new people and new feelings. Anxiety, a close cousin to fear, is more diffuse and perhaps even more powerful for its ability to agitate our nerves even when there's no immediate threat, when we are only imagining how things might possibly go wrong, afraid of what *could be*. But as we move from childhood to maturity, the questions remain basically the same. *Am I safe? What's at risk? Can I afford to make my world a little bigger by embracing something new?*

Newness, in general, almost always requires an extra degree of caution. But here's the thing: We also sometimes over-accommodate our fears. It's easy to misinterpret a jolt of fear or a wash of anxiety as a cue to step back, stay put, and avoid experiencing something new.

As we grow older, our response to fear, stress, and all that's intimidating becomes more nuanced. We may no longer scream and run away like we did as kids, but still we retreat in other ways. Avoidance is the adult equivalent of a child's shriek. Maybe you don't put your name in for a promotion at work. You don't cross a room to introduce yourself to someone you admire. You don't sign up for a class that's going to challenge you or engage in a conversation with someone whose political or religious views you don't already know. In trying to spare yourself the worry and discomfort of taking a risk, you're potentially costing yourself an opportunity. In clinging only to what you know, you are making your world small. You are robbing yourself of chances to grow.

I think it's always worth asking yourself: Am I afraid because I'm in actual danger, or is it simply because I'm staring newness in the face?

Decoding fear involves pausing to consider our own instincts, examining what we step back from and what we might more readily step toward, and, maybe most important, *why* we are stepping forward or back.

These can translate to larger societal questions, too. When we avoid what's new or different and let those impulses in ourselves go unchallenged, we are more likely to seek out and privilege the aspects of sameness in our lives. We may cluster in communities built on sameness; we may embrace conformity as a type of comfort, a means of avoiding fear. And yet when we steep ourselves in sameness, we only become more startled by differentness. We grow less accustomed to anything—or anyone—that's not immediately familiar.

If fear is a response to newness, then we might consider the idea that bigotry is often a reaction to fear: Why did you cross the street at the sight of a Black boy in a hoodie? Why did you put your house on the market after an immigrant family moved in next door? What causes you to feel threatened by two men kissing on the street?

I THINK THE most anxious I've ever been in my life was when Barack told me for the first time that he wanted to run for president of the United States. I found the prospect of it actually terrifying. And perhaps worse, as we carried on a conversation off and on over the course of a few weeks late in 2006, he made it clear that the decision was really up to me. He loved me, he needed me, and we were partners. Which is to say that if I deemed the enterprise too risky or thought it would cause too many problems for our family, I could stop the whole thing.

All I had to do was say no. And, trust me, even as there were all sorts of people around us urging Barack to run, I was pretty ready to shut it down. I knew, however, that before I did, I at least owed him—and us—an honest reckoning with the choice. I had to think my way past that initial jolt. I had to sift out the worries and find my most rational thoughts. I carried this seemingly preposterous and intimidating idea around for a couple of weeks. It was with me on my commute to the office and through hard workouts at the gym. It was there as I tucked our daughters into bed and as I lay in bed next to my husband at night.

I understood that Barack wanted to be president. I was certain he'd make a great president. But at the same time, I myself didn't like political life. I liked my job. I was bent on providing Sasha and Malia with a settled and quiet life. I was not a fan of disruption and unpredictability, and I knew a campaign would bring heaps of it. I knew, too, that we'd be opening ourselves up to judgment. A lot of judgment. You run for president and you are basically asking every American to either approve or disapprove of you with their vote.

Let me tell you, that felt scary.

Saying no would be a relief, I told myself. If I said no, things would stay just as they were. We would remain comfortably in our house, in our city, in the jobs we already had, surrounded by people we already knew. There'd be no change of schools, no change of residence, no changes at all.

And there it was, finally laid bare, the thing my fear was

trying to excuse: I didn't want change. I didn't want discomfort, or uncertainty, or loss of control. I didn't want my husband to run for president because there was no predicting—no imagining, really—what lay on the other side of the experience. I had legitimate worries, of course, but what was it I was actually afraid of? It was the newness.

Realizing this helped me think more clearly. It made the idea somehow less preposterous, less intimidating. I was able to unbundle my worries in such a way that they became less paralyzing. I'd already practiced doing this for years—dating all the way back to my rendezvous with that turtle on Aunt Robbie's stage—and Barack had done the same. I reminded myself that the two of us had moved through plenty of changes, plenty of newness, in the past. As teenagers, we'd left the safety of our families and gone away to college. We'd taken on new careers. We'd survived being the only Black people in plenty of rooms. Barack had won and lost elections before. We'd dealt with infertility and the death of parents and the strain of raising little kids. Had the uncertainties made us anxious? Did the newness create discomfort? Sure, many times. And yet hadn't we proven ourselves more competent, more adaptable each step of the way? We had. We were actually quite practiced at it now.

That's what finally brought me around.

It's strange to think that I could have altered the course of history with my fear.

But I didn't. I said yes.

More than anything, I didn't want to live with the alternative version of that story. I didn't want to be a family that sat around the dinner table, talking about the paths not taken or what might have been. I didn't want to someday have to tell my daughters that there had been a time when their dad might have become president—that he'd had the faith of a lot of people and the courage to try to do something enormous, but that I'd jettisoned the possibility, pretending it was for everyone's good when, really, I was protecting my own comfort with how things were, my interest in staying put.

I felt both a little bound and a little provoked by the legacy of my two grandfathers, proud Black men who had worked hard and taken good care of their families, but whose lives had been circumscribed by fear—often tangible and legitimate fear—and whose worlds were narrowed as a result. Southside, my mom's dad, had difficulty trusting anyone who wasn't family and found it nearly impossible to trust anyone who was white, which meant that he avoided a lot of people, including doctors and dentists, to the detriment of his own well-being. He fretted constantly about the safety of his kids and grandkids, certain we'd be harmed if we ventured too far from home, even as his teeth rotted out and his early symptoms of lung cancer went unaddressed. His house, a few blocks from my childhood home, was his palace, a safe and joyful sphere filled with jazz, where everyone laughed, ate well, and felt loved, but rarely would you see Southside anywhere else.

My other grandfather, Dandy, had a different temperament. He was less playful, less gregarious than Southside, but no less mistrustful of the world. His pain sat closer to the surface, right next to his pride, the two things sometimes getting stirred together and manifesting as rage. Just like Southside, Dandy had been born in the Jim Crow South, had lost his father early, and had migrated to Chicago, hoping for a better life yet encountering not just the Great Depression but the reality that the North was dominated by the same racial caste system that existed in the South. He'd dreamed of going to college, but had instead worked mostly as a day laborer, washing dishes, working in a laundry, and lining up pins in a bowling alley. Fixing, mending, carrying.

Even though both my grandfathers had the intelligence and skills to work trade-union jobs—Dandy as an electrician, Southside as a carpenter—they'd been boxed out of stable employment because unions at the time seldom allowed Black folks to join. While I'd grown up only partially aware of what racism had cost all four of my grandparents—the doors that had been closed on them, the humiliations they wouldn't speak of—I understood that they'd had little choice but to live inside the limits imposed on them. I also saw the impact of those limits, how grooved into my grandfathers' psyches they'd become.

I remember one day early in my teenage years when I'd needed Dandy to give me a ride to a doctor's appointment because my mother was at work. He'd come to pick me up at Euclid Avenue in his car, dressed up for an outing and full of the same bluster and pride he always had when we visited him at his apartment. It wasn't until we started driving toward downtown that I noticed his clenched jaw and tight grip on the steering wheel. He made a timid left turn into traffic on what he thought was a two-way street, until I corrected him. Moments later, he made a sloppy lane change, causing the driver in the car next to us to swerve and blare her horn, prompting Dandy to then run a red light.

If my grandfather had been a drinker, I might have thought he was drunk. But it wasn't that at all. I realized he was petrified, on an unfamiliar mission, in an unfamiliar part of town, his nerves fully jangled. Though he was probably around sixty-five years old at the time, he was thoroughly unpracticed at navigating anything but the several city blocks he passed through during his more routine trips around the neighborhood. It was as if fear itself was driving the car. And it was not going well.

Our hurts become our fears. Our fears become our limits.

For many of us, this can be a heavy inheritance, carried by generations. It's a lot to try to push back against, to try to unlearn.

My parents were products of their own parents, which is to say they were generally cautious, pragmatic people who were careful about taking risks and fully aware of the dangers that came with being Black folks moving in any new direction. But at the same time, I think they'd seen the impact of their parents' limits, the relative smallness of their worlds. It astonishes me now to think of all the opportunities I would have missed out on had I said no to Barack's run for president—all the people I'd never have met, all the experiences I wouldn't have had, and all that I'd never have learned about my country and my world if I'd let my fear get in the way. I credit my parents for doing what they could to break the cycle of fear, to prevent their limits from becoming ours. They wanted more and different for their own kids—a wider sphere of comfort for us to travel—and it showed up in how they worked with us on decoding our fears.

When, as a girl, I used to get freaked out during the violent thunderstorms that rolled through Chicago on humid summer evenings, my father would wrap his arms around me and break down the mechanics of the weather around us. He'd explain that the booms were nothing but clashing pillars of harmless air and that there were ways to avoid getting struck by lightning, like staying clear of windows and water. He never told me to get over my fear, nor did he dismiss it as irrational or dumb. He just used solid information as a means of unbundling the threat and giving me tools to stay safe.

My mother, meanwhile, led by example, appearing deft and unrattled around pretty much everything I found terrifying. She swept nasty-looking spiders off our doorstep. She shooed away the snarly dogs that launched themselves off the Mendoza family's porch any time we walked past it on our block. And early one weekend morning, when Craig and I somehow managed to set a pair of Pop-Tarts on fire in the toaster while our parents were still sleeping, my mother materialized in an instant, unplugged the toaster, and calmly tossed the whole smoking mess into the sink.

Even half asleep in her bathrobe, she was a goddess of competence. And competence, I've learned, is what sits on the flip side of fear.

Craig and I grew up with plenty of threats that were not abstract. The South Side of Chicago was not Sesame Street. We knew to avoid walking down certain dangerous blocks. We'd lost neighbors to house fires. We saw people evicted when their debts rose and their wages didn't. My family had countless reasons to stay alert—more, probably, than I even knew about as a kid. But what my parents showed us was how to parse that alertness thoughtfully—to break down the mechanics of what scared us, to help figure out when fear was serving us and when it was holding us back.

My parents nudged my brother and me forward into competence, creating opportunities for us to feel a sense of certainty and mastery each time we conquered something new. I think as they saw it, competence was a form of safety; knowing how to step forward despite our nerves was protection in and of itself. Their job was to show us it was possible. I was petrified the first few times I had to walk to and from elementary school all by myself, for example, but my mother insisted it was time for me to learn. I was in kindergarten then, five years old—old enough to think that my mother had lost her mind. Did she really believe I could walk to school alone?

But that's exactly why my mom made me do it. She understood the importance of setting aside her fears and allowing me the power of my own competence, even as a kindergartner. And because she had faith in me, I had faith in me, too. As scared as I was, I felt a sense of pride and independence, which became important building blocks in my foundation as an independent human being.

I remember every fraught step I took of that first block-and-a-half trip to school. And just as clearly, I remember the smile on my mom's face as I broke into a sprint on the final stretch of the journey home.

She had been waiting for me, standing out on our front lawn with her neck craned in order to catch sight of me rounding the corner onto our block. I could see that she, too, had been a little anxious about the whole thing. She also had felt a touch of fear.

But fear hadn't stopped her. And now it wouldn't stop me. She had shown me what it felt like to be comfortably afraid.

This idea has stayed with me as I've parented my own two

daughters. It's made me pause to think many times as I've grappled with a ferocious and deeply programmed urge to want to protect my kids from everything scary and hurtful in this world. Every step of the way, I've wanted to shove off their enemies, bat away their risks, and escort them past every threat. It's a basic instinct, I realize, and a product of my fear. So instead, I try to do as my mother did and keep myself planted on that front lawn as they find their own way to becoming confident and independent people, as they create their own safety simply by doing things on their own. I watch them go and wait for them to come back, even as my nerves thrum and my heart pounds out of my chest. Because what my mother showed me is that if you try to keep your children from feeling fear, you're essentially keeping them from feeling competence, too.

Go forth with a spoonful of fear and return with a wagonful of competence. That was the doctrine at 7436 Euclid Avenue. It's what I've tried to carry forward on behalf of my kids, even as I continue to carry my own full and enduring load of worries. I stay comfortably afraid.

WHEN CRAIG AND I weren't watching monster movies as kids, we'd sometimes catch a famous motorcycle stuntman named Evel Knievel on television. He was about as curious an American hero as perhaps there ever was. He dressed in a white leather jumpsuit emblazoned with stars and stripes, modeled himself vaguely after Elvis Presley, and performed dangerous feats like trying to jump his motorcycle over rows of parked cars and Greyhound buses, or trying to rocket himself across a high-walled river canyon in Idaho. He was foolish but captivating. Evel Knievel landed some of his jumps and crashed on others. He broke a lot of bones, suffered a lot of concussions, got run over by his own motorcycle sometimes, but always managed to limp away. Was it a miracle or a disaster? Nobody at the time seemed willing to define it. We just kept watching that man and his big, heavy Harley-Davidson launch and try to fly.

I felt a little bit like this in 2007 after I said yes to Barack's presidential campaign—like suddenly we were airborne on a motorcycle, disregarding the laws of gravity and the pull of common sense.

People talk about "launching" a political campaign, and now I get why. It's exactly what it feels like—a rapid acceleration into thin air. The on-ramp is short and steep. You and your loved ones are launched and launched suddenly, outward, upward, soaring in a way that's deliberately sensational, inviting the eyes of the public.

For me, this was a whole new level of uncertainty. I am, after all, the product of my own parents and grandparents, which is to say I'm not a leaper or a flier, but rather a deliberate, rung-by-rung ladder climber. Like any good Capricorn, I like to get my bearings before making my next move. Up there, however, in the stratosphere of a fast-moving presidential race, there were no easy bearings to be found. The pace was too quick, the heights too dizzying, the exposure too great. Not to mention the fact we'd strapped our two daughters onto that crazy flying motorcycle with us.

It was during this time that I became even more intimately acquainted with my fearful mind, that ruthless, naysaying part of me that was sure nothing ever would—or could—work out. Over and over and over again, I had to coach myself not to listen to it. Because if I did, I knew precisely what would happen: My nerves would fail. My faith would leave. My brain would seize upon the impossibility of everything, and that's when the tip would begin.

I'd look down from those improbable, mind-boggling heights and I'd spot the exact patch of earth where we'd wreck, and then down we would go. With my thoughts alone, I was capable of initiating the plummet.

This is another thing to recognize: Doubt comes from within. Your fearful mind is almost always trying to seize the steering wheel and change your course. Its whole function is to rehearse catastrophe, scare you out of opportunity, and throw rocks at your dreams. It enjoys having you flooded and doubtful. Because then you're more likely to stay home on your couch, nice and passive, taking no risks at all. Which means that defying your fear almost always involves defying a part of yourself. To me, this is a vital aspect of the decoding: You have to learn how to identify and then tame something within. You have to practice past those fears. The more you practice, the better you get at it. Each leap I've taken has only made the next leap easier.

IN AN INTERVIEW with CBS News, Lin-Manuel Miranda once described his pre-performance anxiety as a type of "rocket fuel," recalling that the very first time he ever got on a stage, as a first-grader lip-syncing a Phil Collins song in a school talent show, he'd been hit by an intense stomachache and understood in that moment that he was being presented with a larger choice about what to do with his fear. "I realized I could either fall underneath it, or stand on top of it," he said. "And that's how I think of nerves. They're a fuel source. . . . You can get on top of them and it can power the ship, or don't get on top of them, and they blow up your ship."

It brings to mind the first time Lin-Manuel came to the White House to perform, having been invited to our inaugural spoken word and poetry jam in 2009. He was twenty-nine years old and visibly nervous. He'd hastily finished a song he'd been working on in order to perform it at our event. It was the piece that would eventually become the opening number of the smashingly successful musical *Hamilton,* but Lin-Manuel was at the very beginning of that project, still experimenting, still not entirely certain whether his material would work. This would be his first time ever rapping about Alexander Hamilton in front of an audience—an especially intimidating audience, as he saw it—and he had no idea how it would go over. He had told himself that if the song didn't play well that evening, he might have to throw the whole thing away.

That, I'd like to point out, was his fearful mind speaking. The message is right on brand: *Fail and all will be lost.* The fearful mind loves to show up at moments of peak stress, and with a clear agenda: It wants to veto everything. It is not at all down with your twirl.

That night, when Lin-Manuel got onstage and started to introduce himself and his barely born musical to the two hundred people gathered in the East Room, all of us dressed in fancy clothes, his nerves instantly revved up. His eyes started darting all over the place. He claims that he was looking for the exit signs in case he needed to run. And he was stammering a bit, further startled that his voice seemed to be coming out at an odd pitch.

He later recalled the experience in a podcast interview. "I'm really nervous," he said. "And the first thing I did, which was a mistake, was like, lock eyes with the President of the United States. And I realized, *Can't look at him, that's too scary.*" He apparently then looked at me and deemed me too scary as well. But then his eyes found my mother's. She was sitting in a chair on the other side of Barack, and—no surprise to me—something in her expression told him it was going to be okay.

What happened next felt like a small piece of history in itself. Accompanied by pianist Alex Lacamoire, Lin-Manuel put on an electrifying three-minute rap performance, dazzling the audience with his spitfire showmanship and utterly fresh take on the Founding Fathers. And when he was finished, he smiled, waved, and left the stage, having channeled his fear into something wholly unforgettable, leaving the rest of us speechless and in awe.

What we'd witnessed was someone who'd climbed on top of his nerves.

It was breathtaking to see him do it. And inside of that moment, I think, is a larger message about what becomes possible when we find ways to convert fear into rocket fuel.

There's no getting around the fact that our nerves will ride shotgun with us pretty much any time we approach the unfamiliar, any time we move into a new frontier and feel the stakes get bumped up as a result. Think about it: Who is utterly comfortable on the first day of school? Who doesn't bring a spoonful of fear to the first day of a new job? Or along on a first date? Who doesn't feel a jolt when walking into a room full of strangers or taking a public stance on something important? These are moments of distinct discomfort, foisted upon us routinely by life. But they can be thrilling, too.

Why? Because we don't know what lies on the other side of that initial experience. And the journey to get there might just be transformative.

How will you meet your soul mate if you don't go on that date? How will you get ahead if you don't take that new job, or move to a new city? How will you learn and grow if fear stops you from leaving home to go to college? Or from stepping forward into a room full of new people, or traveling to a new country, or befriending someone whose skin color is different from yours? The unknown is where possibility glitters. If you don't take the risk, if you don't ride out a few jolts, you are taking away your opportunities to transform.

Can I afford to make my world a little bigger? I believe the answer is almost always yes.

TO THIS DAY, I remain a little shocked that Barack and I managed to land our flying motorcycle—that we made it to and through eight years in the White House. But somehow, we did. The bad news is that it hasn't eliminated fear and doubt from my life. The good news is that I'm not so intimidated by my own thoughts anymore.

I've come to believe that it's actually worth getting to know your fearful mind. Why? Well, for one thing, it's never going to leave you. You can't evict it. It's more or less hardwired into your psyche and will accompany you onto every stage you set foot on, into every job interview you go to, and every new relationship you enter into. It's there, and it's not going to shut up. Your fearful mind is the same self-protecting impulse you knew as a child—the same set of instincts that drove you to cry during a thunderstorm or scream bloody murder when forced to sit on a mall Santa's lap—only now, just like you, it's become more grown-up and sophisticated. And given all the times you've forced it to march through uncomfortable situations in life, it's pretty pissed at you, too.

As I've said, it wants you off the motorcycle and at home on the couch.

Your fearful mind is basically a life partner you didn't choose. And to be clear, it didn't choose you, either. Because you suck, you're a failure, you're not very smart, *and* you never get anything right. So, seriously, why would anyone choose you for anything?

Sound familiar? It does to me.

I've lived with my fearful mind for fifty-eight years now. We don't get along. She makes me uneasy. She likes to see me weak. She keeps a giant overstuffed file folder containing every mistake and misstep I've ever made and is constantly scanning the universe for further evidence of my failings. She hates how I look, all the time and no matter what. She doesn't like the email I sent to a colleague. She doesn't like the comment I made at the dinner party last night, either. She can't believe I say such dumb things in general. Every day, she tries to tell me that I don't know what I'm doing. Every day, I try to talk back to her. Or to at least override her with more positive thoughts. But still, she won't go away.

She is every monster I've ever known. And she is also me.

Over time, though, I've become better about accepting her presence. I'm not happy about it, exactly, but I do acknowledge that she's got real estate in my head. In fact, I've granted her full citizenship, if only because this makes her easier to name and thus to decode. Rather than pretending she doesn't exist or constantly trying to defeat her, I've gotten to know my fearful mind as well as she knows me. And this alone has loosened her hold and lessened her stealth. I'm not so easily ambushed when the jolts arrive. To me, my fearful mind is noisy but generally ineffectual—more thunder than lightning—and that's taken the teeth right out of her agenda.

Any time I hear the patter of negativity and self-criticism starting to get loud in my brain, when my doubts begin to build, I try to pause for a moment and call it as I see it. I've been practicing stepping back and addressing my fear with familiarity, offering no more than a half-friendly shrug and a few easy words:

Oh, hello. It's you again.
Thanks for showing up. For making me so alert.
But I see you.
You're no monster to me.

A simple hug is one of the most powerful tools we have for
communicating gladness for another's presence.

CHAPTER THREE

STARTING KIND

I HAVE A FRIEND named Ron who begins his day by saying hello to himself in the mirror. He does this without irony, and he often does it out loud.

I learned about this not from Ron, but from his wife, Matrice.

Matrice says that she has awoken to the sound of her husband delivering a hearty early-morning greeting to his own reflection over the bathroom sink.

"Heeey, Buddy!" is what he says.

Matrice imitates him perfectly, as wives so often do. And in her voice channeling his voice, you can hear the blast of fresh affection Ron finds for himself at the start of a new day. He is full of warmth. It sounds as if he's saying hello to a beloved coworker or an old friend who's turned up out of the blue. As if he's pleasantly surprised by the person who has shown up to join him for whatever the day holds in store.

Matrice says that even for her, overhearing these words from bed is the best way to wake up.

The first time she mentioned this little habit of Ron's, I laughed. It was funny in part because I could imagine it so easily. Ron is a straight-up brilliant and successful man, someone to whom other people are instantly drawn. He's confident without being preening. He exudes warmth and charisma and self-assurance. He's been the mayor of a large city. He has beautiful children and a happy family. He's got a big smile, an easy bearing, and an enviable amount of poise.

As I thought about it, though, I realized that Ron's "Heeey, Buddy!" was more than just an amusing practice. I think there's something important about this type of habit. It's a glimpse of someone locking into his poise, someone choosing to begin the day with kindness toward himself.

Ron, of course, is a man. And as such, we can probably assume that he arrives at the mirror with far fewer hang-ups about his appearance than many of us are conditioned to bring to it. For a lot of people, especially those who are not men, the mirror can be a scary place. Many of us find it tough to approach with any sort of ease, especially first thing in the morning. We can be reflexively harsh in our self-appraisal. We have often absorbed negative comments about our looks, messages that leave us feeling objectified, unworthy, or unseen. Women are also consistently held to higher standards when it comes to grooming and style, requiring more elaborate, more expensive, and more time-consuming preparation before feeling comfortable heading to work or even just stepping out into a new day.

I personally have plenty of mornings when I flip on the bathroom light, take one look, and desperately want to flip it off again. Face-to-face with myself, I'll impulsively start in on cataloging my flaws, seeing only what's dry and puffy, recognizing only the parts of me that could and should be better. In assessing myself, I instantly alienate myself. I start my day divided—one part of me a critic, the other a clown. One of us bites; the other hurts. The feeling is decidedly bad. It's hard to shake off.

And that's what I want to talk about here—the possibility of starting kind. I would guess that like the rest of us, my pal Ron often shows up tired and puffy at the mirror. He, too, has plenty of flaws that surely beg to be inspected and scrutinized. But what he sees first, what he chooses to *recognize,* is a whole person, someone he's genuinely glad to see. Unlike a lot of us, Ron has figured out that self-loathing is hardly a good starting block from which to launch a new day.

Ron's "Heeey, Buddy!" has a certain quiet potency. It's efficient, free of false bravado, and private (or it was until Matrice told me about it). Most importantly, it's not an assessment. It doesn't invite any sort of follow-up, like, "You look like crap," or "Why can't you do more?" Standing at the mirror, Ron is redirecting any impulse to judge or self-denigrate. He refuses to seize on self-criticism and begins instead with a simple message of compassion and approval.

If you think about it, this is exactly the sort of thing many of us rather desperately try to wring out of other people— parents, teachers, bosses, lovers, and so on—and then end up feeling crushed when we don't get it. For me, part of the beauty of "Heeey, Buddy!" is that it's not terribly ambitious. It doesn't really count as a pep talk. It requires no passion or eloquence, nor any sort of belief that the day ahead will be stellar, full of new opportunities and positive growth. It is merely a friendly hello—two words delivered in a warm tone. And for this reason, maybe it's something more of us could try to do.

In a televised conversation for Oprah's Book Club many years ago, the late Nobel Prize–winning author Toni Morrison described something meaningful she'd learned about parenting—and more generally about being an adult in the presence of children, and maybe even about being human. "When a kid walks in the room, your child or anybody else's child," she asked her audience that day, "does your face light up? That's what they're looking for."

Morrison's own two sons were grown at this point, but what she'd learned had stayed with her. "When my children used to walk in the room when they were little, I looked at them to see if they'd buckled their trousers, or if their hair was combed, or if their socks were up," she said. "You think your affection and your deep love is on display, because you're caring for them. It's not. When they see you, they see the critical face. *What's wrong now?*"

As a parent, she'd figured out that the critical face asserts itself ahead of anything else, regardless of how much affection and deep love come attached to it. In a side-by-side contest, the critical face will always win, leaving even a four-year-old wondering what they're getting wrong. Many of us spend a lifetime registering the presence of critical faces around us, feeling bombarded by judgment, asking ourselves what we're getting wrong, and internalizing the answers in harmful ways that stay with us for life. All too often, we turn the critical gaze directly on ourselves. We punish ourselves with *what's wrong* before ever having the chance to even glimpse *what's right*.

Which leads to the second part of Toni Morrison's epiphany: It's okay—even important sometimes—to tip the scales in the other direction. With her kids, Morrison learned to dial back the judgment and instead to lead with something warmer, truer, and more immediate—a lit-up face, an unfettered sense of gladness, a recognition not of the combed hair or pulled-up socks, but of the whole person who'd shown up before her. "Because when they walked into a room, I was glad to see them," she said. "It's just as small as that, you see."

She had learned to put her gladness out front and up first, not just with her kids but with all kids. Like Ron, she made a point of starting kind.

This isn't to say that Toni Morrison coddled her children or lowered her expectations for them. It's not to say that she raised boys who didn't know how to take care of themselves, or who would always be looking for the approval of others. I believe it's quite the opposite, in fact. What Morrison was doing for her kids is what my own parents did for me: She was giving them a simple message of enoughness. She was validating their light, that unique bit of brightness inside each of them—literally showing them it was there and it belonged to them, a power they could carry for themselves.

It's worth saying, of course, that messages of gladness and enoughness can be generally hard to come by in life, and seldom are they delivered up front. In school, in jobs, and even inside of families and relationships, we are routinely asked to prove our worth, conditioned to believe we must pass a series of tests in order to win approval or advance ourselves. Rare is the boss who hands you their full trust on day one, or the coworker who looks at you with gladness each time you show up. And even the most wonderful life partner in the world might not manage to muster a lit-up face for you as they are taking the trash out or heading upstairs to change another diaper.

But the thing is, when someone does light up for us, we remember it. The feeling lands. I can still summon the warmth I felt from my third-grade teacher, Miss Seals, who seemed genuinely happy to see her students each day. When we are given a kind start, when another person greets us with unfettered gladness or trusts our ability to succeed, it can have a lasting, lifting sort of effect. How many of us remember the face of that one teacher, parent, coach, or friend who met us with gladness ahead of all else? Research shows that when teachers take the time to welcome students individually at the door, the level of academic engagement in the classroom goes up by more than 20 percent, while disruptive behavior goes down. It's the simplest concept in the world, really: Gladness is nourishing. It is a gift. When someone is happy to see us, we get a little steadier on our feet. We have an easier time locking into our poise. And we carry that feeling forward.

Children show us how instinctive the need for gladness is all the time. They are like magnets for tenderness. At the White House, we used to host groups of kids each year for Take Your Child to Work Day. A couple hundred of them would come and tour the kitchen, meet our dogs, Bo and Sunny, and get a peek into the armor-plated presidential vehicle known as the Beast. Before they left, I'd sit down with them in the East Room and spend some time answering whatever questions they wanted to ask. Kids would raise their hands and wait for me to call on them. They asked things like "What's your favorite food?" and "Why do you exercise so much?" and "Is there a pool here?" and "Is the president nice?"

During one such visit, a little girl named Anaya raised her hand. When I called on her, she stood up and asked my age (the answer at the time was fifty-one) and then flattered me by saying that I looked too young to be that old. Laughing, I waved her up to the front of the room and gave her a big, enveloping hug.

More hands immediately shot into the air. As the session wrapped up, it seemed that a lot of the remaining questions had vanished, replaced by just one.

"Can I please get a hug?" asked another child I called on.

And another one after that: "Can I have a hug?"

This was followed by a swelling of voices from around the room, a chorus of children calling, "Me too, me too, me too!"

Those kids seemed to understand innately that a hug was the more meaningful takeaway that day—a feeling they'd remember far longer than any words I might have uttered, more than any information I might have had to dispense. They wanted the feeling, the sensation of my straightforward gladness for them, above all else. And the truth is, I wanted it back. Gladness is reciprocal that way. As First Lady, I met more adults than children, but it was the kids who fed my soul and gave me energy on days when I was feeling drained. Meeting them was among the best parts of my role. I knew all too well that for many children in the world, no one had or would ever light up for them. I felt it was one of my duties as First Lady to be that light for every child I encountered, just in case. I lit up for the kids I met the same way I would for my own kids, knowing that I could, with my gladness, show them that they mattered—how valued they were.

In the chapters ahead, we'll look more closely at what it takes to find and nourish relationships built on gladness—how to identify the poise builders in your world and to become one for the people around you. We'll also talk about the challenges not just of being seen with gladness, but of being seen more generally, the fact that many of us struggle with a sense of invisibility or are faced with having to overcome stereotypes in order to be recognized fully as ourselves. For now, though, I want to offer one small reminder, which is that real growth begins with how gladly you're able to see yourself.

SO LET'S RETURN to Ron, saying hello to himself at the start of a new day—his two words delivered in a warm tone. He is making a point of putting his gladness out front and up first, dropping it in ahead of judgment. And with it, he becomes literally self-assured.

It's easy to forget that we can do this for ourselves. We are capable of making a home delivery of approval and kindness, even to the weary and imperfect person who appears before us in the mirror. We can acknowledge our own light, our sense of *what is.* Many books have been written about the power of gratitude, and for good reason: It works. It doesn't take all that much, really. Maybe just some practice. Maybe getting more deliberate about noticing the reflex to tear yourself down, how quickly those thoughts arrive, and making a point of replacing them with your own gentle form of "Heeey, Buddy," whatever that may be.

I have been trying recently to wake up in the morning and give myself some sort of deliberately kind start—to consciously and intentionally take the first self-denigrating or negatively tinged thought that arrives in my head and slide it off to one side. Then I invite a second thought, a better and more tender one, something more intentional, more friendly to self. And I choose that as my launching point. My second thought is usually pretty simple. Often, it's just a quiet but grateful acknowledgment that I have made it once again to the starting line of a new day.

Remember that the bar is pretty low. Starting kind does not necessarily mean starting grand. You don't need to make any declarations about what you're going to do in a day, discover some deep new well of confidence, or pretend that you're invincible. None of this has to be done out loud, and it definitely does not need to be done in front of the mirror. You're just trying, one way or another, to box out the inner critic and push your gladness up front, to meet your own gaze—even metaphorically—with some small speck of warmth, to utter some sort of friendly hello. Maybe it takes getting over a little self-consciousness, or perhaps a chuckling spouse in the next room.

In any event, Ron's still at it. He gets up in the morning and raises something powerful and stabilizing from within. He greets himself with a message that says: *You're here, and that's a happy miracle, so let's get after it.* Which to me is a beautiful thing.

Even so, Matrice and I like to giggle about it. We find it kind of adorable.

"Heeey, Buddy!" we started saying to each other, just for fun.

"Heeey, Buddy!" I called across the room to Ron, the next time I saw him.

And because he's a secure, poised person who knows how to be friendly to himself, he wasn't at all embarrassed.

He just smiled at me and said the words right back.

My height was a difference that was impossible to miss—
there I am in the center of the back row, the tallest girl in my class
at Bryn Mawr Elementary School.

CHAPTER FOUR

AM I SEEN?

HAVE YOU EVER felt like you don't matter? That you exist in a world that doesn't see you?

Everywhere I go, I meet people who tell me they're struggling to be accepted as themselves, whether it's at school, at work, or inside a larger community. They describe the self-consciousness that comes with feeling like you don't belong in the space you're in. It's something I've known and lived with much of my life.

Nearly everyone on earth experiences this sort of feeling at some point—that prickling awareness that you're somehow not suited to your environment, that you're being viewed as a trespasser. But for those of us who are perceived as different—whether due to our race, ethnicity, body size, gender, queerness, disability, neurodivergence, or in any number of other ways, in any number of combinations—these feelings don't just come and go; they can be acute and unrelenting. Living with them takes a lot of work. Trying to understand what causes them and what to do about them can be daunting, to say the least.

Most of my earliest memories of feeling different have nothing to do with being Black. In the neighborhood where I was raised, the color of my skin was basically unremarkable. I went to school with a mix of kids, from a mix of backgrounds, and something about the mix seemed to create more space for who we all were.

But still, I was tall. And tall became something to contend with. Tall stood out. "Tall" became the label that got attached to me first, and it stuck with me right through. It was not something I could shake, not something I could hide about myself. I showed up tall for the first day of kindergarten and grew steadily from there, topping out at where I am now—five foot eleven inches—around the age of sixteen.

In elementary school, I dreaded the teacher's inevitable call any time we headed out for recess, had a fire drill, or got ready for a school performance: "Okay, kids, line yourselves up by height!" The order was implied: *small first, tall last.*

Though I know my teachers didn't intend it this way, these callouts added to the awkwardness I was already feeling, as if I were being publicly assigned to the peripheries. I couldn't help but hear the message as *You belong on the outside.* It created a small wound in me, the tiniest kernel of self-loathing that would keep me from embracing my strengths. As the tall kid, I was relegated to the back of most groups, singing from the last row of the third-grade chorus. I was always bringing up the rear. The attention given to my height brought about a new self-consciousness in me, a slight sense of otherness. There were times when I'd cross a room fully steeped in my own awkwardness, my mind fixed on one thought: *I'm the tall girl, headed to the back of the line.*

I can see now that I was actually delivering myself two thoughts at once, two messages that when combined became especially poisonous: *I stand out.* And *I don't matter.*

My size didn't serve me the way it seemed to serve my brother, who by the age of thirteen was big enough to hold his own against full-grown men on the basketball courts in the park across the street from our house. He was applauded for his strength and athleticism. It became a tool for him to use, helping him to make friends and earn respect in the neighborhood. It helped get him into college, connecting him not just with fellow athletes who smoothed his transition but also to team boosters who acted as mentors and helped him make further connections. Craig's height and strength would end up taking him all the way to a successful career in coaching.

On me, however, this combination of height and strength felt less like an asset and more like a burden. As a girl, I couldn't figure out what I was supposed to do with it. I remember watching the 1976 Olympics and becoming obsessed with the Romanian gymnast Nadia Comăneci, who astonished everyone by scoring the first-ever "Perfect 10" in Olympic-level gymnastics with a flawlessly executed uneven-bar routine. Not only that—she went on to do it six more times, winning on bars and beam and taking the all-around gold medal, too. Her power left me breathless. Her poise was riveting. Watching the gutsy way she went after greatness, I felt something stirring in myself. Before Nadia Comăneci, a Perfect 10 had been nothing more than an idea to reach toward, an ephemeral kind of miracle, but she'd now shown that it was achievable—a whole new level of excellence. What we'd seen was the sports-world equivalent of a moon landing.

Even better, Nadia was just fourteen years old. Actually, technically speaking, she was fourteen and a half, and at the time, I was twelve and a half. I was encouraged by the age gap. To me, it mattered less that I had never even tried gymnastics and more that I had a full two-year on-ramp to get myself into Nadia-style shape, at which point I'd chalk up my hands and bust my way into international competition. Nadia became my new benchmark for aging. All I could think was: *Okay, that's what fourteen and a half looks like.*

And so I decided to aim myself in that same direction, thinking that I, too, would get myself to the moon.

With my mother's blessing, I signed up for once-a-week "acrobatics" classes at Mayfair Academy, the studio where I normally took dance. Mayfair had been founded in the late 1950s by a successful African American tap dancer and choreographer from the South Side who wanted to give kids from his own community the kind of access to dance and movement that he'd seen in wealthier, whiter neighborhoods to the north. That little studio was as close to a gymnastics facility as a person could find on the South Side, but it was not specifically equipped for the sport, which meant there were no balance beams or floor mats, no trainers or sponge pits, no vaults and no bars. There was just a single runner mat on which I and about a dozen other would-be Nadias could practice our tumbling and splits.

For the better part of a whole school year, I dutifully worked on my handstand, my cartwheel, my roundoff. I could sometimes pull off a back walkover, but most of the time not. Something about how my body weight was distributed seemed inherently to complicate the endeavor. I'd spend five minutes stuck in an awkward backbend, arm muscles quivering as I tried fruitlessly to kick my lanky, grasshopper-like legs up and over my arched body, rarely finding the right momentum or fulcrum point. Eventually, I'd just sink flat-backed to the floor.

I began to feel slightly out of place among my fellow acrobats. Harder still was watching new kids—most of them narrow-framed girls at least six inches shorter than I was—arrive in freshly bought leotards and quickly master skills that I couldn't.

It got a little embarrassing. Then it started to get demoralizing.

And then finally, conceding that my moon shot was over, I formally retired from the sport of gymnastics at the age of thirteen.

I was not Nadia. I never would be.

THE TRUTH IS, I wasn't built to be a Nadia. My center of gravity was too high; my limbs were too long for all the tucking and spinning. I was simply too tall to succeed in gymnastics, and beyond that, trying to access the type of specialized equipment and coaching needed to advance would have probably bankrupted my family. It didn't matter how motivated I'd been. It didn't matter that Nadia's string of Perfect 10s had activated some impulse in me, a yearning to prove myself, a feeling that I, too, was capable of doing remarkable things. I'd picked a good hero, but an impossible path.

But what was I supposed to do with my strength? I was a strong kid from a strong family, but "strong" wasn't a label regularly awarded to girls, not in a positive way, anyway. It was not something to cherish or cultivate. I had a strong body, a strong personality, a strong drive. And yet that power didn't seem to make much sense outside the walls of our nurturing home. It felt like something I kept bottled up.

The larger problem was that I didn't know my other options. I couldn't readily find a set of heroes to follow. I struggled to find new outlets for my strength. There were no girls' soccer or softball leagues (that I knew of, anyway) in my neighborhood. I had no easy access to tennis equipment or lessons. I may have been able to find a basketball team to play on, but something in me instinctively rebelled against it. (There was that kernel of self-loathing again.) I didn't want to gravitate to the one sport that tall girls were basically expected to do. Somehow it felt like a concession.

Keep in mind that this was a different time. It was long before Venus and Serena. There was no Maya Moore, no WNBA, no U.S. women's soccer or hockey. Rarely did you see a woman sweat, strive, or play on a team. Wilma Rudolph, a Black track athlete, had briefly caught the world's attention in the early 1960s; the next American superstar sprinter, Florence Griffith Joyner ("Flo-Jo"), had not yet appeared on the scene. Title IX, the landmark civil rights amendment that barred gender-based discrimination in education, ultimately reshaping college athletics and creating a new generation of female athletes, was four years old and only slowly being implemented. Despite the fact that I could flip on the TV and see men playing football, baseball, golf, or basketball practically every day of the week, the only time I saw women competing athletically on TV was in occasional tennis matches. Which is why the Olympics, when they came around every four years, were so utterly transfixing.

Even then, though, the coverage of female Olympians heavily favored sports like gymnastics and figure skating, events featuring petite white women who competed individually and in body-hugging Lycra. They never seemed to sweat, those women, their strength wrapped in a carefully controlled, almost emphatically feminine grace. Though I know they were out there somewhere, in events that didn't make prime time, or from countries the network cameras weren't interested in, I don't recall seeing a Black female athlete on television during my childhood, not once.

It wasn't just sports, either. I came across very few people who looked like me on TV, in movies, or in magazines or books. On television shows, strong women who had a point of view were generally used only for comic relief, as mouthy or shrewish foils to the men. Black people were often depicted as either criminals or maids; almost never did they show up as doctors, lawyers, artists, professors, or scientists. Or they were featured in cartoonish extremes: The Evans family of *Good Times* lived a joke-filled life in a public housing complex, and George and Weezy of *The Jeffersons* had managed to get out of the hood and move on up to a "dee-luxe apartment in the sky." My dad used to roll his eyes any time he saw us laughing at those sitcom families. "Why are they always broke and goofy?" he'd say, shaking his head.

As a kid, I was striving toward some sort of existence I couldn't quite see. Aside from Nadia, my role models were

Mary Tyler Moore, Stevie Wonder, and José Cardenal, an out-fielder for the Chicago Cubs. I suppose if you blended all those people together, it might have resulted vaguely in the kind of person I hoped to be, but you'd have to squint to even imagine it.

I found myself grasping for heroes, anyone who even remotely resembled me, anyone who could light the path forward and show me what was possible: *Okay, that's what a professional woman looks like. That's what a powerful female leader is. That's what a Black athlete does with her strength.*

In life, it's hard to dream about what's not visible. When you look around and can't find any version of yourself out there in the wider world, when you scan the horizon and see nobody like you, you start to feel a broader loneliness, a sense of being mismatched to your own hopes, your own plans, your own strengths. You begin to wonder where—and how—you will ever belong.

BY THE TIME I got to high school, I felt a degree of envy for the kids who could easily blend into a crowd. Though I was happy in my classes and had a good set of friends, I still felt the label of my height. I was aware of it nearly all the time. I was straight-up jealous of the smaller girls, the ones whose body size didn't seem to factor into how they bought their clothes or whether any boy would think twice before asking them to dance.

Many of my free hours went to searching for clothes that worked for my shape and size. Most of the time, I just had to settle for a fit that wasn't quite right. I tried not to get dismayed, watching my smaller friends casually pull pairs of Calvin Klein jeans off the rack, not having to worry for one second that the pant legs would "flood." I spent time agonizing over heel heights, hoping to look cool but not too much taller. I often got distracted in class, tugging at the legs of my pants, trying to keep my ankles fashionably out of view. And the sleeves on my shirts and jackets were never long enough for my arms, so I kept them perpetually rolled up, hoping that no one would notice. I spent energy hiding, adjusting, and compensating for what I wasn't.

I'd go to pep rallies at school and watch the cheerleaders do flips and swish their pom-poms, recognizing that same mix of strength and performative grace I'd seen in the gymnasts, all the while understanding, with a touch of dismay, that some of those girls were approximately the size of one of my legs. At the same time I was waking up to the fact that there were gender dynamics at play—that the girls I envied were underdogs, too. Even small, even classically pretty, they were operating within a narrowed set of choices. As strong and disciplined as those cheerleaders may have been, they were still largely viewed as decorative—as perky sideline mascots playing a supporting role in the larger, more riveting drama of boys' football and basketball. The applause was primarily directed toward the boys.

I kept trying to fit myself into the spaces I was in. All of us were trying to fit. It's part of being a teenager, I now realize. It's what gives many of us our early experiences with failure. Even the popular, confident kids, I used to tell my daughters, are privately scared—just slightly better at hiding their own efforts to fit in. At that age, nearly everyone is wearing some sort of mask.

THIS SORT OF self-consciousness is almost a developmental stage—something to endure, learn from, and try to grow past. But for many people, that feeling of not fitting, of having to exist outside the norms being presented to you, often persists deep into adulthood.

Do I belong?

What do others think of me?

How am I seen?

We ask these questions and will contort ourselves sometimes to get answers that don't hurt. We adjust, hide, and compensate in order to manage our differentness in relation to the spaces we find ourselves in. We wear different masks—brave faces, really—for different situations, hoping to feel more safety or come closer to a sense of belonging, but still never feeling fully like ourselves.

It can be easy to presume that your differentness is the most visible part of you, the thing people perceive first and remember longest. Sometimes this is absolutely true, and other times it's not. The difficult part is that you will rarely know. You have little choice except to keep going, regardless. But the problem is, once you allow the judgment of others inside, it gets distracting. This is a hallmark of self-consciousness, a shift from thinking about yourself to imagining how people are thinking about you. And it can also become a form of self-sabotage, because now suddenly, you, too, are perceiving your differentness first. Instead of focusing on trying to solve the math problem on the board, you're worrying about how you look. You raise your hand to ask a question at a lecture, but you're simultaneously wondering how your voice sounds in a room full of people who are not like you. You're headed into a meeting with your boss, but you're second-guessing the impression you'll make, fretting about the length of your skirt and whether you should have worn lipstick.

You start carrying the load of your label, whatever that label may be. Your differentness attaches to you like a flag.

All this creates an extra burden, extra distraction. It adds another layer of required thinking to situations that for some might be casual, but for you now take energy. It can feel almost as if the world has quietly divided into two right in front of your eyes: those who have to think more and those who can think less.

I HAVE A number of Black friends who were raised in affluent white suburbs. Many of them say that their parents made a conscious choice to bring them up in places with well-resourced public schools, easy access to nature, and reliably clean water and air. Which often meant that they had to move away from their home cities and extended families, marshaling every dollar to land themselves in a new zip code. It sometimes meant that in order to afford these better-off places with better-off schools, they ended up in a tiny rented apartment next to the commuter train station at the very edge of town—but still, it was a toehold into a certain set of advantages. It also nearly always meant that their children would grow up as "onlies," finding few if any other people of color in their classes, on sports teams, in the popcorn line at the movie theater, and in the aisles of the grocery store. In the name of giving their kids better opportunities, these parents put themselves on a sort of racial frontier.

I have a friend—I'll call her Andrea—who grew up as an "only" in a bedroom community of New York, a town richly dotted with country clubs and hilly forest, where fathers rode the train to work in the city and mothers mostly stayed home with their children. Her own parents were successful Black professionals, educated and deeply ambitious. They lived in a nice house and drove nice cars. When it came to wealth, the family fit in plenty well. But this did little to offset the extent to which their Black bodies stood out inside the homogeneity of a white town. Andrea was very young when she started noticing the small hesitancies of people around her, the split-second pause that came as someone new tried to reconcile the sight of a little Black girl in a privileged space, that tiny extra thought: *How'd she get here? What's this all about?* It's not to say that Andrea didn't end up with friends who loved her for herself, or to suggest that she grew up unhappy as a result of where she lived; it was just that from an early age, she was contending with the label of differentness, picking up on the signals of not-belonging, the quiet, beneath-the-surface suggestions that she was somehow trespassing in her own hometown.

These messages of not-belonging create wounds, and the wounds don't easily go away. My friend grew up to become a highly educated, well-off professional herself. She has devoted a good part of her career to diversity and inclusion efforts in corporate spaces, trying to make sure there are fewer "onlies" in the places she works. After so many years of needing to navigate her way through people who viewed her as other, she's developed a set of tools and a suit of emotional armor that seem to work for her. And yet, the old wounds haven't disappeared: Andrea still gets emotional, remembering the way her kindergarten teacher would light up and deliver affectionate hugs to her white classmates, but shy away from ever touching her. She'll still cry, recalling how invisible she felt any time a white friend got a worksheet returned covered with a teacher's encouraging stars and smiley faces, while hers, completed with equal diligence and precision, came back bearing only an impersonal checkmark. It was subtle and unsubtle, one of a thousand tiny cuts.

My own parents seemed to have no interest in the suburbs and whatever toehold they might provide. Their choice was to keep us rooted in our city community, close to aunts, uncles, grandparents, and cousins, even as other families—especially white ones—were starting to move away. This perhaps had less to do with any thought-out agenda and more to do with my mother's general resistance to change, though I do think my parents liked where we were. We knew our neighbors. We were comfortable inside the mix of people, the range of race, class, and culture that existed around us. That mix was shelter. For us, it was never anything but good.

WHAT THIS MEANT, though, is that for the first seventeen years of my life, I was never an "only." It wasn't until I arrived at college that I got my first real taste of racial invisibility. My dad drove me from Chicago to Princeton and suddenly I was walking the bisecting pathways between nineteenth-century stone buildings, ducking Frisbees being tossed across a pristine quad by prep-schoolers in untucked shirts, swallowing my astonishment. I was stunned that such a place even existed, and that I, Michelle Robinson of Euclid Avenue, had made it there.

The place was beautiful and it was also, for me, a little charged. I'd never been in an environment populated mostly by young white men before. (This is not a generalization but rather a statement of fact: More than three-quarters of the students in my university class were white, and nearly two-thirds of them were male.) I'm pretty certain I felt their presence more than they felt mine. As a young Black woman, I was a minority on two fronts. Walking across campus felt like crossing a force field, a kind of frontier. I had to make an effort not to think about how different I was.

Even as I stood out, I quickly realized nobody was paying much attention. I was as inconsequential as a puff of air. There was a kind of imperviousness about Princeton in general. Something about its genteel Gothic arches and more than two hundred years of proud elitism (otherwise known as "academic excellence") created a sense that all of us, regardless of where we'd arrived from, were just visitors passing through. The institution would outlive us all. And yet it also started to become clear that some of my classmates felt more at home in those surroundings, less shocked by the abundance, less concerned with needing to prove themselves. For some, attending Princeton was essentially a birthright—one in eight in my class were legacy admissions, it turns out—the latest in a lineage of fathers and grandfathers who'd passed beneath those same arches and who might reasonably presume that their own kids would someday do the same. (At that point, the school had been co-ed for only twelve years, so alumni mothers and grandmothers weren't yet part of the equation.)

I understood none of this at the time. I hadn't yet grasped the concept of entitlement. It hadn't dawned on me that the certainty and comfort being showcased by some of my peers were fed by an underground spring of generational wealth and deep networks of privilege. All I knew was that I felt different and occasionally diminished. I'd been admitted to the school, but that didn't necessarily grant me a sense of belonging.

There's something unnerving about moving through a place and not seeing people who look like you anywhere. It's haunting, almost, as if your "kind" has been erased from the planet completely. You may have grown up knowing your grandparents, their food, their culture, their way of speaking, but now, suddenly, there's no history of them. Your own reality seems vanished. There are no faces like yours in the portraits lining the walls of classrooms and dining halls; the buildings you spend your days in are all named for white men. Your teachers aren't like you. Your peers aren't like you. Even on the streets of the larger town, there's hardly anyone who looks like you.

What honestly hadn't occurred to me before going to college was that there were giant pockets of America that looked less like where I came from and more like Princeton did, basically devoid of differentness. For a lot of people, this was simply the norm. I started to catch the small hesitation as someone new took in the sight of me, needing that extra second to compute my differentness, my presence in this place. I came to realize that many of my classmates had grown up surrounded by people who looked and acted like them, their lives shaped by sameness, their comfort defined by it, too. Some had never had a peer who was Black or brown. This made me practically unrecognizable to them, as alien as alien can be. No wonder they could so easily stereotype me! No wonder people seemed afraid of my hair, the tone of my skin! A kid like me fit nowhere in their world. Where they came from, people like me literally did not exist.

As time went on, I found refuge and community in certain spaces at college—namely in my dorm room with my friends Angela and Suzanne, and at the campus multicultural center, where students of color tended to hang out. It was a place we could shed our self-consciousness and feel more at home, unworried about what others thought of us. There, I made friends and found a wonderful adult mentor in Czerny Brasuell, the center's director, who became my work-study supervisor and invested herself in my success. What made college survivable for me was the fact that I was able to create an informal council of friends, confidantes, and advisers, people with whom I could joke about anything, including the strangeness of being an "only." Every Black student I knew had a story to tell about the labels they carried, about how "Black" eclipsed "college student" almost every time. I had a friend who was followed more than once by campus security as he walked back to his dorm in the evening. Another talked about how her white roommate was friendly and warm in private, but at parties pretended not to know her.

Maybe because we had no choice, we found ways to laugh about these things. Beneath it, though, I think we were doing something actually useful, pooling our experiences to land upon a helpful and oddly steadying truth: We were not crazy. This stuff wasn't just in our heads. The disconnection and isolation each of us was experiencing individually—what was feeding our self-consciousness—was not made up, nor was it due to some internal flaw or lack of trying on our part. We were not simply imagining the biases that put us on the outside. It was all real. It was all true. Knowing this, recognizing it, even if we didn't quite know how to change it, was important.

My group of friends made me feel less alone, and yet in order to do the work of college, to get the benefits I'd come for, I still had to step out of my at-home circle and into the force field of the broader culture. There'd be times when I'd find myself moving through a campus dining room or lecture hall, wanting to blend in but also hyperaware of my differentness, my mind running simultaneously on two tracks. I'd be focused on finding a seat, but I'd be almost equally focused on the image of me trying to find a seat—on what I assumed were the thoughts running through other people's heads: *There goes the Black girl, looking for a seat.*

In other words, *I stand out. I don't matter.*

It can mess with your head if you let it.

I can still conjure the discomfort of those moments. I felt ungrounded, divided from myself, almost as if I'd been flung out of my own body.

Self-consciousness can do this. It can take away your footing and erase what you know to be true about yourself. It can leave you clumsy and unsure, disoriented about who and where you are. It's as if the world has held up a mirror at an unflattering angle, showing you your unrecognizability to others, all the ways in which you don't belong. Sometimes that image becomes all you can see. Sociologist and civil rights leader W.E.B. Du Bois famously described this tension in his landmark 1903 book, *The Souls of Black Folk*. "It is a peculiar sensation," he wrote, "this double-consciousness, this sense of always looking at one's self through the eyes of others, of measuring one's soul by the tape of a world that looks on in amused contempt and pity."

The feeling is that old, if not a whole lot older.

And it's that common, too. Even now, even still.

The question becomes what to do with it.

MY FATHER, WHOSE shaky demeanor and foot-dragging limp sometimes caused people to stop and stare at him on the street, used to tell us, with a smile and a shrug, "No one can make you feel bad if you feel good about yourself."

It was a brilliantly simple maxim, and for him, it seemed to work. My dad could shrug off nearly anything. He was not reactive, not a firebrand. He was instead modest and level-headed, which is why I think people so often turned up at our house, asking for his input and advice, knowing they'd be met with an open mind. He kept three dollars folded up in the front pocket of his shirt and would hand out two of them to anyone who asked for cash, which apparently happened fairly often. According to my mother, my dad would deliberately hold back the third dollar for dignity's sake, so that the person who'd hit him up could walk away feeling okay, knowing they hadn't taken everything he had.

My father did not worry about how others saw him. He was good with himself, clear about his own worth, centered despite being physically unbalanced. I don't know exactly how he got to this place or what sort of lessons he'd had to learn along the way, but he somehow had figured out how to live unburdened by the judgment of others. This quality in him was so vivid, I swear you could spot it from across a room. It drew people toward him. It surfaced as a kind of ease—and not the ease that comes from privilege or wealth, but from something different. It was ease despite struggle. Ease despite uncertainty. It was ease from within.

It made him noticeable, visible in all the right ways.

My dad did not let the injustices of the world burn him up the way they had burned up his own father. I believe this was a deliberate choice. It was another instance of what he could do *despite*. He'd had plenty of exposure to unfairness himself: He'd been born into the Great Depression, was five when his father disappeared to fight in World War II, hadn't managed to afford college. He'd lived through exclusionary housing and education policies, the assassinations of some of his heroes, and the onset of an incurable, crippling disease. But he'd also seen, in his father—my grandfather Dandy—how fear created limits, the toll bitterness could take.

And so my dad went the other way. He allowed none of it into his soul. He made a point of not holding on to pain or embarrassment, knowing that it wasn't likely to serve him, recognizing that there was a certain power in being able to shake things off, in letting certain moments go. He understood the unfairness was there, but he refused to be brought down by it, recognizing that much of it was not in his control.

Instead, he taught Craig and me to be curious about how the world worked, educating us on issues of equality and justice, sitting at the dinner table and answering our questions about things like Jim Crow laws or the riots that happened on the West Side of Chicago after Martin Luther King Jr. was shot. On election days, he made sure to bring us with him to the polling place located in the church basement across from our elementary school, so we could see how cool it was to cast a vote. He also took my brother and me for Sunday drives in his Buick to show us the South Side neighborhood where wealthier African American people lived, wanting us to have a picture in our heads about the difference a college education could make, a reason for us to persist at school and keep our minds open. It was as if he were driving us to the foot of a mountain and then pointing toward the top. It was his way of saying, *You can get there, even if I can't.*

With his centeredness, my dad was able to look past whatever mirror the world might have held up to him, all the ways a blue-collar Black man walking on crutches might otherwise be made to feel worthless or invisible. He didn't focus on who he wasn't or what he didn't have. Instead, he measured his value by who he was and what he had—love, community, food in the fridge, two tall and noisy kids, and friends knocking on his door. He saw these things as success and as reason to keep going. It was evidence he mattered.

How you view yourself becomes everything. It's your foundation, the starting point for changing the world around you. I learned that from him. My father's visibility helped me to find my own.

NO ONE CAN *make you feel bad if you feel good about yourself.* It took me years to absorb my dad's maxim more fully into my own life. I grew into my confidence slowly, in fits and starts. Only gradually did I learn to carry my differentness with pride.

It began, to a certain extent, with acceptance. At some point in elementary school, I got used to being the tallest girl in my class. Because, really, what choice did I have? And later, at college, I had to adjust to being an "only" in my classes and at campus events. Again—no real choice. Over time, I grew accustomed to being in spaces where men outnumbered and usually outvoiced women. These were simply the environments as they existed. And I began to realize that if I wanted to change the dynamics of those spaces—for myself and for whoever would follow me, to create more room for differentness and broaden the definition of who belonged—I had to first find my own footing, my own solid pride. I learned not to hide who I was, but to own it.

I could not get defeated early or start avoiding situations that might be easier to avoid. I had to become more comfortably afraid. Unless I was going to quit, I had to keep going. My dad's life provided an object lesson in this as well: You take what you have and you march it forward. You find your tools, adapt as needed, and carry on. You persevere, understanding that there are plenty of despites.

My own temperament is different from my father's in certain ways. I can be less abiding. I tend to express my opinions with more force. I'm not able to shrug off unfairness quite the way he did, nor do I necessarily consider that a goal for myself. But the lesson I took from him was about where real steadiness comes from, which is from the inside. And steadiness, I've found, becomes the platform from which you can launch a bigger life.

In part by seeing my father's ease with his differentness, the dignity he carried into nearly every space he entered, I started to figure out what helped keep fear out of my head and better allowed me to stake my own claim over situations I was in. I realized that there was something I *could* choose, I *could* control, and that was what I told myself during moments of discomfort—the messages I allowed into my mind any time I stepped into a new force field, any time I crossed a room full of strangers and felt that prickling awareness that I didn't belong or was being judged.

Whatever the signals in those spaces were—whether people saw me as different, or unentitled to be there, or problematic in some way, even if what I was sensing was unconscious or unintended—I didn't need to let those signals in. I had a choice about it. I could let my own life, my own actions, represent my truth. I could keep showing up and keep doing the work. That poison wasn't mine.

I learned that I could attach better feelings to my differentness. It was helpful to do when entering a new space, a kind of psychological squaring of the shoulders. I could take a second to remind myself of what, inside the walls of my own home, inside the shelter of my friendships, I already knew to be true. My validation came from inside. And it helped to be able to carry that power into a new room.

In my own head, in real time, and for my own benefit, I could rewrite the story of not-mattering:

I'm tall and that's a good thing.
I'm a woman and that's a good thing.
I'm Black and that's a good thing.
I am myself and that is a very good thing.

When you start to rewrite the story of not-mattering, you start to find a new center. You remove yourself from other people's mirrors and begin speaking more fully from your own experience, your own knowing place. You become better able to attach to your pride and more readily step over all the despites. It doesn't remove the obstacles, but I've found that it helps to shrink them. It helps you to count your victories, even the small ones, and know that you're doing okay.

This, I believe, is the root of true confidence and becomes the place from which you can move toward more visibility, more agency, and more ability to create broader change. It's not something you conquer in one, two, or even a dozen tries. It takes work to get yourself out of other people's mirrors. It takes practice to keep the right messages in your head.

It's also helpful to acknowledge what makes this work so difficult. We are tasked with trying to write our own script over layers and layers of already-written ones. We have to try to put our truth over narratives that have long suggested we don't fit, don't belong, or don't register at all. These stories have been enshrined by tradition and cemented in everyday life, in many cases forming the literal backdrop to our days. They unconsciously shape our conception of both self and other. They purport to tell us who is lesser and who is greater, who is strong and who is weak. They have anointed heroes and established norms: *This is who matters. This is what success looks like. This is what a doctor looks like, what a scientist looks like, what a mother looks like, what a senator looks like, what a criminal looks like, what a victory looks like.*

Whether you grew up with the Confederate flag flying over your statehouse, or played in public parks anchored by bronzed tributes to slave owners, or were taught your country's history through a canon formed almost exclusively by whiteness, you have those stories inside you. The Mellon Foundation recently funded a study of monuments around the United States, finding that the vast majority of them honored white men; half were enslavers and 40 percent were born into wealth. Black and Indigenous people made up only about 10 percent of those commemorated; women just 6 percent. Statues of mermaids outnumbered statues of female members of Congress by a ratio of eleven to one.

I'll say it again: It's hard to dream about what's not visible. You can't readily strive toward what you don't see. Rewriting the story of not-mattering takes both courage and persistence. As disheartening as it is, there are people in this world who are more comfortable or feel more powerful when others are made to feel isolated, broken, or unwelcome. They are happy to keep you small. Visibility sits at the center of many of our current and most contentious civic debates. As state legislatures argue about whether to ban teachers from discussing systemic racism in public schools, as school boards vote to remove books about the Holocaust, or racism, or LGBTQ+ people from school libraries, we need to stay aware of whose stories are being told and whose are being erased. This is a battle over who matters, about who gets to be seen.

We are a young country dominated by old narratives. Many of these stories have been lionized, repeated, and left unchallenged to the point that we hardly even recognize them as stories anymore. Instead, we've internalized them as truth. We forget to make the effort to decode them.

When my brother, Craig, turned twelve, for example, he outgrew his bike. He'd been growing so quickly that his old bike—his kid-sized bike—no longer fit his long body, even with the seat hiked as high as it would go. So my parents went out and bought him an adult-sized bike, a bright yellow ten-speed they found on sale at Goldblatt's department store. Craig was thrilled by the new bike. He glided around on it like a king, proud to be on those pedals, excited to have something that fit so well. Until one afternoon he rode the ten-speed to the public lakeshore park not far from our house and was promptly stopped by a city police officer, who accused him of having stolen it.

Why? Because he was a Black boy on a nice bike. It evidently didn't fit with what the officer thought about Black boys and the sorts of bikes they rode—never mind that the officer himself was Black. He had accepted a certain story as truth, internalizing a stereotype that compelled him to separate a boy not just from his bike but also from his pride. (The man later apologized, though only after having been thoroughly scolded by our mother.)

The message the police officer gave my brother was as clear as it is common:

I don't see you as being entitled to what you've got.
I doubt that you belong with this thing that's made you
*   proud.*

This is precisely the sort of doubt many of us sense in the eyes of others when we are crossing an unfamiliar room, when we experience the dynamics of a new force field. We are picking up on some idea that we are seen as trespassers, that our pride requires extra proof. These are the narratives we are left to try to rewrite, not just for ourselves but for a world that won't accept us.

STACEY ABRAMS, the voting-rights activist and politician, tells a story about how after she was named valedictorian of her high school class in 1991, she was invited to join other valedictorians from around her home state of Georgia for an afternoon reception at the governor's mansion in Atlanta to celebrate their success as students. Excited for the opportunity, she and her parents dressed up in their best clothes and rode city buses from Decatur, near where they lived, to Buckhead, the leafy, upscale neighborhood where the mansion was located. They got off the bus, Abrams says, walked partway up the driveway, and were stopped by a security guard, who took one look at them and said, "This is a private event. You don't belong here."

A Black family arriving on a city bus, too poor to own a car, didn't fit with the guard's idea of who might be invited to mingle with the governor.

The message was familiar: *I don't see you as being entitled to what you have. You stand out; you don't matter.*

Lucky for Stacey Abrams, her parents would have none of that nonsense. Her mother, she recalls, gripped her arm to stop her from turning and running back to the bus. Her father started arguing with the guard. The family did eventually make it into the reception—after forcing the man to find Stacey's name at the very top of the alphabetized guest list on his clipboard—but the damage was already done, a drop of poison had escaped; a young woman had been separated from her pride, and it would taint the entire experience.

"I don't remember meeting the governor of Georgia or my fellow valedictorians," Abrams told *The New York Times* years later. "All I remember that day was a man at a gate, telling me I don't belong."

These messages have the power to obliterate, especially when delivered to someone who is young and still forming a sense of self, and especially when coming from someone in authority in a moment when we are feeling open and proud. The people who deliver these messages become almost impossible to forget. They haunt us like ghosts. How many of us remain in a one-way dialogue with someone who demeaned or diminished us even decades ago? How many of us are still silently talking back to that person who tried to erase us from a place we were trying to get to? We return again and again to those gates, telling and retelling the story to ourselves, working hard to reattach ourselves to our pride. In *Becoming,* I wrote about how casually my high school guidance counselor seemed to brush aside my aspirations within ten minutes of meeting me, suggesting that I shouldn't bother applying to Princeton, since, as she saw it, I was not "Princeton material."

I was hurt and angry, destroyed not just by her words but by the indifference and speed with which they were delivered. She'd looked at me, evaluated me, and seen none of my light. Or that's how it felt, anyway. My path from that moment on would be shaped, at least in part, by that one remark—a single off-the-cuff sentence, uttered by a virtual stranger.

This is how powerful messages can be, and why we need to pay careful attention to both how we deliver and how we receive them. It's natural for kids to want others to recognize their light. They crave it. They grow with it. And if they're made to feel invisible, they will often find other, less productive ways to be seen. They'll act out inside the darkness they've been left with. I think about this when reading stories about young people who get caught up in crime and mayhem. If kids aren't given the chance to feel pride, they won't have any reason to respect the spaces they're in or the authorities who have pushed them into the margins. It becomes easier to destroy something that doesn't belong to you.

Thanks largely to other supportive adults in my life, I was able to quickly convert my hurt over the guidance counselor's remark into fuel. I became triply motivated to prove her wrong. My life became a kind of reply: *Your limits aren't mine.* To this day, she gets no gratitude from me, but I was able, in response to her indifference, to discover something in myself, a certain resolve. I set about trying to create an existence that was bigger and more purposeful than anything she would ever have granted me, if I'd allowed her the power to dictate where I belonged or not. Her low expectations became a part of my despite.

It's possible that the guard who stopped Stacey Abrams at the gates of the governor's mansion went home after his shift, had dinner with his family, and never thought about her again. But she, of course, has not forgotten him. He and his message about not-belonging rode along with her as she went to college, got two advanced degrees, authored a dozen books, and launched one of the most successful voter-mobilization efforts in history. And it's surely stayed with her as she's twice run to become governor of Georgia herself, hoping to open those gates even wider. He is part of her despite.

Stacey Abrams still talks about her experience with the guard, viewing it primarily through the lens of what it crystallized for her, her own deep resolve. "I've spent my life, whether intentionally or not, proving him wrong," she has said. "But it wasn't about him. It wasn't about what he saw or didn't see in me. It was about who I am, and who I intend to be."

I imagine that, for her, that guard remains perched at the gate, the same way my guidance counselor will forever sit at a desk in my head. They live quietly in the margins of our minds, along with all our other despites—shrunk down by our excellence, the answers we've provided. They will be remembered only for what they failed to accomplish. Only for what they gave us to step over.

They've become bit players in our larger and more interesting stories about who belongs. Their only power, it turns out, is to remind us of why we persist.

PART TWO

We are each other's
harvest:
we are each other's
business:
we are each other's
magnitude and bond.

— GWENDOLYN BROOKS,
FROM "PAUL ROBESON"

My girlfriends and I lean on one another for strength, solace, and joy.

CHAPTER FIVE

MY KITCHEN TABLE

I AM NOT SOMEONE who takes friendship lightly. I can be serious about making friends and even more serious about keeping them. My friends sometimes joke that I can be a bit of a drillmaster, even, when it comes to maintaining our bonds. They offer this observation lovingly and with an occasional hint of fatigue. And I get it. I accept both their love and their fatigue. It's true that I can be intense about staying connected with those I care about. I am a dedicated planner of group outings, getaway weekends, tennis dates, and one-on-one walks along the Potomac River. I love always having something to look forward to, someone dear I'm expecting to see. For me, friendships are both a commitment and a lifeline, and I hold on to them as such, tightly and deliberately.

I've written before about how, during the White House years, I used to call about a dozen of my girlfriends a few times a year and ask them to join me at Camp David for what I initially billed as a "spa weekend" or "health journey," though soon—after they'd discovered that I'd signed us all up for three workouts a day and arranged for no meat, no junk food, and no alcohol to be served—my friends rebranded our retreats "Boot Camp." They also, in time, began to insist that if I wanted them to keep showing up and exercising like that, we had to fold in at least *some* steak, *some* dessert, and definitely *some* wine. We were all professional women with too little time, which meant that when we kicked back, we wanted everything all at once. Most of us had school-age kids, busy spouses, demanding careers. We were accustomed to squeezing in things like sleep, exercise, fun, and intimacy around the edges of the lives of our many dependents, with decidedly uneven results. Who can relax when your brain is stuffed full of inane, paranoia-inducing questions, the type that ambush you late at night or halfway through a workday meeting with a client? *Did I miss the deadline for summer camp sign-up? Are we out of peanut butter? When's the last time anyone fed the gerbils?*

I saw those weekends as a mighty breath of fresh air, a three-day opportunity for me and my friends to reset our priorities, even if temporarily. Forget kids, partners, jobs. Forget unfinished chores and looming deadlines. Forget the damned gerbils. It would be us first, everything else last. And for me, there is no quicker or more efficient way to obliterate stress and get focused on the present moment than to throw myself into a hard-core, edge-pushing workout. Or even better, a series of them. I guess you might say that vigor is one of my Love Languages. I like who we become when we're feeling a little pushed. I like having friends who enjoy sweating a little, who can see the fun in finding their own inner reservoirs of determination and strength. And who will later flop their tired bodies onto a set of couches in front of the fireplace and talk late into the night.

Or that's what happened once I agreed my ladies could have their wine and snacks back. Which is another important thing to remember about friendship: You're crazy if you think you get to make all the rules. What mattered was that we just kept showing up, in closeness, in commitment, in compromise, and even in fatigue. For me, it's all about showing up.

I am fully convinced that you will get further in life when you've got at least a couple of solid friends around you, when you're reliably and demonstratively invested in them, and they in you. This came into clear focus for me during those years at Princeton, when I learned how important it was to have a group of people who provided emotional shelter, good humor, and a communal energy that I could then take forward with me into the everyday struggles of being a student.

Later, when I married a partner whose work kept him away from home for days at a time, I was bolstered by my friends, especially those whose kids liked to play with mine. We became comrades, carpooling to dance lessons and swim classes, feeding one another's children when someone had to stay late at work, listening sympathetically any time somebody needed to vent, or was hurting, or was trying to make a major life decision. No matter how busy or hectic my own life felt, I had a handful of friends for whom I'd readily drop my own concerns in order to help them out with theirs. We covered for one another, making the ride smoother for all. Among us, the message was always *I got you. I'll be there.*

Having close friendships has also helped to take pressure off my marriage, I've found. Barack and I have never tried to be each other's "everything" in life—to single-handedly shoulder the entire load of care that each of us requires. I don't expect him to want to hear every last one of my stories or thoughts, or to sort through my every worry with me, or to be solely responsible for my day-to-day entertainment and happiness. Nor do I want to have to do all that for him. Instead, we distribute the load. We have other forms of emotional rescue and relief. We are carried by a wide array of friendships—some his, some mine, some ours together—and we do our best to help carry our friends.

I think I became extra intense about my friendships around the time I arrived in Washington early in 2009—a period when I was feeling especially pushed, digging deep into my own reservoir of strength. Barack had been elected president and, within nine weeks, we'd boxed up our belongings in Chicago, pulled Sasha and Malia out of school, and moved ourselves to D.C., a city where I hardly knew a soul. We spent the first couple of weeks ahead of the inauguration living at a hotel, while the girls settled into their new school and Barack worked triple-time to put together his administration-in-waiting. I was making dozens of decisions daily on a future I could still hardly imagine—from choosing what types of bedspreads and flatware to use in the White House to hiring staff for my offices in the East Wing. We were also set to host about 150 personal guests at the inauguration—friends, family, and a lot of kids—all of whom needed itineraries, event tickets, and places to stay.

What I remember most about this stretch of time is the odd new sheen on everything, the sense that so much about our old life was so quickly being replaced. We were in a new city, with a lot of new people, with new jobs, a new life. My days became a surreal mishmash of the mundane and the extraordinary, the practical and the historic. We needed a pencil box for Sasha, a ball gown for me. We needed a toothbrush holder and an economic rescue package. Also, I was quickly realizing, we were really going to need our friends.

I was happy to have so many of them coming to D.C. to help us celebrate, to witness what for America counted as a transfer of political power, but for me also felt like a nerve-racking transfer from one life, one way of being, to another. I needed my own witnesses for that, friends who could revel in the day's glory and all that it said about equity and progress and my husband's hard work, *and* who would find me afterward and hug me tight, knowing exactly how much about our old life I was going to miss. My friend Elizabeth was coming in from New Haven. My friend Verna from law school was coming from Cincinnati. My friend Kelly, who'd been my ride-or-die sidekick through pregnancy and early motherhood and had moved to Washington a year earlier, would be there, along with a big group of other friends coming from Chicago. They'd all been busily shopping for outfits and lining up their plans. I'd arranged for everyone to have seats near the inaugural stage, knowing that I'd be nervous and would want to feel their presence and support, even if I wouldn't know precisely where to look to find them in the crowd. It just mattered that they'd be there, almost like birds in the trees.

MOVING INTO THE White House, I carried this slight but nagging worry that my friendships might never be the same, that all of the relationships important to our family were vulnerable to change, thanks to the strange pomp and grandeur that now surrounded us, the sudden shift in how we were seen. I worried about how Sasha and Malia would manage to connect with other children now that there'd be Secret Service agents following them to every class, soccer practice, and birthday party. I wasn't entirely sure how Barack would ever find time to fit a social life in around all the crushingly urgent crises he was dealing with. And for myself, I wondered how, amid all this new noise and security, I'd be able to keep my close friends close while also making space for at least a few new ones as well.

Until now, most of my adult friendships had been built over time and often in casual ways, through different and often arbitrary combinations of luck, geography, and overlapping interests. I'd met my friend Sandy after we started chatting one day at a hair salon in downtown Chicago, noticing we were both pregnant. I'd met Kelly at work, though it wasn't until later, when we had babies at the same time, that we started hanging out more regularly. My friend Anita, an OB/GYN, had actually *delivered* my babies, the two of us growing close after our husbands started playing a lot of pickup basketball together. The point is, new friends tended to pop up like daisies in my life, and I made the effort to cultivate them. If I encountered someone who seemed interesting, whether at work, or a holiday party, or a hair salon, or, as was increasingly the case, through my children and their activities, I usually made a point of following up, getting that person's phone number or email address, proposing that we grab lunch sometime or meet up at a playground.

Nowadays, when I'm talking to young people, I'll often hear them express fear or hesitation about exactly this moment in a new friendship—that hinge point when you make the move from *Nice to meet you* to *Hey, let's hang out.* They'll say it feels weird and awkward to pursue a potential friend, to ask someone to have coffee or get together outside of work or school, or to try talking face-to-face with someone they've only known online. They worry about appearing too eager, thinking it makes them seem desperate or uncool. They are afraid to take that risk, worried about rejection. Their fears—no surprise—become their limits this way. And the numbers seem to suggest that the limits are real. According to a 2021 survey, one-third of American adults reported that they have fewer than three close friends. Twelve percent said they have none at all.

One of the first things Dr. Vivek Murthy did after Barack appointed him to be surgeon general of the United States in 2014 was to travel the country, asking Americans to talk about their health and well-being. What struck him most was the degree to which people described feeling lonely. "Men, women, children. Highly trained professionals. Tradespeople. Minimum-wage earners. No group, no matter how educated, wealthy, or accomplished, seemed to be exempt," Murthy wrote in his 2020 book *Together: The Healing Power of Human Connection in a Sometimes Lonely World,* which came out just as the pandemic hit. Even before the coronavirus took a wrecking ball to our patterns of friendship and sociability, Americans were consistently reporting that what was missing from their lives was a sense of belonging, a simple feeling of being "at home" with other people.

So many of us are looking for a sense of home. I understand that finding it is not easy. Murthy (who later returned as surgeon general under President Biden) also found that people tend to feel embarrassed and shameful about acknowledging their loneliness, especially in a culture where self-reliance is considered a national virtue. We don't want to appear needy or inadequate, or to admit to feeling like we're on the outside of things. And yet many of us give ourselves over to systems built to send exactly that message: One dip into Instagram will tell you that everyone's figured out how to be happy, loved, and successful—except you.

Making a genuine connection with another person does help to counteract all this. And I'm not talking about making Instagram or Facebook "friends" here, but rather one-on-one, face-to-face, IRL relationships. These are what open us to the actual lives of others, not just the filtered and curated existences we're likely to encounter online. In a true friendship, you remove your filters. My real friends know what I look like without makeup on, and in bad lighting and at unflattering angles. They've seen me messy. They probably even know what my feet smell like. But more important, they know my truest feelings, my truest self, and I know theirs.

Reading the statistics, I've started to wonder whether, as a culture, we've fallen out of practice with developing and using certain skills around friendship. Surely the pandemic hasn't helped on this front, but perhaps it goes deeper than that. I think about how many of us, myself included, have raised children with all sorts of good intentions but also driven by a touch of anxiety about whether we're providing enough. We pre-arrange every playdate and pack our kids' schedules full of structured activities—sports, lessons, educational enrichment, whatever we're able to find and afford—but in doing this, even in what we assume is for their own safety, we have taken them away from looser, more improvisational situations where they might be called upon to work a broader range of social tools.

If you've ever been a kid allowed to run around a neighborhood full of other kids who have free time on their hands, you probably know what I'm talking about. Most folks of my generation grew up in communities that felt a little more like the Wild West, where children were left to find their own friends, forge their own alliances, settle their own conflicts, and earn their own victories. All this without clear rules. All this without adults overseeing and influencing the interactions, and without anybody handing you a trophy just for showing up. This environment can get messy sometimes, yes, but it's also where learning happens. The experiences aren't always comfortable or rewarding—not the way karate or piano lessons might be—but I think it's part of what we've forgotten: Discomfort is a teacher. Lack of reward is a teacher. Dealing with these things gives us practice at life, helping us figure out who we are when we're a little pushed. When that tool is missing from your toolbox, it gets harder to navigate the adult world and the intricate dance of friendship.

Which is why I think we must continue to practice the art of opening ourselves and connecting with others. The simple truth is that making a friend involves taking a risk, which of course means swallowing a little fear. Friendship can be, at least at first, an emotional gamble—much like dating. You need to show something of yourself in order for it to work. And in showing yourself, you open yourself to being judged or even rejected. You have to be willing to accept the possibility that maybe, for any number of good reasons, you won't end up friends with this person after all.

Every friendship has an ignition point. By necessity, it involves a deliberate extension of curiosity from one person to another, and I believe this is an offer you should never be ashamed to make. To say *I am curious about you* is a form of gladness, and gladness, as we've established, is nourishing. Yes, it can be awkward to express for the very first time that you might actually be glad to see someone if they were to meet you for coffee or maybe show up at your birthday party, but when they *do* show up and you *do* feel glad, you both get the gift. You're finding the light in another person, creating something new together. You are building a sense of home.

HERE'S A FUNNY story. One of my very first encounters with my friend Denielle happened to be in the driveway of the White House when she came to pick up her daughter Olivia from a playdate with Sasha. Our two daughters were in the slightly awkward, early stages of a new friendship, getting to know each other at school and playing on the same rec-league basketball team. I had also spotted Denielle across the room at a couple of school events I'd attended, taking note of the way she hung back in a crowd, and, if I'm honest, appreciating how little interest she seemed to have in meeting me.

I was not just new to Washington, a stranger among strangers, but I was also still trying to get used to the idea that as First Lady, I'd become an object of keen interest to others. My presence tended to change the dynamics in a room, not because of who I was but because of *what* I was. For this reason, I tended to find myself a little less interested in the people who eagerly made a beeline for me and more interested in those who hung back.

At this point, my social concerns were still mostly about our daughters, anyway. I'd been thrilled that Sasha had wanted to invite Olivia and a couple of other girls over to spend a Saturday running around the residence and then watching a movie in the in-house theater. I had passed much of the morning pretending to do other things while silently hovering on the periphery of their playdate, quietly overcome with emotion any time a new peal of laughter erupted from Sasha's room. After months of sweating the details of our transition to the White House, I felt a gush of relief. It was a sign of normalcy, a kind of watershed moment for our family: *Friends were in the house.*

Denielle, meanwhile, had been sweating her own details. She'd been given detailed drop-off and pick-up instructions for the playdate via email from one of my aides. And she had been asked, as all visitors were, to submit her Social Security number and license-plate information days in advance, so that the Secret Service could clear her entry onto the grounds. Just getting a child to our doorstep was a process. And God love her, Denielle was trying to play it cool, like it was no big thing that her third-grader had been invited to run around the president's home on a Saturday. But of course it was. Years later, when we could laugh about it, she told me that knowing she'd be driving the family car up the stately access road that rings the massive

South Lawn of the White House, she had gone out and gotten it washed. She'd also gotten her hair done. And her nails. Never mind that the instructions had made clear she wouldn't be setting foot outside the car.

This was another strange facet of our new life as First Family: People felt compelled to try to match themselves to the glamour of our surroundings. I felt embarrassed that anyone would ever, for one second, think they needed to fix themselves up on our behalf. I understood but didn't love the fact that showing up at my home, just *driving up* to my home, stressed people out. But that was us, a family of once-regular folks from Chicago now living in a 132-room palace, surrounded by guards. We weren't exactly approachable. Little was casual, and absolutely nothing was arbitrary. I was still trying to adjust, still wrestling with how to build as much realness into our lives as possible, when at the end of the playdate, I decided to walk little Olivia downstairs so I could say hello to her mom.

This was something of a breach in the protocol, as a White House usher would normally escort visitors to and from the residence. But I also had my own version of normal, which involved ending playdates by greeting a child's parent and giving them a report on how things had gone. I didn't care what my title was; it was the decent thing to do. And so I made it happen. I was finding, a bit to my surprise, that any time I decided to switch up the established White House protocol, people rushed to accommodate my wishes, even though it tended to create a stir. I'd hear it in the rustling around me, Secret Service agents speaking suddenly into their wrist microphones, the quickening of footsteps behind me if I turned in an unexpected direction.

Walking out into the sunlight with Olivia that day, I saw Denielle sitting inside her freshly washed, highly buffed car, trying to take in what was happening as a heavily armed Secret Service Counter Assault Team materialized from nowhere and positioned itself around the vehicle.

This, too, was protocol. Any time Barack or I stepped out of the building, these teams went into heightened alert.

"Hey there!" I called, motioning for her to get out of the car.

Denielle paused for a second, eyeballing the guards clad in helmets and black battle dress—recalling the officers at the gate who had specifically and firmly instructed her to "remain in the vehicle at all times, ma'am"—and then very, very slowly opened the car door and got out.

As I remember it, the two of us chatted for just a few minutes that first day. But it took only that long for me to have a sense of what Denielle might be like as a friend. She had big brown eyes and a gentle smile. Managing to ignore the weirdness around us, she asked how the playdate had gone. She talked a little about the kids' school and her work in public broadcasting. After making sure Olivia was buckled into her seat, she then got back into her car, gave a nonchalant wave, and drove off, leaving me both happy and curious.

Lo and behold, another daisy had popped up.

I STARTED SITTING next to Denielle when I went to the girls' basketball games, and soon after that, I asked her to come hang out with me the next time Olivia came over to play. Even when you are First Lady, even when you have butlers serving lunch to your new friend, you still contend with the slightly stilted, get-to-know-you phase. For me, there was also a new wrinkle now that we lived in the White House: I had to worry about gossip. I was aware that anything I said to a new person could be fed outward to others, any impression I made or casual comment I dropped, positive or negative, accurate or not, could become a story to tell. It was yet another thing I understood but didn't love about this new existence: My private life had a certain currency. Was I a bad mother? Was I a bratty, fit-pitching First Lady? Did I really love my husband? Did he really love me? There were people out there always eager for proof that we were somehow a sham. This added a layer of caution to how I operated, what I showed to whom. I knew we couldn't afford a single stumble, an ounce of misinterpretation. I was still counting the steps, always a little bit scared.

It wasn't exactly easy to lower my guard, not only with Denielle but with anyone new who came into my life during this time. But I also understood what would happen if I didn't. I knew I'd end up feeling isolated, a little paranoid, and stuck in place with a limited view of the world outside my walls. If I didn't drop my fears and open myself to new friends and new people, it would impact my ability to engage in my children's lives in a normal way. I wouldn't feel at home at school functions and potluck dinners. People wouldn't feel at home with me. And if others didn't feel at home with me, how would I ever be an effective First Lady? Staying open to people felt to me like a vital part of this new job.

Research has shown that loneliness actually can compound on itself. A lonely brain becomes hyper-tuned to social threats, which can lead us to isolate further. Disconnection from others makes us more susceptible to conspiratorial and superstitious thinking. And this, in turn, can leave us mistrustful of those who are not like us. Which, of course, becomes another way of getting stuck.

Despite feeling vulnerable in my new role, I was bent on not going in that direction. This was something Barack and I had talked about together, a goal we had not just for ourselves but also for the White House in general: To the greatest extent possible, we wanted to be open rather than closed. We wanted to invite more people in, which is why we expanded the number of tours available to the public, nearly doubled the size of the annual Easter Egg Roll, and started throwing Halloween parties and state dinners for children. We saw openness as the better choice.

In my personal relationships, I moved a little more slowly, though with the same aim. For me, friendship tends to happen gradually. It's a little bit like sliding down your car window to talk to someone new. Maybe at first, you're conversing across an opening of just a few inches—a little cautiously, careful about how much you share. If you feel safe, if your new friend is hearing you, you might lower your window another inch or two and share more. And if that's good, you open it farther, until eventually the window is fully down and the door gets opened and suddenly there's nothing but fresh air between you.

I don't know at what point Denielle grew comfortable enough to quit getting her car washed and her hair done ahead of her visits with me. But it started to matter less what either of us looked like, what sort of impression was being made. Slowly, we shifted into realness, no longer viewing each other across a gulf of nerves or expectations, happy to sit on the couch with our shoes kicked off. Each time we got together, we dropped our guards a little bit more, finding the same unselfconscious rhythms our daughters had during the hours they spent playing with Polly Pockets or climbing trees on the South Lawn. Denielle and I laughed more easily, spoke more earnestly about our feelings. The risks diminished. I no longer needed to worry about whatever I had shared, whether it was a small and stupid gripe or a deep and real concern.

I was safe with her, and she was safe with me. We were friends now, and would stay that way.

A COUPLE OF years ago, *black-ish* actress Tracee Ellis Ross wrote a touching tribute to her friend, the fashion editor Samira Nasr, on Facebook. She described how the two of them had met and bonded while working together at a magazine. Tracee had caught sight of Samira across a room and thought, "She has similar hair . . . I bet we could be friends." And it turned out she was right. They've been besties for more than twenty-five years now. "I couldn't do this life thing without her," Tracee wrote in her post. "I am a barnacle on her life."

I thought this was beautifully put. I've come to appreciate my friends as daisies and birds in my life—brighteners to my every day—but this is another apt way to think about them. If you've ever spent time by the ocean and encountered these bump-sized, hard-shelled crustaceans melded to undersea rocks and the bottoms of boats, you'll know there's nothing more stubborn or solid than a barnacle. The same might be said of an exceptional friend. If you're lucky, you might end up with at least a few melded into your life, people who become stalwart and unshakable, the friends who accept you without judgment, show up for the hard stuff, and give you joy—not just for a semester, or for the two years you live in the same city, but over the course of many years. Barnacles are not showy, either, which I see as also true of the best friendships. They need no witnesses. They are not trying to accomplish something that can be measured or cashed in upon; the substance mostly happens behind the scenes.

My friend Angela is one of my barnacles. We met early on in college and eventually roomed together, along with our other pal, Suzanne. Angela was a fast-talking kid from D.C. with a ferocious intellect and the preppiest wardrobe I'd ever seen. Before meeting Angela, I had not encountered many Black girls in pink cable-knit Ralph Lauren sweaters. But that's the beauty of college; it's a widening of the boundaries. It dumps a lot of new people in front of you, rearranging your notions of what's possible, often blowing the lid off whatever you thought didn't or couldn't exist. Angela had a boisterous laugh and a penchant for getting up at five A.M. to study and napping at midday. I learned from her, and she learned from me. We were camp counselors together one summer in rural New York. I started going home with Angela at Thanksgiving and on certain holiday weekends, since it was too expensive to travel to Chicago, getting to see her in the context of her family, which it turned out was not so different from mine. After college, she was the first of my friends to marry and have kids, managing motherhood even as she was going to law school, and seeing her settle in as a parent—the calm and patient way she diapered, fed, and soothed her two sons—helped me feel that I'd eventually be able to do it, too.

Over time, our friendship became more rugged and enduring—more barnacle-like—marked not just by how we could still fall apart laughing like college kids, but also by all the ways life could get somber—all that we'd lost and would still need to survive. We lost our other roommate, Suzanne, to cancer five years after we graduated. I lost my father not long after that. There were times early on in my relationship with Barack when the phone would ring late at night, and I'd hear Angela sighing on the line. Her marriage was slowly disintegrating, and she needed to talk. She saw me through infertility; I saw her through divorce. We were pushed in so many ways, and we kept showing up.

Any time I started to feel low at the White House, I'd see if Angela could come for a visit. And she turned up every time, dressed in sunny colors and carrying a bright purse, unfazed by all the security and odd grandeur, her mouth moving before she'd even gotten through the door. Inside her purse, she carried a crumpled piece of paper with a running list of all the things she'd thought of while we were apart and now wanted to talk about. It's been like this for decades now, our conversation never finished.

Angela is part of this wider circle of friends that has carried me through several phases of life now, some of them older friends, some of them newer—the people who always show up. In psychology, this is sometimes referred to as your "social convoy," the set of essential relationships that travel with you through time, protecting you from all sorts of things, as convoys do. Finding and maintaining healthy friendships may not always be the easiest undertaking, especially now that a pandemic has made casual interactions more fraught, but the benefits have been well-established. If you have strong social ties, research shows that you are likely to live longer and with less stress. Scientists have linked having a robust social support system to lower rates of depression, anxiety, and heart disease. Even small social interactions—the kind you have while buying a cup of coffee or out walking a dog—have been shown to boost mental health and create stronger ties inside a community.

I'm not sure how friendship, or even just engaging with another person in the three minutes it takes to buy your morning cup of coffee, has come to feel like a small act of bravery. But increasingly it seems that way. Perhaps, as I mentioned earlier, it's because we now carry with us little rectangular shields against face-to-face sociability—our phones—which I think also shield us from serendipity. Any time we avoid even a small real-life connection, we are to some extent avoiding possibility. We scroll through news or play Candy Crush while waiting for coffee, unaware of and visibly incurious about those around us. We stuff speakers into our ears and tune out the people in the dog park or the grocery store, signaling outwardly that our minds are in other places. As we move through life engaged with our phones, we are also blocking out dozens of tiny but meaningful pathways for connection. We shut out the vibrant life all around us, limiting our access to the up-close warmth of other people. If I'd been staring at Twitter on my phone during my hair appointments, I'd probably never have bothered to speak to Sandy, who is now one of my dearest friends. If Angela had shown up at Princeton focused on keeping Snapchat streaks going with her full crew of preppy high school pals, we may never have grown so close.

I recognize, of course, that there are arguments to be made on the other side. A smartphone is a tool, after all, and the internet is nothing if not a doorway into a giant, practically boundless universe of potential connection. It's introduced many of us to new perspectives, elevated previously unheard voices, and encouraged collaboration and efficiency across all sectors of society. At its very best, it allows us to see more deeply into the world, letting us bear witness to both atrocities and acts of courage or kindness we'd otherwise remain naïve about. It's given us more opportunity to hold powerful entities accountable and to feel empathy and connection across borders and cultures. I've talked to many people who've found online communities that have become vital lifelines to information, comfort, and kinship, helping them to feel less alone.

All this is generally wonderful. And yet, even with this thrumming portal for connection perpetually in our grasp, we remain lonely—maybe lonelier than ever—lost in a stew of content. A great many of us struggle to know what and whom we should believe.

The Edelman Trust Barometer, an annual survey measuring public sentiment in twenty-eight countries around the world, recently concluded that distrust has become "society's default emotion." Meanwhile, social media has been deliberately engineered to leave us thirsty, sending both our youngest and our greatest minds tirelessly questing for likes, clicks, and approval. What this means is that the images we see and the messages we get are often shaped less by what's true and more by what sort of response they'll yield. Outrage sells. Impulsivity is entertaining. As the social psychologist Jonathan Haidt has pointed out, thanks to the design of social media, we are performing more often than we are connecting. And through this, we're being manipulated away from what's real about other people and often what's most real in ourselves.

I happen to believe that our phones don't give us the kind of data we need to overcome our mistrust of other people and other points of view, at least not enough of the time. I often say that it's much harder to hate up close. When we drop our fears about newness and open ourselves to others, even through quick and casual interactions, even while masked—saying hello to someone in an elevator, for example, or chatting in a grocery line—we are practicing an important form of micro-connection. We're signaling a general okayness between us, adding just a drop of social glue to a world that desperately needs it.

When we take time to really engage with others, we are likely to find, too, that our differences are not nearly as profound as we might think, or what certain media channels or well-known personalities would want us to believe. Real-world connections most often tend to cut against stereotypes. They can be remarkably calming, in fact—a small but potent way to reset a bad mood or challenge broader feelings of mistrust. The only thing is that in order to get there, you do first need to lay down your shield.

MY OWN STANDARDS for sociability are fully old-school, tracking back to my childhood kitchen on Euclid Avenue. This was the place I was always allowed to be myself, where my feelings—however silly they may have seemed at the time—were never squelched. I could breeze in from the Wild West of the neighborhood social scene and air out the details of every petty dispute, immature crush, and newly drawn tribal line—knowing that I was in the right place to do it, that I was safe, accepted, and at home. Our kitchen at Euclid functioned like a magnet for others, too: Neighbors dropped by, cousins came over to eat, my brother's gangly teenage friends would plunk themselves down and ask my father for advice, and my mother served peanut butter and jelly sandwiches to all my friends, letting us play jacks on the floor and gossip about school while she worked on dinner. The room itself was tiny, maybe ten feet by ten feet, low-ceilinged, and anchored by a small table with four chairs and a vinyl tablecloth, but the comfort and security it gave me was vast.

I try to provide the same thing for my friends now: a sense of home, a sense of safety and belonging, a sympathetic ear. And it's what I look for inside of friendships, that same enveloping feeling. I refer to my friend group as my "Kitchen Table," the people beyond my family whom I trust, delight in, and rely on most—and for whom I would do anything. These are the friends I've asked to pull up a chair and sit with me in life.

I've also learned that support, love, and validation can come from any- and everywhere—not just from your home. Some of the most important people who've sat at my table are those who are older than I am, who took the time to mentor me when I was young, opening their own lives as examples of what's possible, supplementing what my parents could not offer. Czerny, my high-energy work-study supervisor at Princeton, took me under her wing and let me observe her movements as a single parent and professional woman, providing me with a meaningful, up-close lesson on how to find balance in a busy life. Valerie Jarrett later helped me to make the most important career transition of my life, moving out of corporate law and into public service, and has become like a big sister to me, personally and professionally. She has shepherded me through all sorts of transitions, counsels me when I'm trying to make decisions, and calms me down when I'm upset. She's allowed me to be a barnacle on her life.

My table also includes a broad circle of younger people whose voices I value, who help keep my perspective fresh and challenge me to keep up with what's new. They talk to me about everything from what's cool in nail design to how to appreciate a dembow beat. They have attempted to help me understand both Tinder and TikTok. And they'll call me out when I say something that strikes them as old-school or unenlightened. My young friends keep me learning all the time.

A Kitchen Table, in general, is never stagnant. Friends will come and go, taking on more or less importance as you move through different phases of life. You may have a small group of friends, or just a few one-on-one friendships. All of that is okay. What matters most is the quality of your relationships. It's good to be discerning about who you trust, who you bring close. With new relationships, I find myself quietly assessing whether I feel safe and whether, inside the context of a budding friendship, I feel seen and appreciated for who I am. With our friends, we are always looking for very simple reassurances that we matter, that our light is recognized and our voice is heard—and we owe our friends the same. I want to say, too, that it's okay to step back from or downsize a difficult friendship. Sometimes we have to let certain friends go, or at least diminish our reliance on them.

Not all of the people who sit at my Kitchen Table know one another well; some have never even met. But collectively, they are powerful. I lean on each individual at different times and in different ways. Which is another thing worth recognizing about friendship: No one person, no one relationship, will fulfill your every need. Not every friend can offer you safety or support on every day. Not everyone can, or will, show up precisely when or how you need them to. And this is why it's good to always continue making room at your table, to keep yourself open to gathering more friends. You will never not need them, and you will never stop learning from them. I can promise you that.

The best way to be a friend to someone, as I see it, is to revel in their uniqueness, to appreciate each person for what they bring, receiving them simply as themselves. This sometimes means letting friends off the hook for what they can't or don't bring. I have active friends who want to climb mountains and take trips, and others who are happiest to laze on the couch with a cup of tea. There are some I'd call in a crisis and some I would not. Some friends give advice; others regale me with stories of their dating lives. A few love nothing more than a great late-night party; others go to bed religiously at nine P.M. I have friends who are excellent about remembering birthdays and meaningful dates, and friends who are scattershot about keeping track of that stuff but who will give you the gift of their sincere and full attention when with you in a room. What matters is that I can see and appreciate them, and they can see and appreciate me. My friends give me perspective. They help show me who I am. As one of the characters in Toni Morrison's novel *Beloved* says of another, "She is a friend of my mind. . . . The pieces I am, she gather them and give them back to me in all the right order."

Over time, too, a number of friends from different parts of my life have come to be close with one another, in part due to my drillmaster tendencies, my insistence that we gather as a group whenever anyone can swing it. Together, we have formed what I think of as a circle of well-wishers, a group in which we each are always rooting for one another's success. We announce our victories and get feedback on our challenges. We push through the hard stuff and nudge one another in small ways, through encouragement, through thoughtful listening. With my friends, the conversation is never finished. We are all guests at one another's tables, sharing the privilege of intimacy and honesty.

"Don't do life alone," I often tell my daughters. Especially for those who live with differentness, it's important to create spaces where you feel safe and at home in order to survive. It's worth working to find people with whom you can remove your armor and shed your worries. With your closest friends, you can say all the things you've held back in other spaces. You can show your unbridled anger, your fear of injustices and slights. Because you can't hold it all in. You can't process the challenges of being different all on your own. It's just too big, too painful, to keep inside. To try to carry it alone can be corrosive, draining.

Your Kitchen Table is your safe haven, a place to rest in the storm. It's where you can pause the endless and exhausting pursuit of overcoming everyday challenges and safely dissect the barrage of indignities that comes your way. It's where you can scream, yell, cuss, and cry. It's a place to lick your wounds and replenish your strength. Your Kitchen Table is where you go for oxygen so that you can breathe again.

WHEN BARACK WAS president, he was surrounded by wonderful colleagues in the West Wing—dialed-in, super-intelligent cabinet members and staffers who together made a high-functioning team and an excellent support system. But still, I saw the loneliness of the presidency up close—the massive weight my husband carried as chief decision maker, how the stresses mounted without relief. He'd pour himself into addressing one crisis only to have another emerge. He was routinely blamed for things he couldn't control, sometimes excoriated by those impatient for change. He was dealing with a contentious Congress, a country wounded by a recession, and all sorts of issues overseas. I would watch him head off to his study in the evenings after we'd had dinner, knowing he'd be at his desk until two in the morning—alone, awake, and trying to stay on top of it all.

He wasn't lonely, exactly—life was too full for that—but he did need escape. I worried about the unrelenting nature of the job, what the stress might do to his health. A few years into the presidency, I surprised Barack for his birthday by inviting about ten of his guy friends to Camp David for a weekend to celebrate and have some fun. It was August. Congress was not in session. He would still, of course, be traveling with a consort of advisers and getting his daily briefings, but I figured that at least he could try to unplug a little.

And unplug he did. I'm not sure I've ever seen someone dive so quickly into having fun as my husband did on that weekend, which I took to be a clear indication of how badly he'd needed the reprieve. His high school pals had come from Hawaii; some college friends came, as did some of his best pals from Chicago. What did they do? They played. As Sasha, Malia, and I, along with a handful of other wives and kids who'd come, mostly hung out by the pool, the men hurled themselves into every activity Camp David had to offer.

It was like they'd been given a get-out-of-jail-free card that sprung them from their work and family obligations, and much as it was with my friends and our Boot Camp weekends, they weren't going to waste a second of that time. They played basketball. They played cards and threw darts. They did some skeet shooting. They bowled. They had a home-run derby and a football toss. They kept score on every last thing, trash-talking their way through each event, boisterously reviewing various plays and upsets late into the night.

"Campathalon," we came to call it, and it's become an institution in Barack's life, an annual gathering we now host on Martha's Vineyard, which has grown to include trophies and an opening ceremony. For my hardworking, sober-minded husband, it's a reprieve he now counts on, a return to the lightness of childhood, a chance to catch up and be silly with those he holds dear. It's like a schoolyard recess, a time to run free and a little wild, playing with his friends. It connects him to his joy.

Life has shown me that strong friendships are most often the result of strong intentions. Your table needs to be deliberately built, deliberately populated, and deliberately tended to. Not only do you have to say *I am curious about you* to someone who might be a friend, but you should also invest in that curiosity—setting aside time and energy for your friendship to grow and deepen, privileging it ahead of the things that will pile up and demand your attention in ways that friendship seldom does. It helps, I've found, to create rituals and routines around friendship—weekly coffees, monthly cocktails, annual gatherings. My friend Kathleen and I keep regular morning dates to walk by the river. I have a group that's done an annual mother-daughter ski weekend for more than a decade, and the event is cemented into everyone's calendars and protected at all costs, even by our daughters, who now understand what having a Kitchen Table can mean in their own lives. My Boot Camp weekends have become less frequent and also less rigorous than they once were, but still, I like it when we sweat together.

Researchers at the University of Virginia once set out to explore a certain theory about friendship. They strapped heavy backpacks onto a group of volunteers and one by one positioned each person in front of a big hill, as if they were going to climb it. Each volunteer was asked to estimate how steep it was. Half of them stood alone in front of the hill; the other half stood next to someone they'd identified as a friend. And consistently, those who were with a friend viewed the hill as less steep, the climb ahead less difficult. When people who'd been friends a long time stood in front of the hill, the results became even more pronounced: The slope only seemed to flatten out more. This is the power of having others alongside you. It's a reason to tend to your friends.

And that's what I most want to tell those who might be sitting with hesitancy at the edge of any new friendship, who are holding themselves back. It's what worries me when I hear from young people who feel too nervous to take the risk or endure the awkwardness of finding and getting to know new friends. I want to tell them that there is both richness and safety to be found in other people if you're willing to extend your curiosity that way, if you can keep yourself open to it. Your friends become your ecosystem. When you make them, you are putting more daisies in your life. You are putting more birds in the trees.

Barack is my best friend, my true love, and my life's greatest disrupter.

CHAPTER SIX

PARTNERING WELL

L AST YEAR, OUR two daughters rented an apartment together in Los Angeles. They both happened to be living in the city—Sasha going to college, Malia working in an entry-level writing job—and they'd gone out and found a small place in a quiet neighborhood that was convenient for them both. I was charmed by the fact that they'd chosen each other as room-mates. It makes me happy to think we've raised siblings who, now in their early twenties, have also managed to be friends.

On the first day of the first month of their new lease, the two of them moved their belongings into the empty apartment. Most of what they had, it seemed, was clothes. Like many peo-ple their age, our daughters had until that point been largely itinerant, aside from those months spent locked down by the pandemic. They'd moved between college dorm rooms and furnished sublet apartments, never traveling with more than could reasonably fit into the trunk of a car. A few times a year, one or both of them would land back at home with us for a week or two of vacation, swan-diving into the comforts of our grown-up existence, reveling in the full fridge, the absence of roommates and easy access to laundry, the loafing sweetness of a resident dog. During these interludes, they'd fuel up on food, sleep, privacy, and family time. Then they'd stash a few belongings in a closet, swapping out a set of winter clothes for a set of summer clothes or vice versa, and leave again, fluttering off like migratory birds.

Now, though, things were changing. They'd found a grown-up place for themselves, something that felt a little less temporary. Our daughters themselves were starting to appear more grown-up, more anchored into adult life.

For the first month or so, I caught glimpses of their home-decorating efforts over our video calls. I'd notice a cute new chair they'd picked up somewhere, or some framed photos hung artfully on the wall. They got themselves a vacuum cleaner. They bought throw pillows, towels, and also a set of steak knives, which I found amusing since neither of them was all that big on cooking or eating meat—or cooking much at all, really. But the point was, they were building a home, deliberately and proudly. They were learning for themselves how "home" is done.

One night I was talking to Sasha over FaceTime but quickly got distracted by Malia, who was moving around in the background, running a Swiffer duster over a shelf loaded with trinkets and books. She was dusting their belongings! It looked so adult, even if I couldn't help but notice that she hadn't yet learned to pick up or move the objects on the shelf so that they could be dusted on all sides.

But hey, she was halfway dusting! My heart felt ready to burst.

As soon as we were able, Barack and I went out to L.A. for a visit. Sasha and Malia showed us around their new apartment with glee. They'd done a nice job with it, having poked around yard sales and shopped at a nearby IKEA, watching their budget. They were sleeping on box springs and mattresses with no bed frame, but they'd found some pretty bedspreads to cover it all. They'd picked up a set of quirky end tables at a flea market. They had a dining room table, though hadn't yet found affordable chairs.

We were all going out to eat dinner at a restaurant, but first they insisted on serving us a drink. As Barack and I sat on the couch, Malia produced a charcuterie board she'd put together, announcing that she'd never before understood how outrageously expensive cheese can be.

"And I didn't even get any of the super-fancy ones!" she said.

Sasha attempted to fix us a couple of weak martinis—*Wait, you know how to make martinis?*—and served them in water glasses, first laying down a couple of newly purchased coasters so that we wouldn't mark up their brand-new coffee table with our drinks.

I watched all this with some astonishment. It's not that I'm surprised that our kids have grown up, exactly, but somehow the whole scene—the coasters, in particular—signaled a different sort of landmark, the type of thing every parent spends years scanning for, which is evidence of common sense.

As Sasha set down our drinks that night, I thought about all the coasters she and her sister hadn't bothered to use when they were under our care, all the times over the years I'd tried to get water marks out of various tables, including at the White House.

But the dynamics had changed. We were at *their* table now. They owned it, and they were protecting it. Clearly, they had learned.

HOW DO ANY of us turn into adults, with real grown-up lives and real grown-up relationships? Mostly through trial and error, it would seem. By just figuring it out. Many of us, I think, puzzle out our identities only over time, figuring out who we are and what we need in order to get by. We approximate our way into maturity, often following some loose idea of what we believe grown-up life is supposed to look like.

We practice and learn, learn and practice. We make mistakes and then start over again. For a long time, a lot feels experimental, unsettled. We try on different ways of being. We sample and discard different attitudes, approaches, influences, and tools for living until, piece by piece, we begin to better understand what suits us best, what helps us most.

I've been thinking about this a lot recently as I watch our girls settle into their West Coast life, stocking up on housewares and cutlery, dusting the furniture as best they know how.

They are practicing. They are learning. They are mid-process, partway to where they'd like to get. Each day, in some small way, they refine their conception of who they are as individuals and how they want to live, trying to understand where and how and with whom they feel most settled and safe.

Socially speaking, Sasha and Malia are in that slightly wild, slightly ragtag flea-market stage of life, where new friends are exciting treasures that can be found almost anywhere. I remember this phase from my own early twenties. The hunt is fun, the bazaar is always colorful, and the sense of discovery is generally pretty thrilling. At the same time, though, they are unconsciously engaged in a more serious, more commonsense pursuit: They're learning who they can lean on and who they enjoy, which relationships they most want to invest in and which will carry them through life. They are beginning to build their own Kitchen Tables.

It's no different with romantic relationships. Malia and Sasha have been doing precisely what Barack and I were each doing at their age, which is dating around. (I'm told, by the way, that "dating around" is no longer the sort of terminology used by people my kids' ages.) What I mean by it, in general, is that they've gone out with different people and tried on different styles of relationships. It's just one part of the life-building that's happening for them these days, a piece of the larger puzzle.

The truth is that I'm hoping our daughters won't rush out of the flea market too quickly. I hope they will instead linger a while, allowing their relationships to remain fluid and youthful. What I want more than anything is for them to prioritize learning the skills of independence—how to make a living, how to keep themselves healthy, fed, and happy—well ahead of signing up for a lifetime spent with another person. I tell them to focus on becoming whole people, able to stand on their own. When you know your own light, you are then better prepared to share it with another person. But you have to practice your way through all of it.

I'm rooting for my daughters to learn their way into maturity in their relationships, not worrying about wringing some clear result from it. I don't want them to see marriage as some sort of trophy that must be hunted and won, or to believe that a wedding is the sort of spectacle they need to properly launch a fulfilling life, or to ever feel that having children is any sort of requirement. My hope instead is that they'll experience different levels of commitment, figuring out how to end relationships that aren't working and how to start new ones that seem promising. I want them to know how to navigate conflicts, to understand the heady thrills of intimacy, and to have a sense of what it's like to get your heart shaken up. When and if my kids do choose someone, finally, to be with for life, I want them to do it from a place of strength, truly knowing who they are and what they need.

I won't reveal any more about my kids' romantic lives here, out of respect for their privacy (and because surely they would kill me). But I will say that it's been beautiful to watch them practice and learn.

What do I most hope for them?

I hope they find home, whatever that ends up looking like.

PEOPLE OFTEN REACH out to me seeking relationship advice. They remark on photographs they've seen of me and Barack together—the two of us laughing, or sharing a look, appearing content to be side by side—deducing that we enjoy each other's company. They ask how we have managed to stay both married and unmiserable for thirty years now. I want to say, *Yes,*

truly, it's a surprise to us, too, sometimes! And really, I'm not joking. We have our issues, of course, but I love the man, and he loves me, now, still, and seemingly forever.

Our love is not perfect, but it's real and we're committed to it. This particular certainty sits parked like a grand piano in the middle of every room we enter. We are, in many ways, very different people, my husband and I. He's a night owl who enjoys solitary pursuits. I'm an early bird who loves a crowded room. In my opinion, he spends too much time golfing. In his opinion, I watch too much lowbrow TV. But between us, there's a loving assuredness that's as simple as knowing the other person is there to stay, no matter what. This is what I think people pick up on in those photos: that tiny triumph we get to feel, knowing that despite having spent half our lives together now, despite all the ways we aggravate each other and all the ways we are different, neither one of us has walked away. We're still here. *We remain.*

Over the course of my adult life, I've lived in a number of places, but as far as I'm concerned, I've only ever had one real home. My home is my family. My home is Barack.

Our partnership is something we have created together. We inhabit it every day, making improvements to it as we're able, sometimes letting it exist "as is" for stretches when we're preoccupied with other concerns. Our marriage is what we launch from and land in, a place where we can each be thoroughly, comfortably, often annoyingly ourselves. We've come to accept that this sphere we dwell in together, the energy and emotion between us, may not always be tidy and ordered, or exactly how one or both of us wants it, but the plain and reassuring fact is, it endures. For us, it's become a solid piece of certainty in a world where certainty seems exceptionally hard to come by.

A lot of the questions I get from people over social media or in letters and emails seem to revolve around this premise of certainty in relationships, how much of it we're supposed to feel, at what point, and with what sort of vigor and degree of fluctuation. How am I supposed to know when I've found the right partner, the sort of person who is worth committing to? Am I wrong to sometimes dislike my partner? How do I do a good job loving someone when my own parents provided a not-so-great example? What happens when there's conflict, irritation, hardship, challenge?

I hear from some who are pondering marriage, thinking that getting married will fix certain problems in their relationship. Or they're pondering having a baby, thinking that'll fix their marriage. I hear sometimes from those who are pondering divorce, wondering whether to stay with or run from a relationship that feels sour or troubled. I hear from still others who think that marriage, in general, is a boring, patriarchal, and outmoded tradition. And I hear from young folks who are worried about making mistakes in relationships, or have *already* made mistakes and are now wondering what to do.

"hey mrs michelle," a young woman named Lexi wrote me from Alabama not long ago, "i'm having a lot of boy problems . . ." And she poured her heart out from there.

The honest truth is, I don't have answers to these questions or prescriptions to offer for anyone's individual challenges. The only love story I know is the one I happen to live inside every day. Your path toward certainty—if that's even what you're after—will look different from mine, just as your conception of home and who belongs there with you will always be unique to you.

Only slowly do most of us figure out what we need in intimate relationships and what we are able to give to them. We practice. We learn. We mess up. We sometimes acquire tools that don't actually serve us. Many of us make a few questionable investments early on. We might, for example, buy a bunch of steak knives, assuming that's just what we're supposed to do.

We obsess, overthink, and misplace our energy. Sometimes we follow bad advice or ignore good advice. We retreat when hurt. We armor up when scared. We might attack when provoked or yield when ashamed. You may also decide, as many do, that you are perfectly happy and fulfilled when not paired up with anyone. And if this is the case, I hope you'll celebrate it for what it is—a completely valid and successful life choice. A lot of us, too, will unconsciously mimic the relationships we were raised around—whatever version of home we knew as kids—and this, of course, can work out either beautifully, or horribly, or somewhere in the middle. Real and lasting love, I think, happens mostly in the realm of in-between. Together, you are answering the question: *Who are we and who do we want to be?*

THESE DAYS, I'LL sometimes catch sight of my husband from a slight distance and feel as if I'm peering through the scrim of time. What I see is a gray-haired, slightly less scrawny, slightly more world-weary version of the twenty-seven-year-old guy who arrived as a summer associate at my corporate law office decades ago, damp from a rainstorm, having traveled without an umbrella, and only a little bit sheepish for having shown up late to his first day of work. What made his smile so memorable? Why did his voice sound so good?

He was charming then. He is charming now. He was minorly famous then—a law student whose intellect was creating something of a stir in legal circles—and he is, I suppose, majorly famous now. But all that said, he's really the exact same person, with the same poise, the same heart and hang-ups, the same perennial struggle to be punctual or to remember something as basic and functional as an umbrella on a rainy day. He's that same quixotic, alternately smooth and geeky person I found in the waiting area of the law firm all those years ago, whose hand I shook, whose lanky height and unusual countenance I took in for the first time, not yet understanding that I was looking at my truest love and my life's greatest disrupter.

Like a lot of people, I had ideas about what marriage would be like, and few of them turned out to be right. When I was a kid, my friends and I used to play fortune-telling games like MASH, which forecast where we'd live, what kind of car we'd drive, and how many kids we'd have, or another that involved folding up a piece of paper, origami-style, covered with hidden options for who we would marry written under the flaps. We'd giggle and gasp at the various results: Would I really marry Marlon Jackson from the Jackson 5, live in California, and drive a station wagon? Would my friend Terry actually have nine kids with our classmate Teddy and live in a mansion in Florida?

What I knew was that the possibilities seemed both grand and endless. What I *thought* I knew was that the end result would be a dreamy spectacle of a wedding followed by years of hot bliss and a passionate, never-settle-for-less style of living. Because wasn't that how it was supposed to be? I was too young, still, to see my own parents' marriage as something I wouldn't mind having for myself one day. They were committed and companionable, running a serviceable and friendly joint operation, governed by common sense. They made each other laugh. They got all the chores done. At Valentine's Day and on my mom's birthday every year, my dad would drive over to the Evergreen Plaza shopping center and buy her a fancy new outfit, delivering it to her gift-wrapped with a bow.

I understood they were generally happy, but I had also watched a lot of *All My Children,* absorbing the legendary hot-and-cold passions of Erica Kane, which made the union between my parents seem quiet and a little uninteresting. I instead let myself imagine the fantasy-dream version of marriage and family life for myself, more resembling the glamorous romances my friends and I used to act out with our Barbies and Kens. I also knew, having observed my grandparents, that marriages didn't always work out. My mom's parents had separated long before I was born and, as far as I knew, never spoke to each other again. My dad's parents had lived apart for most of his childhood but then had somehow, surprisingly, patched things up.

I can see now that the examples were all around me, the indications that long-term partnership is rarely glamorous or smooth. My mother still describes the first shouting match she ever had with my dad, which occurred soon after their wedding in 1960, when she was twenty-three and he was twenty-five. Following a short honeymoon, they'd moved in together for the very first time and realized, rather suddenly, that they were arriving into this bonded partnership with two sets of habits, two baked-in ways of doing things. What was their first fight about? It was not about money, or having children, or anything that was happening in the world at the time. No, it was about which way the toilet paper should hang on its roller in the bathroom—whether the loose end should be draped over the top of the roll or fall beneath it.

Dad came from an "under" house, whereas Mom was raised in an "over" house, and at least for a short while there, the conflict felt epic and unsolvable. With only two options available, one of them would have to concede and accept the other's way of doing it. An argument can seem petty, but in many instances, what's behind it is not. In merging your life with someone else's, you are suddenly looking at—and often being asked to adapt to—another family's history and patterns of behavior. In the case of the Great Toilet Paper Dispute of 1960, it was my mother who ultimately relinquished her position, deciding it was far too stupid a thing for anyone to be yelling about. She simply chose to let it go. Our family thereafter lived peaceably as an "under" family. The issue was never revisited, at least not until Craig and I each grew up and found partners of our own. (The Obamas are "over" people, as it turns out, and remain so to this day.) Marriage is full of high-stakes/low-stakes negotiations like this.

In *Becoming,* I wrote about how despite the generally steady nature of their relationship, my mom used to consider the possibility of leaving my father. Every so often, she'd put herself through a kind of thought exercise, letting herself daydream about what would happen if she chose to walk out the door on Euclid Avenue and find herself a different life, with a different man, in a different place. What would have happened if her origami fortune-telling game had unfolded a different way? What if she'd ended up with a millionaire, or a mysterious man from the South, or a certain boy she'd known in junior high school?

She allowed herself these thoughts usually in the springtime, having endured another icy cold winter, another season of dark days spent largely indoors in our cramped little space. Different sounded pretty nice about then. Different was akin to the fresh air floating in through the windows when it finally got warm enough to open them again. Different was an engaging sort of reverie, a pretend honeymoon going on in her head.

And then she'd laugh to herself, imagining what kind of fresh hell a mysterious man from the South would have wrought in her life, knowing that the boy from junior high had his own pile of messes, and that any millionaire would surely show up with plenty of issues as well.

And with that, the pretend honeymoon would end, and she'd go back to real life, back to my dad.

It was her way, I think, of quietly renewing something in her heart, remembering the decent and loving home she had, her reasons to remain.

IF YOU CHOOSE to try to make a life with another person, you will live by that choice. You'll find yourself having to choose again and again to remain rather than run. It helps if you enter into a committed relationship prepared to work, ready to be humbled, and willing to accept and even enjoy living in that in-between space, bouncing between the poles of beautiful and horrible, sometimes in the span of a single conversation, sometimes over the course of years. And inside of that choice and those years, you'll almost certainly come to see that there's no such thing as a fifty-fifty balance. Instead, it'll be like beads on an abacus, sliding back and forth—the math rarely tidy, the equation never quite solved. A relationship is dynamic this way, full of change, always evolving. At no point will both of you feel like things are perfectly fair and equal. Someone will always be adjusting. Someone will always be sacrificing. One person may be up while the other is down; one might bear more of the financial pressures while the other handles caregiving and family obligations. Those choices and the stresses that go along with them are real. I've come to realize, though, that life happens in seasons. Your fulfillment—in love, family, and career—rarely happens all at once. In a strong partnership, both people will take their turns at compromise, building that shared sense of home together, there in the in-between.

Regardless of how wildly and deeply in love you are, you will be asked to onboard a whole lot of your partner's foibles. You will be required to ignore all sorts of minor irritations and at least a few major ones, too, trying to assert love and constancy over all of it—over all the rough spots and inevitable disruptions. You will need to do this as often and as compassionately as you can. *And* you will need to be doing it with someone who is equally able and willing to create the same latitude and show the same forbearance toward you—to love you despite all the baggage you show up with, despite what you look like and how you behave when you are at your absolute worst.

It's an insane and seemingly against-the-odds proposition,

if you think about it. And it doesn't always work. (It *shouldn't* always work: If you are being harmed inside a relationship, it is time to remove yourself from it.) But when it does work, it can feel like an actual, honest-to-god miracle, which is what love is, after all. That's the whole point. Any long-term partnership, really, is an act of stubborn faith.

When Barack and I committed to a life together, it wasn't because there was some set of established guarantees. I couldn't really have forecast much about how anything would go. We weren't yet financially secure; we both had years' worth of student loans still to pay off. There were no predictable outcomes, on any front. I married him, in fact, knowing that he was a swerver, someone who would always—predictably!—choose the less-certain route toward fulfillment. You could count on the guy to reject any sort of standard path and challenge anything that came too easily. He was committed to juggling different jobs, turning down cushy corporate positions because he wanted to write books, teach, and stay aligned with his values. Neither one of us had wealth in our families to fall back on. We soon learned that even our ability to have children came with a question mark, beginning a rough several years of fertility struggles. And then, too, there was that wild, flying motorcycle ride of his political career.

We entered into all that chaos together, certain of only one thing, and that was that we'd be better off facing it as a team.

I LEARNED EARLY on that a partner is not a fix for your issues, or a filler of your needs. People are who they are; you can't make someone become something they don't want to be, or into a type of person they have never had modeled for them. I wanted a mate who was led by his own values, independent of my love. I wanted someone who was honest because he valued honesty, faithful because he valued faithfulness.

I tell this to my daughters now: You don't want to settle down with someone because you're looking for a breadwinner, or a caregiver, or a parent for your kids, or a rescue from your problems. Those arrangements, in my experience, rarely work out well. The goal, instead, is to find someone who will do the work *with* you, not for you, contributing on all fronts and in all ways. When someone wants to play just one role, declaring anything like "I make the money, so don't expect me to change diapers," my advice would be to start running for the hills. I tell my girls that a successful partnership is like a winning basketball team, made up of two deft individuals with fully developed and interchangeable sets of skills. Each player has to know not just how to shoot, but also how to dribble, pass, and defend.

That doesn't mean there aren't weaknesses or differences you'll compensate for in each other. It's just that together, you'll have to cover the full court, keeping yourselves versatile over time. A partnership doesn't actually change who you are, even as it challenges you to be accommodating of another person's needs. Just as Barack hasn't changed much in the thirty-three years since we met, neither have I. I am still the same sensible striver who first shook his hand, and he remains the bookish optimist who thinks on three planes at once.

The change is in what's between us, the million small adjustments, compromises, and sacrifices we've each made in order to accommodate the close presence of the other, this hybrid energy of him and me together—us two—now seasoned and battle-tested over decades. Whatever small stirring happened between us on that first day of our acquaintance, whatever seed of mutual curiosity got planted in the moment we shook hands and started to talk, *that's* the thing we have grown and matured over time into certainty. That's the ongoing miracle, the conversation still under way, the home in which we live. He's him. I'm me. It's just that we now know each other. Really, really, really well.

I've always tried to help people see past the glittery side of my life with Barack and get a better look at our realness. I've made a fairly deliberate effort to blow holes in the myth that my husband is a perfect man, or ours is a perfect marriage, or that love, in general, is any sort of breezy endeavor. I've written about how Barack and I went to—and desperately needed—couples counseling as we began to get prickly and distant with each other when our kids were young and we were both feeling maxed out. I've joked about all the times I've been fed up enough with my husband that I felt like pushing him out a window, all the regular and petty resentments I am capable of nursing, even now, probably forever. True intimacy can be aggravating. And yet we stay.

As much as I've spoken often and openly about our unpolished parts, some seem to prefer the façade. I once got lambasted by a *New York Times* columnist for discussing the fact that my husband was not a god, but rather a mortal who sometimes forgets to pick his socks up off the floor or put the butter back in the fridge. My personal feeling about this remains unchanged, and I think it's true of people in general: We only hurt ourselves when we hide our realness away.

I HAVE A friend whom I'll call Carissa, who recently spent more than a year dodging a lot of realness with a man she was dating. Carissa is in her thirties, a gorgeous African American woman who owns her own business, has lots of friends, and is by all measures a successful person. The only thing was, she didn't like being single. She wanted a partner. She hoped eventually to have kids. She'd met this guy online and liked him a lot. They started going out. They took a whirlwind trip to the Caribbean and had a great time. They came home and continued to see each other, though they were also both busy with their jobs and their own set of friends. The idea was, Carissa said, that they were "keeping it casual."

What she didn't fully realize until later was that she and this man were essentially having the same first date over and over again, resisting any impulse to grow closer emotionally. They were stuck inside of "casual," having fun to be sure, but never risking something as simple as a small disagreement or a probing conversation, something that might break either of them open or possibly require follow-up. Casual was supposed to mean easy. Being together was supposed to involve no work or discomfort. But the thing is, the "real" always shows up. It will find you, one way or another.

More than a year into their relationship, Carissa invited both her man and one of her closest girlfriends to dinner one evening at her apartment, introducing them for the first time.

Over the course of the meal, she watched as her naturally out-going friend innocently peppered the guy with earnest questions, almost methodically surfacing all sorts of information that was brand new to Carissa. He'd had a troubled relationship with his father, it turned out. He'd felt unloved as a child. He'd struggled to commit in past relationships.

None of this was necessarily a problem. It was just all new, a layer of this person Carissa had never before seen. She'd been too afraid to go looking for it, she realized. She'd never asked him much of anything, nor had he asked her anything deep or real about herself. For months now, they'd been hooking up while also avoiding emotional intimacy, each of them trying to stay invulnerable. Carissa had convinced herself that she was good with "casual," even if casual went against her own life goals. And did the guy actually want casual? She didn't even know. They had never really discussed any of it in depth. It felt too late to even start. It was like they'd just spent a year eating candy instead of meals.

What Carissa came to see was that she'd hidden herself behind a façade, pretending that she wasn't yearning for more or better, all the while thinking that the mere passage of time somehow counted as progress in the relationship.

Later, after they'd finally broken up, she told me she'd held herself back from showing too much curiosity or asking about commitment because she was convinced it would make her seem "high-maintenance" and therefore radioactive. She could be ambitious in her career, fastidious about the details of her everyday life, but when it came to being with a man, those same qualities would, she felt, work against her.

Carissa hadn't wanted to show herself as willing to put effort into a relationship, worried it would somehow make her unworthy of further attention from a guy it turned out she hardly knew, anyway.

"I didn't want to seem thirsty or needy," she said. "I was just trying to play it cool."

But playing it cool, in the end, had gotten her—gotten them—nowhere.

I TALK TO young people sometimes who have made an art of embracing the casual and playing it cool, avoiding the fact that being real and vulnerable is a pillar of true intimacy. They haven't grasped the idea that there's room for depth and real-ness in relationships, even during the flea-market phase of life. They may spend their twenties hooking up but not practicing the basics of commitment and good communication, the no-tion that it's possible to share real feelings and real vulnerabil-ity. They eat a whole lot of candy but build no muscle. And then when it's time to get serious, when they are imagining a family life and a more settled existence, they are suddenly, often frantically, learning these skills for the first time, realizing that there is little that's casual or cool about a lasting commit-ment.

What stood out right away about Barack was that he had no interest in being casual. His forthrightness with me was even a little startling at first. Before meeting him, I had dated men who were less sure of themselves and what they wanted. I'd gone out with a player or two—guys who were nice to look at and exciting to be around, but who were often peering over my shoulder, trying to see who else was in a room, what further connections could be made. My early loves taught me the same lessons as anyone's: I'd been cheated on and lied to a few times. This was during my own flea-market stage of life, when I myself was trying on different ways of being, working to equip myself for the life to come. I was uncertain in those first relationships. I could be noncommittal. I was still learning, figuring my own self out, trying to make sense of my own needs and wants.

Barack was different from anyone I'd known before. He was direct and clear about what he wanted—unusual in his certainty, at least when it came to me. If I hadn't had a handful of practice relationships already, I probably wouldn't have recognized how unusual it was.

"I like you," he told me, several weeks after we first met and had gone out for a few professional lunches. "I think we should start dating. I'd love to take you out."

Even as I waffled over whether to cave in to my growing attraction to him, fretting about the propriety of an office relationship, Barack was unflappable and quietly persistent, convinced we were a good match. He gave me the space to think it over, but remained clear on the fact that I was interesting to him, that he liked being around me, that he wanted more. He shared his point of view in much the same manner I'd see him do years later when occupying the Oval Office, tenting his fingers together and laying out his thoughts like a set of well-reasoned bullet points:

Number one, he thought I was smart and beautiful.

Number two, he was pretty sure I liked talking to him, too.

Number three, this would hardly count as an office romance because he was just a summer hire.

Number four, he wanted to spend time with me and nobody else. And given that he'd be back at law school in eight weeks or so, our time was actually short.

So really, why not?

With him, there would be none of the standard cat-and-mouse romantic gamesmanship. He was uninterested in playing around. Instead, he took the guesswork right out of it. He put his feelings on the table and left them there, as if to say, *Here's my interest. Here's my respect. This is my starting point. We can only go forward from here.*

This mix of candor and certainty was, I have to admit, flattering and refreshing. It was also sexy as hell.

His certainty became our foundation. I'd never gone out with anyone who was so intentional before, so free of doubt, so utterly unconcerned with playing it cool. He asked me questions about my feelings, my ideas, my family; he answered all my questions about his. With him, I could be thirsty—for his story, his affection, his support—without feeling unsure about it, because he, too, was thirsty. Neither one of us was cool in the least. For me, this felt like a whole new world opening up. The inquisitiveness between us helped to erase my self-consciousness. Gone were the days when I'd waste energy wondering if the person I was dating was going to call me back. Gone were the insecurities I might bring to a party, or into the bedroom, or to a deep conversation about what I wanted from life. I was suddenly stronger inside myself. I felt liked. I felt respected. I felt seen.

Were we in love? It was too soon to say. But we were madly and deeply curious. And it's that curiosity that drove us forward through that summer and into the fall, when Barack went back to school on the East Coast, and I tunneled once again into the grind of my legal work. But I was walking around a little differently now, feeling as if some new switch had been flipped on. This guy, his curiosity, added light to my world.

A few months into our relationship, Barack invited me to come home with him to Honolulu over Christmas, so I could see the place where he'd grown up. I immediately said yes. I'd never been to Hawaii. I'd never even imagined getting myself to Hawaii. My only conception of the place was a kind of pop-media fantasy involving ukuleles, tiki torches, grass skirts, and coconuts. My impressions were largely if not entirely derived from the Brady Bunch's three-episode visit to Oahu in 1972, in which Greg took up surfing, Jan and Marcia wore bikinis, and Alice threw out her back learning to hula.

I incorporated what I thought I knew about Hawaii into my daydreams about what spending Christmas there would be like. Barack and I were still in the fantasy stage of our new relationship, so it all felt fitting. We hadn't yet had a fight. Our phone calls were for the most part gooey and joyful, loaded with a certain anticipatory lust. I'd hang up with him, knowing that Hawaii, of course, would be the perfect setting for our first holiday together. As Christmas approached, the air in Chicago grew bitingly cold, the sun setting a bit earlier each day. I left for work in the dark and came home in the dark, all the while stoking my heart with thoughts of what lay ahead, the warm breezes and wafting palm trees, naps on the beach and early-evening mai tais, a series of languorous vacation days spent idly falling in love.

THROUGH THE WINDOW of the airplane, Oahu appeared dreamy and just as I'd imagined it, the reality sliding over the fantasy in a near-perfect overlay. As we circled Honolulu on a late-December afternoon, I had Barack sitting next to me and paradise down below. I could see the glittering aquamarine waters of the Pacific, lush green volcanic mountains, and the curving white arc of Waikiki Beach. I could hardly believe it was happening.

From the airport, we caught a taxi to the apartment building on South Beretania Street where Barack had lived with his grandparents during his teenage years while his mother was mostly away, doing anthropological fieldwork in Indonesia. I remember on that car ride being struck by how surprisingly big and urban Honolulu seemed to be, a city stacked next to a body of water not unlike Chicago was. There was a freeway, traffic, and skyscrapers, none of which I remembered seeing during the Brady Bunch's visit, nor had they factored into my daydreams. My mind clicked furiously, taking everything in, processing it like data. I was twenty-five years old and seeing this place for the first time, alongside this guy whom I felt I knew and yet didn't fully know, trying to make sense of what all of this was. We passed a series of tightly packed high-rise apartment complexes, where you could see terraces cluttered with bikes and potted plants, people's laundry strung up and drying in the sun. I remember thinking, *Oh, right, this is real life.*

Barack's grandparents' building was also a high-rise, though not a huge one. It was modernist and blocklike, made of functional concrete. Across the street was a historic church with a wide green lawn. We took an elevator to the tenth floor, carrying our bags through the humid air along an outdoor corridor on the exterior of the building, until finally, after many hours of travel, we stood at the door to their apartment, the home Barack had lived in the longest so far in his life.

Within minutes, I'd met the family: Barack's mom, his grandparents—Toot and Gramps—and his younger sister, Maya, who was nineteen at the time. (A year or so later, I'd meet the Kenyan side of his family, including his sister Auma, with whom he'd grown especially close.) They were friendly to me, curious about me, but above all they seemed thrilled to have Barack—"Bar," they called him (short for Barry and pronounced "Bear")—back in the house.

Over the next ten days, I got to know Honolulu a little and Barack's family a lot. He and I stayed in the back room of an apartment belonging to one of Maya's friends. In the mornings, we would walk hand in hand over to the high-rise on South Beretania and remain there for a couple of hours, chatting as everyone worked intently on a jigsaw puzzle or sat outside on the small lanai that overlooked the church across the street. The apartment was cozy and compact, decorated with a mix of Indonesian batiks and Midwestern trinkets that reminded me of Dandy and Grandma's old apartment back in Chicago. One of the first things I realized, seeing Barack's home, was that he'd grown up in circumstances as modest as mine had been. The apartment had a galley kitchen and was too small to fit a table anywhere, so we ate our meals on TV trays in the living room, with Toot serving tuna sandwiches dressed with French's mustard and sweet pickles, much like we'd eaten at home on Euclid Avenue.

WE WERE DIFFERENT and we were alike, Barack and I. I could see it all better now. As he reconnected with his family after a full year apart, I studied the spaces in between what was familiar and what was not.

Barack and his mom reconnected by having intense, winding conversations about geopolitics and the state of the world. Gramps, meanwhile, liked to joke around. Toot, who had retired from a bank job a few years earlier, was struggling with back pain, which caused her to be a little gruff, but she liked to play cards. She was no-nonsense, I could see, having largely carried the weight of supporting the entire family for many years. Maya was buoyant and sweet, telling me stories about her first year of college in New York and asking Barack for advice on which courses to take.

Their family, to me, appeared like a constellation of stars spread across the sky, each person fixed in arrangement with the others, the group of them spaced in a five-point pattern that was wholly unique to them. Family life had always been carried out comfortably across oceans and continents. Among the five of them, they had three different last names. Barack and Maya had different fathers, from two different cultures. Their mother, Ann, was a cerebral free spirit, the child of two white Kansans with conservative roots, and had been obstinate about picking a different path. In Barack, I saw someone who'd found his place between all those other pulses of light. He'd inherited his mother's rebellious spirit, his grandmother's thrift and deep sense of responsibility, his grandfather's whimsy. He'd inherited his own father's absence, the legacy of one Barack Obama Sr., who'd barely been present in his son's life but still managed to leave behind an utterly fierce set of expectations involving intellectual rigor and discipline.

Unlike in my family, Barack's family members hugged one another a lot. They said "I love you" so often it almost made me uncomfortable, for the sheer fact that this sort of declarative intimacy was new to me. In some ways, it helped explain Barack's refreshing directness with his feelings. His family used words demonstratively, in a way that my family did not. I came to realize this was probably due to the fact they'd spent years relying on words to stay close, communicating through sporadic letters and long-distance phone calls, their love pronounced over the ether, echoing longer for how emphatically it was declared. It was the same with the hugging, the intense conversations, the hours of dedicated jigsaw-puzzling. They were pouring a year's worth of love through a funnel, knowing they had only ten days together. Each time they saw one another, there was always a sense it would be many months before it happened again.

The constellation of my family was arranged entirely differently. With most everyone not just planted in Chicago but living inside a relatively tight grid on the South Side, we were less expansive, more densely packed. Everyone more or less had settled within a fifteen-minute drive. Even as a young professional, I was living literally on top of my parents, occupying the second floor of the house on Euclid, and still saw my brother and an array of cousins for macaroni and ribs on Sundays. In my family, we weren't given to saying "I love you" or getting eloquent with our feelings. Instead, we just shrugged and said, "Okay, well, see you Sunday," knowing full well that everyone would turn up. It was rote and repeated and reliable. For the Robinsons, consistency was love.

In years to come, this would be something Barack and I would end up needing to unpack, largely through trial and error—our competing and often conflicting ideas about what a commitment looked like, the relative positioning of our two stars in the sky, our ability to handle all the uncertainty that lay in between. I hated it when he was late or cavalier about his obligations to be somewhere. He resented it when I crowded him or made too many plans for us, involving too many people. Which gaps did we try to close? Which did we simply acknowledge and let be? Who made the adjustments or tried to unlearn what they knew?

It took us some time and a lot of practice to figure out how to work through our disagreements. Barack, it turns out, is an on-the-spot fixer. He likes to jump right in and try to hash out a relationship problem immediately when it surfaces. He tends to be economical with his emotions. I think this is again probably because his family had tried to fit so much into their ten days or so of time together each year. I will see him wanting to move through the hard stuff quickly sometimes, rapidly deploying his full arsenal of rational insight, eager to push through to the warmth and reconciliation on the other side of a conflict. Much as he had to as a child, he packs it all in, conducting himself efficiently, keen for a resolution.

I, on the other hand, run a lot hotter and slower than my husband does. I boil over with irritation and then have to work my way gradually back toward reason, which is perhaps a by-product of the latitude I was given as a child, the fact that I was encouraged to speak every thought in my head. Time was never short in my family. My brain will sometimes implode at the outset of a conflict, and the last thing I want to do is engage in some instantly rational, bullet-pointed debate about who's right or what the solution is. When feeling cornered, it turns out, I am capable of saying some stupid, hurtful things. There have been times in our relationship when Barack has pushed for an immediate conversation and promptly gotten burned by the steam of my anger.

We've had to learn our way through it. We've had to practice responding to each other in ways that take into account both of our histories, our different needs and ways of being. Barack has figured out how to give me more space and time to cool off and process my emotions slowly, knowing that I was raised with that sort of space and time. I have likewise learned to become more efficient and less hurtful while doing that processing. And I try not to let a problem sit too long, knowing that he was raised not to let things fester.

We have found that there is no right or wrong way to get through. There's no rigid set of partnership principles we live by. There is only what we can work out between us, two intensely specific individuals, day by day and year by year, through pushing and yielding, drawing from deep wells of patience as we try to understand each other a little more. I value physical presence over words. I treasure punctuality, time put in, routine and regularity—which were less important in the home he was raised in. Barack values having space to think, being able to resist any form of establishment, and living lightly and with a high degree of flexibility—which were less important in the home I was raised in. It's always helped when we are able to name our feelings and situate some of our differences inside of personal history rather than present blame.

DURING THE AFTERNOONS over that Christmas vacation, Barack and I would leave his grandparents' apartment and walk several miles to the quieter side of Waikiki Beach, stopping at a convenience store to pick up snacks along the way. We'd find an empty spot by the water and spread a rattan mat out over the sand. It was in these moments I felt finally as if we were on vacation, far away from both work and home, fully present with each other. We'd take dips in the ocean and then lie out to dry off under the sun, talking for hours at a time, until finally at some point, Barack would stand up, towel the sand off his body, and say, "Well, we've got to get back."

Oh right, I'd think, with a touch of dismay. *This is real life.*

The truth is, what I wanted just then was the fantasy version of Hawaii. Rather than schlepping the few miles back to South Beretania Street for a no-frills dinner with the grandparents in front of the evening news, rather than watching Barack sit up late helping Maya figure out her tuition payment plan or talking with his mother about her perpetually-behind-schedule doctoral dissertation about the economics of blacksmithing in rural Indonesia, I would have loved to have sat, just the two of us, unhitched from all obligations in the velvet evening air on the patio of a nearby restaurant, drinking mai tais as the sky over the Pacific went from pink to purple to black. I would have loved, finally, to have tripped off a little giddily to some top-floor honeymoon suite in a hotel.

That was how I'd dreamed about Hawaii, back in my office in Chicago as I'd submitted my request to take these precious vacation days off from work. That was what I was trying not to pout about as Barack rolled up the rattan mat and we began the long walk back.

See, I was young still. I had a balance sheet in my head—my gains on one side, my sacrifices on the other. I didn't yet know, though, what was truly precious. I was still piecing together what I'd need for the years and the life ahead, what exactly would keep my heart stoked for the long haul.

I can tell you now that it is not mai tais or honeymoon suites. It is not pretty sunsets in faraway places, or having a showy wedding, or having money, or maintaining a glittery presence in the world. It's none of those things at all.

It took me some time to realize what I was being shown. It took not one evening sitting inside that small high-rise apartment on South Beretania Street but rather ten straight evenings there to fully understand what I was seeing, what a gain on my personal balance sheet it would ultimately become. I was with a man who was doggedly devoted to his family, who went back every morning and every night, knowing it'd be a year before he'd be able to return. I was seeing his version of constancy, the way his sky was arranged. Later, after we'd moved in together, I'd realize that even when physically separated, Barack remained at the center of his family, filling a role that neither of his mom's husbands ever had, attentively counseling Ann and Maya through various crises, problem-solving with them by phone any time issues arose.

The fact that I'd seen all this would end up helping us during what became the toughest stretch of our marriage, when our daughters were still tiny and Barack was spending three or four nights away from home each week in order to do his job as a politician. I'd been raised around a different kind of constancy and closeness, and it meant that I was left feeling vulnerable and unsteady, a little abandoned by his absence. I worried there was a gap between us that might eventually grow too big to close.

But when we were able to talk about it, and especially with the help of a counselor, we were reminded of what we had, the platform already built. I knew Barack's story and he knew mine. It helped us to understand that we would survive the gaps, so long as we stayed conscious of them. We could live in the in-between. We both knew that distance was something he was accustomed to, even if I wasn't. He knew how to love even while far away. He'd had no choice but to practice it his whole life. The girls and I would remain at the center of his universe, no matter what. I'd never be abandoned. He'd shown it to me on that very first trip.

Night after night in the Honolulu apartment, through our first Christmas and New Year's holiday together, I'd watched Barack clear and scrape the dinner plates, do the crossword with his granddad, recommend books to his sister, and read all the fine print on his mother's financial statements to make sure she wasn't getting rooked. He was attentive, patient, and present. He wouldn't leave until the day was fully done, the dishes finished, the conversations all run out and everyone yawning.

I may have been selfishly longing for the honeymoon suite and this man's full attention, but he was instead allowing me to see the real, showing me some version of how our own future might unfold if we chose it to. We weren't casual, and we weren't playing it cool, which is how I began to understand that we would end up being far more than tourists in each other's lives.

This is where certainty begins, inside an elevator on your way down from the tenth floor very late one night. You slip your hand into his as you step out into the balmy Honolulu night with a vault of stars overhead, hit suddenly by the realization that you have made it home.

BARACK AND I return to Hawaii together now every year. Usually, we go back at Christmastime and meet our grown-up daughters there, the two of them arriving fresh from their own place, their own lives. We gather with Barack's sister, Maya, and her family, visit with his old pals from high school, and host various friends from the mainland. After more than thirty years of traveling to Oahu, I no longer gasp when I see the wafting palm trees out the plane window or feel quite as awed by the sight of Diamond Head, the volcanic mountain that sits like a massive green bulwark southeast of Waikiki.

What I feel now is the exhilaration of familiarity. I am oriented to this place in ways I'd never have imagined for myself as a kid. Though I remain just a visitor, I do know this one island very well, just as I know this one man who introduced me to it, through our regular and committed returns. I feel like I know every bend in the highway that leads from the airport to the North Shore. I know where to go for excellent shave ice and Korean barbecue. I can recognize the scent of plumeria in the air and take delight in the underwater shadow of a manta ray flapping its way through shallow water. I'm well-acquainted with the quiet waters of Hanauma Bay, where we first showed our toddlers how to swim, and the windy sea cliffs at Lanai Lookout, where my husband goes to remember his beloved mother and grandmother, whose ashes he scattered there.

A couple of years ago, to celebrate our wedding anniversary, Barack and I made a special trip to Honolulu, and he surprised me with a celebratory dinner out on the town. He'd rented a private space on the rooftop terrace of a hotel by the ocean and hired a small band to play.

The two of us stood for a while, taking in the view. It was early evening, and we could see the entire stretch of Waikiki Beach. There were surfers floating languidly on their boards, awaiting the perfect wave, and old men playing chess in the park below. We could see the zoo where we used to take our girls on our annual Christmas trips and the bustle of Kalakaua Avenue, where we'd often stroll with them to watch the jugglers and other sidewalk performers who entertained tourists at night. We pointed out the various hotels we'd stayed in over the years, once we'd had enough money to not have to rely on Barack's family to find us a borrowed room, realizing that we were looking out at the span of all the years we'd now spent returning together to this place. It was a full-circle moment.

That naïve dream I'd once had about visiting Hawaii had come true. I was on a rooftop, alone at sunset with the person I loved.

Barack and I then took a seat and ordered a couple of martinis. We spent some time talking about his family, remembering that very first visit to South Beretania Street and how young we'd both been—how, in retrospect, it seemed like we'd hardly known each other at all. We recalled the rattan mat and all those long walks to get to the beach and then back to his grandparents' place again.

We laughed, recognizing it had been kind of a slog.

Then we clinked our glasses together and watched the sky turn pink.

My mother steadies us all.

CHAPTER SEVEN

MEET MY MOM

AFTER BARACK WAS elected president, word got out that Marian Robinson, my seventy-one-year-old mother, was planning to move to the White House with us. The idea was that she'd help look after Sasha and Malia, who were seven and ten at the time, at least until they were settled. She'd make sure that everyone adjusted okay and then move back to Chicago. The media seemed instantly charmed by this notion, requesting interviews with my mother and producing a slew of stories, dubbing her "First Granny" and "Grandmother-in-Chief." It was as if a new and potentially exciting character had been added to the cast of a network drama. Suddenly, my mother was in the news. She *was* news.

If you've ever met my mother, however, you'll know that the last thing she wants is to be well-known. She agreed to do a handful of interviews, figuring it was just part of the larger transition process, though she said, again and again, that she was surprised that anyone would care.

By her own measure, my mom is nothing special. She also likes to say that while she loves us dearly, my brother and I are not special, either. We're just two kids who had enough love and a good amount of luck and happened to do well as a result. She tries to remind people that neighborhoods like the South Side of Chicago are packed full of "little Michelles and little Craigs." They're in every school, on every block. It's just that too many of them get overlooked and underestimated, so too much of that potential goes unrecognized. This would probably count as the foundational point of my mom's larger philosophy: "All children are great children."

My mother is now eighty-five. She operates with a quiet and mirthful grace. Glamour and gravitas mean nothing to her. She sees right through it, believing that all people should be treated the same. I've seen her talk to the pope and to the postman, approaching them both with the same mild-mannered, unflappable demeanor. If someone asks her a question, she responds in plain and direct terms, practicing a kind of amused detachment and never catering her answers to suit a particular audience. This is another thing about my mother: She doesn't believe in fudging the truth.

What this meant as we transitioned into the White House was that any time a reporter posed a question to my mom, she would answer it candidly rather than soft-pedaling her thoughts or hewing to any set of talking points generated by nervous communications staffers. No, we learned right away that if Grandma was going to talk to the media, Grandma was going to speak her truth and get it over with.

Which is how she surfaced in the national news, describing how she'd been dragged kicking and screaming from her quiet little bungalow on Euclid Avenue and more or less forced, by her own children, to live at the nation's most famous address.

She was not being ungracious; she was just being real. How my mom expressed herself to the reporters on this matter was no different than how she'd expressed herself to me. (Both the postman and the pope would have heard the same.) She had not wanted to come to Washington, but I had flat-out begged her. And when begging hadn't worked, I'd enlisted Craig to further twist her arm. My mother was the rock of our family. She steadied us all. Since the time our daughters were babies, she'd helped us out around the edges of our regular childcare arrangements, filling the gaps as Barack and I often improvised and occasionally flailed our way through different career transitions, heavy workload cycles, and the ever-burgeoning after-school lives of our two young girls.

So, yes, I did kind of force her to come.

The problem was that she was content at home. She had recently retired from her job. She liked her own life in her own space and was uninterested in change more generally. The house on Euclid had all her trinkets. It had the bed she'd slept in for more than thirty years. Her feeling was that the White House felt too much like a museum and too little like a home. (And yes, of course, she voiced this observation directly to a reporter.) But even as she made it known that her move to Washington was largely involuntary and intended to be temporary, she affirmed that her love for Sasha and Malia, her commitment to their growth and well-being, in the end eclipsed everything else. "If somebody's going to be with these kids other than their parents," she told a reporter, giving a shrug, "it better be me."

After that, she decided she was pretty much done giving interviews.

ONCE SHE'D MOVED in, my mother became very popular in the White House, even if she wasn't looking to be. She became the belle of the ball, really. Everyone referred to her simply as "Mrs. R." People on staff enjoyed her precisely because she was so low-key. The butlers, who were mostly Black, liked having a Black grandma in the house. They showed her photos of their own grandkids and occasionally tapped her for life advice. The White House florists who came to change out the flower arrangements would linger to chat with my mom. Secret Service agents kept tabs on her on days when she wandered out the gates and headed to the CVS on Fourteenth Street, or over to Filene's Basement in the other direction, or when she dropped by Betty Currie's house—Betty being Bill Clinton's former secretary—to play cards. The staff housekeepers were often trying to get my mother to let them do more for her, though Mom made it clear that nobody should wait on or clean up after her when she knew perfectly well how to do all that herself.

"Just show me how to work the washing machine and I'm good," she said.

Aware of the favor she was doing us, we tried to keep her duties light. She rode with Sasha and Malia to and from school, helping them adjust to the new routine. On days I was busy with FLOTUS duties, she made sure the girls had snacks and whatever else they needed for after-school activities. Just as she had when I was an elementary school student, she listened with interest to their tales about what had unfolded over the course of the day. When she and I had time alone together, she'd fill me in on anything I'd missed in the kids' day and then she'd do the same sort of listening for me, acting as my sponge and sounding board.

When she wasn't looking after the girls, my mom made herself deliberately scarce. Her feeling was that we should have our own family life, independent of her. And she felt that she, too, should have a life independent of us. She liked her freedom. She liked her space. As a rule of thumb, she tended to be hands-off. She had come to D.C. with only one intention, and that was to be a reliable support to Barack and me and a caring grandmother to our two kids. Everything else, as far as she saw it, was just fuss and noise.

Sometimes we would host VIP guests for a dinner party in the White House residence. They'd look around and ask where my mother was, wondering whether she'd be joining us for the meal.

I'd usually just laugh and point up toward the third floor, where she had a bedroom and liked to hang out in a nearby sitting room, which had big windows that looked out at the Washington Monument. "Nope," I'd say, "Grandma's upstairs in her happy place."

This essentially was code for, "Sorry, Bono, Mom's got a glass of wine, some pork ribs on her TV tray, and *Jeopardy!* is on. Don't for one second think you could ever compete . . ."

OVERALL, THE ARRANGEMENT seemed to work. My mom ended up staying with us in the White House for the whole eight years. The consistency of her presence, her low-drama, low-key approach to life, served us all well, especially as so much around Barack's job was high-key and high-drama. Grandma kept us grounded. She was not there to track what was happening with Ebola, or the filibuster, or who was stirring up trouble by launching test ballistic missiles over the Sea of Japan.

She was there simply to keep loose tabs on whether our family was holding up okay. And we needed it. We needed her. She was our ballast.

Over the course of those eight years, our girls morphed from wide-eyed elementary-schoolers into teenagers in full bloom, intent on achieving independence and the privileges of adult life. As teenagers do, they tested a few limits and did some dumb things. Someone got grounded for missing curfew. Someone posted an eyebrow-raising bikini selfie on Instagram and was promptly instructed by the East Wing communications team to remove it. Someone once had to be dragged by Secret Service agents from an out-of-hand, unsupervised high school party just as local law enforcement was arriving. Someone talked back to the president of the United States when he had the audacity to ask (undiplomatically) how she could possibly study Spanish while listening to rap.

An episode of even mild disobedience or misbehavior from our adolescent daughters would set off a ripple of unsettling worry in me. It preyed upon my greatest fear, which was that life in the White House was messing our kids up. Which of course would be their parents' fault. In these situations, my old friend, the fearful mind, would rev right up, triggering a cascade of doubt and guilt. (Have I mentioned that the fearful mind loves children? It knows all your soft spots and will go after them accordingly.)

One tiny thing would go wrong, and my mother-guilt would kick in. I'd start second-guessing every choice Barack and I had ever made, every fork in the road we'd ever come to. Self-scrutiny, as we've talked about, is something women are programmed to excel at, having been thrust into systems of inequality and fed fully unrealistic images of female "perfection" from the time we were kids ourselves. None of us—truly none—ever live up. And yet we keep trying. Much as it is with marriage and partnership, the fantasy versions of being a parent sit at the forefront of our cultural imagination, whereas the reality is way, way, way less perfect.

For mothers, the feelings of not-enoughness can be especially acute. The images of maternal perfection we encounter in advertisements and across social media are often no less confusing or fake than what we see on the enhanced and photoshopped female bodies—starved, carved, and injected with fillers—that are so often upheld as the societal gold standard for beauty. But still, we are conditioned to buy into it, questing after not just the perfect body, but also perfect children, perfect work-life balances, perfect family experiences, and perfect levels of patience and calm, despite the fact that none of us— again, truly none—will ever live up. The doubt generated by all this artifice can be potent and undermining. It's hard not to look around as a mother and think, *Is everyone doing this perfectly but me?*

I am as prone to this type of self-laceration as the next person. At any sign of conflict or challenge with our kids, I would instantly and ferociously start scanning for my own mistakes. Had I been too tough on them or too indulging? Had I been too present or too absent? Was there some parenting book I'd forgotten to study fifteen years earlier? Was this a bona fide crisis, a sign of bigger problems? Which critical life lessons had I failed to impart? And was it too late now?

If you are in any way responsible for the life of a child, you are surely acquainted with this particular brand of fear and worry, the sleep-stealing torment of fretting about your kids—that haunting, lost-in-the-woods sense that you have somehow not done enough for them, or that you've done everything wrong, and they are now paying the price for your negligence or poor decision-making. It's something I believe many of us feel intensely and almost unremittingly, beginning with those very first moments when we take in the precious and innocent perfection of a little newborn face and think: *Please, oh please, don't let me screw you up.*

As a parent, you are always fighting your own desperation not to fail at the job you've been given. There are whole industries built to feed and capitalize on this very desperation, from baby brain gyms and ergonomic strollers to SAT coaches. It's like a hole that can't ever be filled. And as a great many parents in the United States struggle with the high cost of childcare (which can consume about 20 percent of an average worker's salary), the stresses only grow. You can become convinced that if you pull back even a little, thanks to one tiny advantage you didn't figure out how to provide or afford, you've potentially doomed your own child.

I'm sorry to say that this doesn't end with any one milestone, either. The desperation doesn't go away when your kid learns to sleep or walk, or goes off to kindergarten, or graduates from high school, or even moves into their first apartment and buys a set of steak knives. You will still worry! You will still be afraid for them! As long as you are still breathing, you'll be wondering if there's something more you can do. The world will forever seem infinitely more sinister and dangerous when you have a child, even a grown one, walking around in it. And most of us will do nearly anything to convince ourselves that we've got even a modicum of control. Even now, my husband, the former commander in chief, can't help but to text cautionary news stories to our daughters—about the dangers of highway driving or walking alone at night. When they moved to California, he emailed them a lengthy article about earthquake preparedness and offered to have Secret Service give them a natural-disaster-response briefing. (This was met with a polite "No thanks.")

Caring for your kids and watching them grow is one of the most rewarding endeavors on earth, and at the same time it can drive you nuts.

OVER THE YEARS, I've had one secret weapon to help stem the tide of parental anxiety, though—and that's my own mother. She's been my backstop, my Buddha, a calm and nonjudgmental witness to my various shortcomings and, as such, a vital source of sanity. For the entirety of our daughters' young lives, my mother has stood secondary watch over their growth and development, never meddling in the choices Barack and I have made along the way.

What she offers is perspective and presence. She is an engaged listener, someone who can quickly banish my fear to the back of the room or rein me in when I'm getting a little "extra" with my fretting. She tells me that it's important to always presume the best about children—that it's preferable to let them live up to your expectations and high regard rather than asking them to live down to your doubts and worries. My mom says that you should grant kids your trust rather than making them earn it. This is her version of "starting kind."

Throughout the White House years, Mom was there to give me on-the-spot reality checks. She would reflect Sasha's and Malia's adolescence back to me through the unblinking eyes of a septuagenarian, reminding me that whatever was happening was not a failure but rather developmentally appropriate and within the realm of expectation—and that I'd done some of those same dumb things once myself. Her pep talks were brief and understated, in keeping with her character, but they were also reassuring.

"Those girls are all right," my mom would say, with one of her shrugs. "They're just trying to learn life."

What she was telling me was that I, too, was all right, that I could calm down and trust my own judgment. This has always been at the core of my mom's message.

IF YOU'RE AROUND her enough, you will start to notice that my mother is prone to dropping such little pearls of wisdom into everyday conversation. Usually, they're connected to her belief that it's possible to raise decent children without drama or fuss. These are never blustery proclamations delivered with fury or passion. Instead, you almost have to lean in close and listen for them. They tend to be wry thoughts that just slip out quietly, almost like stray pennies falling from her pocket.

For years now, I've been collecting these pennies, stuffing my own pockets full of them, using them for guidance and as a tool to offset my own doubts and worries as a parent. For a while, I was thinking that maybe my mother should write her own book, that she could tell her life story and share some of the insights that I personally have found to be so valuable. But when I suggested it, she just waved me off, saying, "Now, why on earth would I do that?"

She has given me permission, however, to share a few of her more tried-and-true maxims here, some of the points she's made that have helped me to become a slightly calmer, slightly less guilt-ridden, slightly more decent parent to my own kids. But only if I attach the following disclaimer, which comes direct from my mom herself: "Just make sure they know I'm not in the business of telling anybody how to live."

1. Teach your kids to wake themselves up.

WHEN I WAS five years old and starting kindergarten, my parents gifted me with a small electric alarm clock. It had a square face, with little green glow-in-the-dark hands that pointed toward the hour and the minute. My mom showed me how to set my wake-up time and how to turn the alarm off when it buzzed. She then helped me work backward through all the things I'd need to do in the morning—eat my breakfast, brush my hair and teeth, pick out my clothes, get my shoes tied, and so on—in order to calculate how many minutes it would take to get myself up and out the door to school. She was there to provide instruction, she'd furnished me with the tool, but the challenge of using it effectively became mine to figure out.

And I freaking loved that alarm clock.

I loved what it gave me—which was power and agency over my own little life. My mom, I realize now, had passed on this particular tool at a deliberately chosen window early enough in my development, before I was old enough to be cynical about having to get up for school in the morning, before she'd ever have to start shaking me awake herself. It spared her the hassle in some ways, but the real gift was to me: I could wake myself up. *I could wake myself up!*

If I ever did sleep through my alarm, or otherwise get lazy and drag my feet about going to school, my mother was not interested in doing any nagging or cajoling. She remained hands off, making clear that my life was largely my own. "Listen, I got my education," she'd say. "I've already been to school. This isn't about me."

2. It *isn't* about you. Good parents are always working to put themselves out of business.

THE ALARM-CLOCK APPROACH was representative of an even more deliberate undertaking on my parents' part, and that was to help us kids learn to get on our feet and stay on our feet, not just physically but emotionally. From the day she birthed each of her children, my mother was striving toward a singular goal, and that was to render herself more or less obsolete in our lives. Given how I've just finished describing how much I have

needed my mother's calming presence in recent years, I suppose it's clear she has yet to fully get there. But it's not for lack
of trying.

My mom made no bones about the fact that especially when
it came to day-to-day practical tasks, her plan was to become
as unnecessary in our lives as possible, as quickly as possible.
The sooner that time arrived, the sooner she felt that Craig and
I could handle our own business, the more successful she'd
deem herself to be as a parent. "I'm not raising babies," she
used to say. "I am raising adults."

It may sound scandalous to say, especially in an era when
helicopter-parenting has become de rigueur, but I'm pretty
sure that most of my mom's decision-making was guided by
one basic question: *What's the minimum I can do for them
right now?*

This was not a cavalier or self-serving question, but rather
a deeply thoughtful one. In our home, self-sufficiency mattered
above all else. My parents understood that they were operating
on a limited budget—of money, space, access to privilege, and,
in the case of my dad's health, not just energy but time left
on earth—which led them to be economical on all fronts. My
dad's point of view was that we were lucky and should never
take any piece of that luck for granted. We were taught to appreciate what was in front of us, the gifts we'd been given,
whether it was a bowl of ice cream or a chance to go to the
circus. He wanted us to savor the moment we were in, to resist
the impulse to always start looking for the next indulgence or
thrill, or to envy what others had.

His reprimands were gentle and teasing, but the lesson was
earnest: "Never satisfied!" he'd say lightly if someone tore

open a birthday gift and then hurriedly looked for the next. "Never satisfied!" he'd say if we asked for a second helping of ice cream before the first was done. He pushed us to be thoughtful about our wants.

Teaching us to rely on ourselves and to think clearly about what we needed was pretty much the only advantage our parents could convey. They couldn't provide us with shortcuts, so instead they worked on giving us skills. Their hopes for their kids were wrapped up in this one idea: If Craig and I were to travel further in life than they had, we would need big engines and full tanks of fuel, not to mention the ability to do our own repairs.

My mom believed that her hands only got in the way of our hands. If there was something new we needed to learn, she'd show us a way to do it and then quickly step aside. This meant that with the aid of a step stool, Craig and I learned how to wash and dry the dishes long before we were tall enough to reach the sink. We were required to make our beds and do our own laundry as a matter of habit. As I've mentioned, Mom nudged me into walking to and from school by myself, allowing me to find my own way. These were small skills, all of them, but they represented a daily practice in self-reliance and problem-solving, a step-by-step overcoming of doubt and fear, until there was less overall to doubt, less to fear. It became easier to both explore and discover. From one solid habit, we were able to build more.

We did a fair amount of this stuff imperfectly, but the point was we were doing it. Nobody was doing it for us. My mother wasn't stepping in. She didn't correct our errors or squelch our way of doing things, even if our way was slightly different from hers. This, I believe, was my first taste of power. I liked being trusted to get something done. "It's easier for kids to make mistakes when they're little," my mom told me recently when I asked her about this. "Let them make them. And then you can't make too big a deal out of it, either. Because if you do, they'll stop trying."

She sat by and allowed us to struggle and make mistakes—with our chores, our homework, and our relationships with various teachers, coaches, and friends. None of it was tied to her own self-worth or ego, or done for bragging rights. It was not about her at all, she would say. She was busy trying to wash her hands of us, after all. This meant that her mood didn't rise or fall on our victories. Her happiness wasn't dictated by whether we came home with A's on our report cards, whether Craig scored a lot of points at his basketball game, or I got elected to student council. When good things happened, she was happy for us. When bad things happened, she'd help us process it before returning to her own chores and challenges. The important thing was that she loved us regardless of whether we succeeded or failed. She lit up with gladness any time we walked through the door.

My mom remained quietly watchful over what was happening in our lives, but she did not immediately offer to fight our battles. A lot of what we were learning was social, developing skills to understand who we wanted to surround ourselves with, whose voices we allowed into our heads and why. When she could, she found time to volunteer in our classrooms at school, which gave her a useful window on our everyday habitats and in turn probably helped her to recognize when we truly needed help versus when we were just "learning life," which seemed to be most of the time.

On days when I came home stewing about something a teacher had done (and I'll admit, this happened with some regularity), my mom would stand in the kitchen and listen to whatever tirade I had to unleash about the unfairness of some teacher's remark, or the stupidity of an assignment, or how Mrs. So-and-So clearly didn't know what she was doing.

And when I was finished, when the steam of my anger had dissipated to the point that I could think clearly, she'd ask a simple question—one that was fully sincere and also, at the same time, just a tiny bit leading. "Do you need me to go in there for you?"

There were a couple of instances over the years when I did genuinely need my mom's help, and I got it. But 99 percent of the time, I did not need her to go in on my behalf. Just by asking that question, and by giving me a chance to respond, she was subtly pushing me to continue reasoning out the situation in my head. How bad was it actually? What were the solutions? What could I do?

This is how, in the end, I usually knew I could trust my own answer, which was "I think I can handle it."

My mother helped me to learn how to puzzle out my own feelings and strategies for dealing with them, in large part by just giving them room and taking care not to smother them with her own feelings or opinions. If I got overly sulky about something, she'd tell me to go do one of my chores, not as punishment, exactly, but rather as a means of right-sizing the problem. "Get up and clean that bathroom," she'd say. "It'll put your mind on things other than yourself."

Inside of our small home, she created a kind of emotional sandbox where Craig and I could safely rehearse our feelings and sort through our responses to whatever was going on in our young lives. She listened as we worked through our problems out loud, whether it was a math equation or a playground issue. Her advice, when she gave it, tended to be of the hard-boiled and practical variety. Most often, it was a reminder to keep perspective and to think backward from the end result we were hoping for—to always stay focused on that.

Once, when I was in high school and unhappy about having to deal with a math teacher who struck me as arrogant, my mom heard my complaint, nodded understandingly, and then shrugged. "You don't have to like your teacher, and she doesn't have to like you," she said. "But she's got math in her head that you need in yours, so maybe you should just go to school and get the math."

She looked at me then and smiled, as if this should be the simplest thing in the world to grasp. "You can come home to be liked," she said. "We will always like you here."

3. Know what's truly precious.

MY MOM REMEMBERS that the house she grew up in on the South Side had a big coffee table at the center of the living room, made of smooth, delicate glass. It was breakable, and so everyone in the family was forced to navigate around it, almost on tiptoe.

She was a studious observer of her own family, my mother. She sat squarely in the middle of seven children, which gave her a lot to watch. She had three older siblings and three younger ones, plus two parents who appeared to be polar opposites and didn't much get along. She spent years absorbing the dynamics around her, quietly and perhaps unconsciously formulating her ideas about how she would someday raise a family of her own.

She saw how her father—my grandfather Southside—tended to baby his kids, especially her three older sisters. He drove them around in his car so that they wouldn't need to take the bus, afraid of what lay beyond his control. He woke them up in the mornings so they wouldn't need to set an alarm. He seemed to enjoy their dependence on him.

My mom took note.

My grandmother Rebecca—my mom's mom—meanwhile, was stiff and proper, patently unhappy and possibly (my mother believes now) clinically depressed. When she was young, she dreamed of being a nurse, but apparently her mother, a washerwoman who'd raised seven kids in Virginia and North Carolina, had told her that going to nursing school cost a lot of money and Black nurses rarely got good jobs. So Rebecca married my grandfather and had seven children instead, never seeming terribly content with what her life had yielded. (She'd also eventually grow unhappy enough to leave, moving out of the house when my mom was about fourteen, supporting herself by becoming a nursing aide. Southside later ran a more relaxed household without her.)

The governing edict in Grandmother Rebecca's house was that children should be seen and not heard. At the dinner table, my mom and her siblings were instructed to stay silent, to listen mutely and respectfully to the adult conversation around them, never contributing to it themselves. My mother vividly remembers the feeling of having a whole bunch of unexpressed thoughts piling up in her head. It was uncomfortable. She didn't like it at all. Even psychologically, they were all on tiptoe, careful about how and where they stepped.

When her mother's friends came to visit their home, my mom and her siblings were required to join the adults in the living room. All of them—from toddlers to teens—were expected to sit politely at the edges, permitted to say nothing more than hello.

My mother describes long evenings spent in that room with her mouth clamped shut in agony, hearing plenty of adult-speak she wanted to engage with, plenty of ideas she'd want to quibble with or at least better understand. She spent hours trying to hold back her opinions, all the while staring at that glass coffee table, which was kept pristine and gleaming at all times, without so much as a single smudge or fingerprint on it. It must have been during these hours that my mother arrived at the idea, even unconsciously, that her own kids someday would be not just allowed but encouraged to speak. Years later, this would become the established creed on Euclid Avenue. Any thought could be expressed, every opinion was valued. No earnest question would ever be disallowed. Laughter and tears were permitted. Nobody would need to tiptoe.

One night when someone new stopped in for a visit, my mom remembers the woman surveying all the young faces and restless bodies packed into the living room and finally posing a logical question: "How possibly could you have a glass table like this and all of these kids?"

She doesn't recall how my grandmother responded, but my mom knew in her heart what the real answer was: Her own mother had, in her opinion, missed a fundamental lesson about what was precious and what was not. What was the point of seeing children without hearing them?

No child in her family would ever dare touch that glass table, the same way none of them would dare to speak, knowing they'd get punished for even trying. They were being held in place rather than being allowed to grow.

One evening, finally, when my mom was about twelve, some grown-up friends came over to their house to visit and for some foolish reason, one of them happened to sit down on the table. To my grandmother's horror, and as her children watched silently, it shattered into pieces on the floor.

For Mom, it was a bit of cosmic justice. Even today, this story still cracks her up.

4. Parent the child you've got.

THE APARTMENT MY parents raised us in had nothing resembling a glass table. We had very little in our lives that was delicate or breakable at all. It's true that we couldn't afford anything too fancy, but it's also true that in the wake of her own upbringing, my mother had no interest in owning showpieces of any sort. She was never going to pretend that anything under our roof was actually precious, beyond our bodies and souls.

At home, Craig and I were permitted to be ourselves. Craig was a natural caretaker, and a bit of a worrier. I was feisty and independent. Our parents saw us each as different and treated us that way. They geared their parenting toward fostering our individual strengths, to drawing out what was best in us, rather than trying to fit us into any sort of preordained mold. My brother and I were respectful of our elders and abided by some general rules, but we also spoke our minds at the dinner table, threw balls indoors, cranked music on the stereo, and horsed around on the couch. When something did break—a water glass or a coffee mug or, every once in a while, a window—it was not a big deal.

I tried to carry this same approach into my parenting of Sasha and Malia. I wanted them to feel both seen *and* heard—to always voice their thoughts, to explore in an unrestrained way, and to never feel like they had to tiptoe in their own home. Barack and I established basic rules and governing principles for our household: Like my mom, I had our kids making their beds as soon as they were old enough to sleep in beds. Like his mom, Barack was all about getting the girls interested early in the pleasure provided by books.

What we learned quickly, however, was that raising little kids followed the same basic trajectory we'd experienced with both pregnancy and childbirth: You can spend a lot of time dreaming, preparing, and planning for family life to go perfectly, but in the end, you're pretty much just left to deal with whatever happens. You can establish systems and routines, anoint your various sleep, feeding, and disciplinary gurus from the staggering variety that exist. You can write your family bylaws and declare your religion and your philosophy out loud, discussing everything ad nauseam with your partner. But at some point, sooner rather than later, you will almost surely be brought to your knees, realizing that despite your best and most earnest efforts, you are only marginally—and sometimes *very* marginally—in control. You may have spent years captaining your own ocean liner with admirable command and antiseptic levels of cleanliness and order, but now you must face the fact that there are pint-sized hijackers on board, and, like it or not, they're going to tear the place up.

As much as they love you, your children come with agendas of their own. They are individuals and will learn lessons their own way, regardless of how carefully you may have planned them. They are bubbling with curiosity to explore, test, and touch what's around them. They will penetrate the bridge of your ship, put their hands all over every surface, and unwittingly break whatever is fragile, including your patience.

Here's a story I'm not necessarily proud of. It happened one evening when we still lived in Chicago, when Malia was about seven years old and Sasha was just four. I was home after a long day of work. As was often the case in those days, Barack was across the country in Washington, D.C., in the middle of a Senate session that I was probably feeling resentful of. I had served the kids dinner, asked how their days had gone, supervised bath time, and was now cleaning up the last of the dishes, sagging a little on my feet, desperate to be off duty and find even just a half hour to sit quietly by myself.

The girls were supposed to be brushing their teeth for bed, but I could hear them running up and down the stairs to our third-floor playroom, giggling wildly as they went.

"Hey, Malia, Sasha, it's time to wind down!" I called from the foot of the stairs. "*Now!*"

There was a brief pause—three whole seconds, maybe—and then more thundering footsteps, another shriek of laughter.

"It's time to settle down!" I yelled again.

Yet it was clear I was shouting into the void, fully disregarded by my own kids. I could feel the heat starting to rise in my cheeks, my patience disintegrating, my steam building up, my stack preparing to blow.

All I wanted, in the whole wide world, was for those children to go to bed.

Since the time I was a kid myself, my mom had always advised me to try to count to ten in moments like these, to pause just long enough that you might grab on to some reason—to respond rather than react.

I think I got as far as counting to eight before I couldn't stand it another second. I was cooked. And I was angry. I ran up the stairs and shouted for the girls to come down from the playroom and join me on the landing. I then took a breath and counted the last two seconds, trying to quell my rage.

When the girls appeared, the two of them in their pajamas, flushed and a little sweaty from the fun they'd been having, appearing fully unmoved by all the orders I'd been shouting up the stairs, I told them I quit. I was resigning from the job of being their mother.

I summoned what little calm I could find in myself and said, not very calmly at all, "Look, you don't listen to me. You seem to think you don't need a mother. You seem perfectly happy to be in charge of yourselves, so go right ahead. . . . You can feed and dress yourselves from now on. And you can get yourselves to bed. I am handing you your own little lives and you can manage them yourselves. I don't care." I threw my hands in the air, showing them how helpless and hurt I felt. "I am done," I said.

It was in this moment that I got one of my life's clearest looks at who I was dealing with.

Malia's eyes grew wide, her lower lip starting to tremble.

"Oh, Mommy," she said, "I don't want that to happen." And she promptly hustled off to the bathroom to brush her teeth.

Something in me relaxed. *Wow,* I thought, *that sure worked fast.*

Four-year-old Sasha, meanwhile, stood clutching the little blue blankie she liked to carry around, taking a second to process the news of my resignation before landing on her own emotional response, which was pure and unfettered relief.

No sooner had her sister shuffled obediently off, Sasha turned without a word and scampered back upstairs to the playroom, as if to say, *Finally! This lady is out of my business!* Within seconds, I heard her flip on the TV.

In a moment of deep fatigue and frustration, I'd handed that child the keys to her own life, and it turned out she was plenty happy to take them, long before she was actually ready to. Much as I liked my mom's idea about eventually becoming obsolete in my kids' lives, it was far too early to quit. (I promptly called Sasha back down from the playroom, marched her through the tooth-brushing, and put her to bed.)

This one episode provided me with an important lesson about how to proceed with my children. I had one who wanted more guardrails from her parents and one who wanted fewer, one who would respond first to my emotions and another who would take my words at face value.

Each kid had her own temperament, her own sensitivities, her own needs, strengths, set of boundaries, and ways of interpreting the world around her. Barack and I would see these same dynamics manifest over and over again in our children as they grew. On the ski slopes, Malia would make measured, precise turns while Sasha preferred to bomb straight downhill with her jacket flapping. If you asked how Sasha's day at school had been, she'd answer with five words before bouncing off to her bedroom, whereas Malia would offer a detailed breakdown of every hour she'd spent away. Malia often sought our advice—like her dad, she likes to make decisions deliberately and with input—whereas Sasha thrived, just as I once had as a kid, when we trusted her to do her own thing. Neither was right or wrong, good or bad. They were—and are—simply different.

As a mother, I came to rely less on parenting books and the anointed advice givers and more on my own instincts, drawing from my own mom's timeless reminder to just calm down and trust my judgment. Barack and I learned gradually to read our own kids for cues, adapting to what they each were showing us, trying to interpret their development through what we understood about their individual gifts and needs. I started to think of parenting as being an art that's practiced a little like fly-fishing, where you stand for hours knee-deep in a swirling river, trying to calculate not just the water current but the movement of the wind and the position of the sun, a practice in which your best maneuvers are executed only through delicate flicks of the wrist. Your patience matters, as does your perspective, as does your precision.

In the end, the child you have will grow into the person they're meant to be. They will learn life their own way. You will control some but definitely not all of how it goes for them. You can't remove unhappiness from their lives. You won't remove struggle. What you can give your kids—what we can give all kids, really—is the opportunity to be heard and seen, the practice they need to make rational decisions based on meaningful values, and the consistency of your gladness that they are there.

5. Come home. We will always like you here.

MY MOTHER SAID this to me and Craig not just once, but often. It's the one message that stood out above all else. You came home to be liked. Home was where you would always find gladness.

In these chapters, I've written a lot about the idea of home. I understand that I was lucky to know a good one early on. I got to bathe in gladness as a child, which gave me a distinct advantage as I grew and developed as a person. Knowing what gladness felt like, I was able to go out and look for more of it, to seek friends and relationships and ultimately a partner who helped bring even more light, more gladness, into my world—which I then tried to pour into the lives of my own children, hoping to give them that same lift. The practice I've had in finding and appreciating the light inside other people has become perhaps my most valuable tool for overcoming uncertainty and dealing with hard times, for seeing through thickets of cynicism and despair, and—most important—for keeping my hopefulness intact.

I recognize that for many folks, "home" can be a more complicated, less comfortable idea. It may represent a place, or set of people, or type of emotional experience that you are rightfully trying to move past. Home could well be a painful spot to which you never want to return. And that is okay. There's power in knowing where you don't want to go.

And then there's also power in discovering where you want to head next.

How do we build places where gladness lives—for ourselves and for others, and most especially for children—and to which we will always want to return?

You may need to courageously remake your idea of home, scraping together a shelter for yourself, fostering the parts of your flame that may have gone unrecognized or unkindled when you yourself were a child. You may need to cultivate a chosen family rather than a biological one, protecting the boundaries that keep you safe. Some of us will have to make bold changes in our lives, rebuilding and repopulating our spaces many times over before we discover what home truly feels like, what it means to be accepted, supported, and loved.

My mom moved (yes, kicking and screaming) to Washington with us, in part to help with our kids, but also in part because I needed her gladness. I am nothing but a grown-up child myself, someone who at the end of a long day comes through the door feeling worn-out and a little needy, looking for solace and acceptance and maybe a snack.

In her wise and plainspoken way, my mother built us all up. She lit up for us every day, so that we could in turn light up for others. She helped make the White House feel less like a museum and more like a home. During those eight years, Barack and I tried to throw open the doors of that home to more people, of more races and backgrounds, and particularly to more children, inviting them in to touch the furniture and explore what was there. We hoped they could connect themselves to history while also understanding that they mattered enough—they were precious enough—to be able to shape its future themselves. We wanted it to feel like a palace of gladness, fueled by a sense of belonging and telegraphing one simple, powerful message: *We will always like you here.*

Mom will take no credit for any of it, of course. She'll be the first to tell you—still—that she's nothing special, and it's never been about her, anyway.

Late in 2016, about a month before a new president was sworn in, my mother happily packed her bags. There was little fanfare and, at her insistence, no farewell party, either. She just moved out of the White House and went back to Chicago, returning to her place on Euclid Avenue, to her old bed and old belongings, pleased that she'd gotten the job done.

PART THREE

What we don't see, we assume can't be.
What a destructive assumption.

—OCTAVIA BUTLER

Shortly after the events of January 6 at the U.S. Capitol shook me
to my core, it was affirming to participate in the democratic ritual of the
January 20, 2021, inauguration of President Joe Biden.

CHAPTER EIGHT

THE WHOLE OF US

I SOMETIMES READ PROFILES of high-earning, successful women who purport to both have and do it all. They tend to give off a certain effortless vibe—well-groomed, well-dressed, excellent at running whatever empire they happen to run, while also appearing as if they make dinner for their kids at night, fold every piece of laundry in the house, and still have time for yoga and trips to the farmers market on weekends. Sometimes we get tips on how they pull it off—tricks for time management or life hacks involving mascara or which incense to burn or what to put in an acai smoothie. All this gets offered alongside a list of five super-literary books they've just finished reading.

I am here to tell you that it's more complicated than this. Most often, what you are seeing in those profiles is the person who happens to sit on top of a symbolic pyramid, appearing graceful, balanced, and in control. But first of all, any balance is likely only momentary. And second of all, it's only thanks to the collective efforts of a team that often includes managers, childcare workers, housekeepers, hairstylists, and other professionals who have devoted themselves to that person's efficiency and care. Many of us, myself included, are propped up by the quiet and often unsung efforts of others. Nobody becomes successful all on their own. I think it's important for those of us who have behind-the-scenes help to make a point of mentioning it as part of our story.

If you know me, then you will also know the exceptionally talented and even-keeled people who have been on my team over the years. They are the solvers of many problems, the trackers of myriad details, the boosters of my own efficiency and ability to operate. While in the White House, I had the assistance of two energetic young women—Kristen Jarvis during the first term and Kristin Jones in the second—who were by my side for nearly every step I took in public, helping to keep me moving forward and equipped for whatever moment was at hand. To this day, they are like big sisters to Sasha and Malia.

Since leaving the White House, I've taken on a variety of new projects, from writing books to executive-producing television shows to helping manage the Obama Foundation, while also continuing my advocacy work on issues like voting rights, girls' education, and children's health. None of it happens without the guidance of Melissa Winter, who left a job on Capitol Hill in 2007 to help me during Barack's presidential campaign, then became an important deputy in the East Wing, and is still with me fifteen years later, now holding down the position of chief of staff, expertly running my office and managing a wide load of responsibilities across every aspect of my professional life. It's hard to overstate how much I rely on her.

For the first five years after leaving the White House, I was fortunate to have a supremely capable assistant named Chynna Clayton, who joined my East Wing staff in 2015 and then agreed to stay on with me as I transitioned into life as a private citizen. Chynna acted as my air-traffic controller, the coordinator of my day-to-day, moment-to-moment life. When a friend wanted to see if I was free to come over for dinner the following Tuesday, I'd usually laugh and say, "You gotta ask my mom." Mom being, of course, Chynna, and Chynna being the one running the calendar.

Chynna kept my credit cards. She had my mother's phone number. She talked to my doctors, scheduled my trips, collaborated with my Secret Service detail, and set up my outings with friends. She could adapt in all types of environments, remaining unflappable in the face of change. On any given day, I might go from having a conversation with a group of students at a school to filming a television show or recording a podcast. I could meet with a world leader or the head of a philanthropic organization and then have dinner with A-list celebrities. It was Chynna facilitating every move.

Her job meant we were together practically all the time. We rode in the car together. We sat together on the plane. In hotels, we stayed in adjoining rooms. The miles we traveled made us close. Chynna cried with me when we lost our sweet old dog Bo. I celebrated with her when she bought her first house. Chynna became not only integral to my life, but dear to my heart.

WHICH IS WHY I got suddenly nervous when, about a year after we'd left the White House, Chynna asked if the two of us could have a formal, one-on-one meeting. Given how much time we already spent together, it was an unusual request, and Chynna had seemed anxious when making it, promptly sending me spinning into anxiety myself. I figured the meeting could only mean one thing: She was going to tell me she was quitting.

As Chynna came into my office and took a seat, I braced myself for the news.

"Uh, ma'am?" she said. (Calling me "ma'am" is a curious hangover from the White House days, a habit of respect that a number of our longtime staffers insist on keeping.) "I've been wanting to tell you something . . ."

"Okay, I'm listening."

"Well, it's about my family."

I watched her shift uncomfortably in her chair. "All right," I said.

"About my dad, specifically."

"Go on . . ."

"Well, I guess I've never mentioned it, but I feel like I probably should. He went to prison."

"Oh, Chynna," I said, figuring it must be fresh news. I knew Chynna's mom, Doris King, but had never met her father, nor had she told me anything about him. "That sounds rough. I'm so sorry. When did this happen?"

"Well, he got locked up when I was three."

I paused for a second, doing the math in my head. "You mean, twenty-five years ago, he went to prison?"

"Yeah, something like that. He got out when I was thirteen." She gave me a searching look. "I just felt like you should know, in case maybe it was a problem."

"A *problem*? Why would it be a problem?"

"I don't know. I just worried it could be."

"Wait," I said. "Have you been worried about this the whole time you've worked for me?"

Her smile was gentle, sheepish. "A little bit. Yes."

"And that's why you wanted to have this meeting?"

Chynna nodded.

"So, you're not quitting?"

She looked shocked by the suggestion. "What? No."

The two of us stared at each other for a few seconds then—struck silent, I think, by mutual relief.

Finally, I started to laugh. "You know, you almost killed me with that one," I said. "I thought you were leaving."

"No, ma'am, not at all." Chynna was laughing now, too. "I just needed to share that one thing with you. It felt like it was time."

We sat and talked for a while after that, both of us recognizing how much "that one thing" actually mattered.

For Chynna, telling that part of her story turned out to be a kind of unburdening, a letting go of something she'd been holding for a long time. She explained to me that her entire life, she'd been ashamed to tell people that her father was incarcerated. She'd hidden it from her teachers and friends when she was young, not wanting to be judged or stereotyped for how her family was built or what they were going through. As she went on to college and then started working among a bunch of seemingly fancy people at the White House, she'd felt the stakes only getting higher, the gulf between the circumstances of her childhood and where she now found herself only growing wider. How do you casually explain to your seatmate on Air Force One that as a kid you'd seen your dad only during visits to a federal penitentiary?

For her, it had become a matter of both habit and strategy just to leave that part of her story out. And yet, the work it sometimes took for her to detour around it, to avoid getting into any sort of conversation that might go in the direction of her childhood, had, over many years, left her conditioned to feel guarded and cautious, wearing an extra layer of armor. She'd been living quietly with a fear that she'd be somehow declared a fraud. Which of course she wasn't.

THAT DAY IN my office, I couldn't possibly reassure Chynna enough that her story—her whole story—was completely okay with me. I was grateful to know it. If anything, it only deepened my respect for her, giving me more insight into the supremely competent young woman who sat before me. The fact that she'd successfully navigated the stress of having a parent in prison throughout her childhood spoke to her resilience, her independence, her ability to persist. It offered a window into how she'd come to be such a wiz with problem-solving and logistics, having learned to think quickly and on multiple levels very young. Her struggle to know what to do with that part of her story perhaps also explained why she'd remained one of the quieter members of our staff. I wasn't just looking at one part of this person I respected now, but all of her—or more of her, anyway. I was seeing someone whose story had many chapters.

I knew that Chynna had grown up in Miami, raised by a determined mother who'd done the job of parenting alone, taking the graveyard shift at work so that she could be present for her daughter after school, encouraging her to seize every opportunity. I'd been able to meet Doris a few times over the years and had seen firsthand how deeply proud of her daughter she was. Chynna's path, her career, her smarts and maturity, were a triumph. Her successes were in part a testament to her mother's investment and hard work.

I also understood from my own upbringing how this kind of support can sometimes translate into added pressure, even if your loved ones aren't intending it as such. When you're breaking new generational ground in your family—the first to leave your neighborhood, the first to go to college, the first to own a house or get any sort of toehold into stability—you travel with the pride and expectations of everyone who came before you, everyone who waved you toward the mountaintop, trusting that you'll get there even if they couldn't.

As wonderful as this is, it also becomes something extra to carry, something that's precious, something you can't afford to be casual about. You leave home knowing that you're holding a tray stacked high with the hopes and sacrifices of others. And now you're trying to walk that tray across a tightrope as you navigate school and work environments where you're seen as different, where your belonging is never guaranteed.

Amid all that effort and all that precariousness, you could be forgiven for not wanting to risk more by sharing a lot of your personal story. You could be forgiven for your inwardness, your caution, your layers of armor. All you're trying to do, really, is to focus, hold your balance, and not fall.

These days, Chynna describes that conversation between us as having helped to unlock something in her, allowing her to shed some of that fear and let go of the sense she was an impostor in her own professional life. Inside the safety of our close relationship, the trust we'd built over time, she chose to let a certain part of herself out of the vault and into the light, a portion of her history that had always made her feel vulnerable, a piece of her *despite*.

I recognize that, for her, sharing felt like a risk, even though the two of us had a relationship that was far more personal and up close than most people have with their bosses. And I also recognize that in many workplaces, or for someone newer to her position, or if Chynna had been more alone as a woman or person of color on our team, this sort of risk would have felt even greater. What we choose to share in professional settings, what we show of ourselves and when, is not only personal but also inherently complicated—an often-delicate matter of timing, circumstance, and careful judgment. We need always to be mindful of what's at stake and who is there to receive our truth. There's no single rule of thumb that will ever apply.

WE'LL TALK MORE in the next chapters about the questions of *when* and *how* to share yourself in authentic and effective ways. But I want to begin with *why* I think it matters that we look for these opportunities to get more comfortable with ourselves and our stories, and, just as importantly, to create space and acceptance for the stories of others—whether it's at work or in our personal lives, or, in an ideal world, both.

On a very basic level, it can be relieving when you take a calculated risk and let something out of the vault, releasing yourself from the obligation to keep it hidden or from trying to compensate for whatever might make you different from your peers. Often, it means you are starting to integrate the left-out parts of yourself into your larger concept of self-worth. It's a means of finding your own light, which will often help others then see it as well. For some, this can be a very private process, done with the help of a counselor, shared inside only the safest of relationships. Sometimes it takes years to arrive at the right moment and set of circumstances to open up. A lot of us wait too long to begin even trying to know or give voice to our own stories. What matters most is that we find ways to examine what's there in the vault and to think about whether or not it's serving us to hold it inside.

After telling me more about her upbringing, and realizing that it did nothing to change the high regard in which I held her, Chynna says she started to feel more confident and comfortable speaking about this part of her story with others in her life, prompting her to then fear a little bit less and to feel more confident and comfortable in general. She also began to understand how much of her energy had gone, even unconsciously, into the withholding.

For years, she'd lived with a fear of being judged for something that was entirely beyond her control and is also remarkably common in this country. Working in the rarefied air of the White House, she had assumed that having had an incarcerated parent made her a type of "only." And yet this likely wasn't the case. Government statistics show that more than five million children in the United States have had a parent in jail or prison at some point—about 7 percent of all youth. It stands to reason that Chynna was probably less alone than she thought. But, of course, nobody was talking about it. And why would they? We often—and given the culture of judgment we live in, rightfully—believe we're safer when we keep our vulnerabilities locked away.

What this means, though, is that a lot of us are left to assume that we're an "only" when perhaps we are not. Our vaults can leave us lonely, isolated from others, exacerbating the pain of invisibility. And that's a tough way to go. The amount we hold there, hidden out of sight and guarded by instinctive feelings of fear or shame, can contribute to a larger sense that we don't belong or don't matter—that our truth will never comfortably fit with the reality of the world we're living in. In keeping our vulnerabilities private, we never get the chance to know who else is out there, who else might understand or even be helped by whatever it is we're holding back.

A year or so after our initial conversation, Chynna came on as a guest to a podcast series I was hosting on Spotify, joining a discussion about the relationships between mentors and mentees. In the course of the conversation, she spoke about having grown up with a father in prison, saying that she'd learned to let go of the shame she'd always assumed belonged with this part of her story and had come to see how it was an experience that helped shape her into the successful person she is today.

In making her story more visible, Chynna turned out to have done something not just for herself but for others. Immediately after the episode dropped, messages started to flood in from all around the country, a bright and beautiful chorus of people who wanted to say something back to her. They thanked her for what she'd said. Many people—older, younger, even some kids—wrote in to say they understood precisely the feelings she had described, having themselves had to navigate the stresses of having a loved one in prison and figuring out how to share the story, how to incorporate it into their own path.

The fact that Chynna spoke not with shame but rather with poise and pride in herself was especially significant. That part of her story was also theirs. In some ways, it lifted them all, creating a wider sphere in which they could feel visible and know they belonged. The idea that a little girl who'd seen the inside of the family-visit room at the federal penitentiary had also seen the inside of the White House meant something to them, too.

WHEN SOMEONE CHOOSES to lift the curtain on a perceived imperfection in her story, on a circumstance or condition that traditionally might be considered to be a weakness, what she's often actually revealing is the source code for her steadiness and strength. And as we've seen plenty of times in our history, the strength of one resolute soul can become the strength of many. I thought about this when I had the privilege of being present on the inaugural stage on January 20, 2021, as a young writer named Amanda Gorman stepped up to the microphone in a sunny yellow coat and electrified an audience of millions by reciting a poem that was perfectly tuned to one of the most fraught and complicated moments in recent history.

Just two weeks earlier, stirred up by the outgoing president, a mob of about two thousand people had overrun the U.S. Capitol in an attempt to prevent Congress from certifying Joe Biden's electoral win. They'd smashed windows, pounded down doors, attacked and injured police officers, and broken into the chambers of the Senate, terrorizing our country's leaders and putting democracy itself in jeopardy. Barack and I had watched in shock as it unfolded live on the news. The events of that day rattled me to the core. I'd understood that our country was grappling with a toxic level of political discord, but seeing the rhetoric tip into reckless, rageful violence aimed at overturning an election was devastating. Watching an American president encourage a siege on his own government was perhaps the most frightening thing I'd ever witnessed.

As citizens, we hadn't always agreed with our elected decision makers. But as Americans, we had historically trusted in the greater enterprise of democracy, a set of ideals in which we'd banked our faith. As First Lady, I'd met scores of diligent and thoughtful government workers, people who'd devoted their lives to public service, a great many of them providing expertise and continuity through multiple presidential administrations, regardless of which party was in charge. I'd seen the same with state government in Illinois during Barack's time as a legislator there, and in city government, when I'd worked for the mayor's office in Chicago. Leaders came and went, they were voted in and voted out, but the government itself—a peaceful, participatory democracy built on the notion of free elections—always stayed and always functioned, like a steady and slow-rotating wheel. None of it was perfect, but that was the pact of our union, our United States. It's what made and kept us free.

Though order was eventually restored and congressional leaders managed to certify the election that same night, the damage done on January 6 was immeasurable; it felt as if the nation's psyche had been torn apart. The pain was palpable and the trauma was real. Tension remained high as Inauguration Day approached. The FBI issued a bulletin that warned of further potential violence, putting all fifty states on alert. Quite honestly, I was afraid of what might happen.

It felt clear, though, that there was a choice to be made between fear and faith, not just for those of us who would sit on the inaugural stage to witness the swearing-in of a newly elected president, but for the citizenry more generally. What sort of stance would we take? Even with uncertainty buzzing in the background, would we show up for our own democracy? Could we remain calm and resolute? Four years earlier, I'd participated in this same ritual for a president whose candidacy I hadn't supported and whose leadership I didn't trust. I hadn't been happy about it, but I'd shown up, anyway. I was there to uphold and dignify the larger process, to help reinforce a higher creed. Inaugurations were just that, a ritual recommitment to the pursuit of our ideals, a call to adapt to whatever reality our broader electorate had delivered, and to carry on.

This time, the stakes felt higher than ever. Could we shut out the background noise and remember our trust?

Weeks earlier, with the help of my longtime stylist Meredith Koop, I'd chosen an outfit for the inauguration, one that was comfortable and practical, a plum-colored wool coat over a matching turtleneck and pants and pulled together by an over-sized gold belt. I picked out a pair of block-heeled boots and some black gloves. I wore a face mask (of course) and didn't carry a purse. Barack and I had received multiple security brief-ings ahead of the event and set off for the Capitol that day feel-ing reasonably assured of our safety. As a precaution, I told Chynna—who normally would have accompanied me and waited in a backstage holding room during the ceremony—to stay at home.

I held Barack's hand and walked onto the inaugural plat-form, trying to inhabit the boldness that seemed to be called for. As we took our seats, I did what I'd done at three succes-sive inaugurations before this: I took a breath and channeled my calm.

I swear, you could feel everything in the air that morning on the National Mall—the tension and the determination, the profound longing for change, the anxiety wrought by the pan-demic, the specter of the violence we'd endured at the Capitol, the wider worries about where we were headed, the sunshine of a new day. It was all there, lingering and unspoken, contra-dictory and a little unsettling. We'd gathered once again in the name of history. Through the democratic process, we'd been given yet another chance to tell the American story, to let the wheel turn. But nobody had yet voiced it into truth.

Until, that is, one woman stood up and gave us her poem.

Amanda Gorman's delivery that day was effervescent. Her voice was pure power. She has oratory skills that are rare for anyone, let alone a twenty-two-year-old, and she used her words that day to boost hope for a sagging, grieving nation. *Don't give up,* the poem told us. *Keep working.*

Here is a part of the poem's final rallying cry. As is the case with any piece of poetry, it's worth reading out loud:

> So let us leave behind a country better than the one we
>   were left.
> With every breath from our bronze-pounded chests,
> We will raise this wounded world into a wondrous one.
>
> We will rise from the gold-limned hills of the West!
> We will rise from the windswept Northeast, where our
>   forefathers first realized revolution!
> We will rise from the lake-rimmed cities of the
>   Midwestern states!
> We will rise from the sunbaked South!
>
> We will rebuild, reconcile, and recover . . .

Her poem retold our nation's story at a moment when we needed to remember our resilience. With it, she managed to settle a lot of nerves. I think for a lot of us, she managed to shift the mood and almost miraculously dissipate a good deal of fear that day, inspiring not just hope but courage.

What I didn't know until later was that Amanda Gorman had grown up with an auditory-processing disorder and, as a result, had spent most of her life wrestling with a speech impediment—one that caused her to have particular difficulty pronouncing the sound of the letter r. It wasn't until she was about twenty years old that she could even accurately say her own last name.

You might now want to go back and reread the passage

above, keeping every *r* in mind. See what that does for your awe.

WHEN I HAD the chance to interview Gorman not long after the inauguration, she explained that she'd come to view her speech impediment less as a disability and more as something she was ultimately glad for. The challenges she'd faced over years of struggling to pronounce words had been difficult to be sure, but they'd also driven her deeper into a practice of exploring and experimenting with sound and language, first as a child, then as a teen, and now as a lionhearted young poet. The work she'd had to do to overcome the impediment had pushed her to discover new abilities in herself.

"For a long time, I looked at it as a weakness," she said. "Now I really look at it as a strength." She'd converted what felt like a vulnerability into a unique asset, something potent and useful. The condition she'd had all her life—what made her different from other kids at school, what most would see as a disadvantage—had also enabled her to become who she was.

What we'd seen in her commanding performance on the inaugural stage was a young woman reaching a pinnacle. But that was just one day in her life, one part of her story, and she wanted to make sure others understood something about the hill she'd climbed. Now that she's in the public eye and being celebrated as a dazzling talent, Gorman has made an effort to emphasize the fact that her success was not instantaneous and that she's leaned on others—family members, speech therapists, teachers—for support along the way. "I want to highlight that this took a lifetime, and it took a village," she told me. Her most visible victory came only after years of small setbacks and incremental progress. With every *r* she managed to master, she took another step forward. And with each new step, she became better acquainted with her own power and agency. She had pronounced her way into assuredness, and in the process of doing the work, she found the source code for her strength.

Now that she knew it, she knew how to own it. It was hers to keep and use forever. And there were still plenty of other pinnacles she intended to reach.

"Especially for girls of color, we're treated as lightning or gold in the pan—we're not treated as things that are going to last," she said. "You really have to crown yourself with the belief that what I'm about and what I'm here for is way beyond this moment. I'm learning that I am not lightning that strikes once. I am the hurricane that comes every single year, and you can expect to see me again soon."

Many successful people I know have learned to use their despites this way. They use them as a training ground. This doesn't necessarily mean that the most successful among us have somehow vanquished every obstacle or are walking around seeing rainbows and unicorns where others see systems of oppression or walls that are simply too high to scale. It often just means that they've done precisely what Gorman's poem urged all of us to do: *Don't give up. Keep working.*

All around me, I see smart and creative folks who are working their way step-by-step into greater power and visibility, in many instances having figured out how to harness rather than hide whatever sets them apart. When we do this, we start to acknowledge all the contradictions and influences that make us unique. We normalize differentness. We reveal more of the larger human mosaic. We help make everyone's story a little more okay.

One of my favorite comedians to watch is Ali Wong, an acerbic, truth-spitting talent. She first caught my attention in 2016 when she put out a stand-up special called *Baby Cobra* on Netflix. In it, she struts the stage at seven and a half months pregnant, wearing a short, body-hugging dress and red horn-rimmed glasses, appearing fantastically and almost defiantly female while delivering a raunchy, no-holds-barred monologue about sex, race, fertility, and motherhood. She manages to be fierce, sexy, and real all at once—led by, encumbered by, and at the same time utterly unfazed by the orb of her belly. To riveting effect, she shows us her whole self.

A writer for *The New Yorker* once asked Wong what she says to younger comics when they want to know the secret for making it in the world of comedy, where, as an Asian American woman and the mother of young children, she remains in a deep minority. Wong replied that the key for her was to not view any of those things as obstacles. "You just shift your perspective and think, 'Wait a minute: I'm a woman! And most stand-up comics are male,'" she said. "You know what male comics can't do? They can't get pregnant. They can't *perform* pregnant. So my attitude is, just *use* all those differences."

Our differences are treasures and they're also tools. They are useful, valid, worthy, and important to share. Recognizing this, not only in ourselves but in the people around us, we begin to rewrite more and more stories of not-mattering. We start to change the paradigms around who belongs, creating more space for more people. Step by step by step, we can lessen the loneliness of not-belonging.

The challenge is to shift our perspectives and celebrate the value of differentness in ourselves and in others, seeing it as reason to step forward rather than back, to stand up rather than sit down, to say more rather than less. The work is challenging. It often requires boldness. And there are never any guarantees on how it will be received. But every time someone pulls it off, every time another tightrope gets crossed, we see even more perspectives begin to shift. It matters when a pregnant Asian American comic makes millions of people laugh. It matters when a twenty-two-year-old Black woman stands up and almost single-handedly resets the mood of a nation. It matters when someone who is Muslim becomes CEO, or someone who is trans becomes class president. It matters when we feel safe enough to show ourselves without shame and find ways to speak openly of the experiences that made us into the people we are. And, as we've seen in recent years, it matters when we have opportunities to affirm a brave voice and diminish another person's isolation with words as simple as "me too."

All these stories widen the view on what's possible. And they also sharpen our understanding of the component parts of being human. Because of them, there's suddenly more to see. The world we live in begins to appear bigger and more nuanced—a truer reflection of the big and nuanced place that it is.

DON'T GIVE UP. Keep working. It's a worthy mantra, but I can't continue without also addressing the inequity buried inside this message. The work of visibility is difficult, and it's distributed unevenly. There's nothing fair about it, in fact. I happen to be well-acquainted with the burdens of representation and the double standards for excellence that steepen the hills that so many of us are trying to climb. It remains a damning fact of life that we ask too much of those who are marginalized and too little of those who are not.

So please keep this in mind as I tell you to see your obstacles as building blocks and your vulnerabilities as strengths. I say none of it casually. I see none of it as simple.

My own experience has shown me that the risks are real, and the work doesn't end. Not only that, but many of us are already in a place where we are justifiably tired, cautious, afraid, or sad. As I've mentioned, the obstacles you face often-times have been deliberately placed; they are land mines hidden inside of systems and structures whose power is premised on the belonging of some but not all people. It can feel like a whole lot to try to overcome, especially if you believe you are doing the work alone. Once again, I'd remind you of the power of small actions, small gestures, small ways you might allow your-self to reset and restore. Not everyone will be a lion or a hur-ricane. But that doesn't mean your work won't count. Or that your story shouldn't be told.

The plain truth, too, is that for many of us, there will be disappointments. You can work your butt off to get yourself into a position of visibility and relative power in this world and yet still feel your heart sink at what you find upon arrival. You may hike all the way up to whatever mountaintop it is you're hoping to reach—a job, a school, an opportunity—nobly carrying the hopes and expectations of your loved ones, batting away messages of shame and otherness like a superhero as you go. And when the climb finally ends and you arrive, exhausted and sweating, to that high place with a pretty view that you've long dreamed about, there's one thing you're almost always guaranteed to encounter, and that's an air-conditioned luxury tour bus and a group of people who did none of the work, having been driven straight up an access road, their picnic blankets already laid out, their party well under way.

It's a demoralizing feeling. I've seen it and I've felt it myself.

There will be times—perhaps a lot of them—when you'll need to take a deep breath and steady yourself all over again. You may look around and have to remind yourself that you are, in fact, stronger and leaner for having made the trek, for having carried the weight on your back. You can tell yourself that the uneven ground you've had to traverse has made you nimble, and you may feel better for your nimbleness.

It still doesn't make it fair.

But when you do the work, you own the skills. They can't be lost or taken away. They are yours to keep and use forever. That's what I hope you'll most remember.

There's one last irony and it's this: For whatever effort you make and wherever you get yourself, there may be people who will accuse you of having taken shortcuts or of being unworthy of your spot on the hill. They'll have an arsenal of phrases—*affirmative action,* or *scholarship kid,* or *gender quota,* or *diversity hire*—and they'll use them as weapons of disdain. The message is deeply familiar: *I don't see you as being entitled to what you've got.*

All I can say is don't listen. Don't let that poison inside.

Here's a story to consider: About twenty years ago, executives at NBC decided to adapt a popular British sitcom for American television. The network hired a group of eight writers to begin working on the scripts. The group included only two people of color, one of whom, perhaps uncoincidentally, happened to be the only woman as well. She was twenty-four years old. It was her first TV writing job, and she was petrified. Not only was she a double minority, but she was wrestling with an extra layer of self-consciousness, having been brought in through a relatively new diversity initiative at NBC. She worried that as a diversity hire, she was being viewed less as a talent and more as someone whose presence was meant simply to check a certain box.

"For a long time, I was really embarrassed about it," this writer later told an interviewer. "No one said anything to me about it, but they all knew. And I was acutely aware of that." She likened the feeling to wearing a scarlet letter, something that kept her on the outside.

Her name was Mindy Kaling. The show was *The Office*. She ended up spending eight seasons as one of its stars. She also wrote twenty-two of its episodes, more than any other writer on the show, and became the first woman of color ever to be nominated for a comedy-writing Emmy Award.

Kaling now speaks often and proudly about having been a diversity hire, saying that it's a meaningful part of her story and important for others to know what it took for her to get to where she is professionally. It's not something to keep in the vault. She was able to drop her self-consciousness and shove off the doubts, she says, once she started to better understand the advantages her colleagues had arrived with in the first place, the connections that came through the familiarity and privilege of being white and male inside a system built and maintained largely by others just like them. She says, "It took me a while to realize that I was just getting the access other people had because of who they knew."

She might have stepped back, but instead she stepped forward. She endured the discomfort of being an "only," drilled down on the work, and through it was able to make more space for others coming up behind her, creating room for more storytellers and more stories. She literally wrote her way into visibility. Kaling has since, of course, become a powerhouse in her field, creating, producing, writing, and starring in multiple hit TV shows and movies, nearly all of which feature the stories of women of color. With her work, she's widened the sphere for belonging.

WHEN WE SHARE our stories with fullness and honesty, we often discover that we're less alone and more connected than we might ever have believed. We create new platforms between us. I've had different points in my life where I've felt this in profound ways, one of the most humbling being in the months after I published *Becoming*. I was amazed by the number of people who showed up at my events, eager to connect over what we had in common. They came with their stories. They showed their hearts. They knew what it was like to have a parent with MS. They'd suffered through miscarriages, lost friends to cancer. They knew what it was like to fall in love with someone who sends your life swerving in a wild new direction.

"Language is a finding place, not a hiding place," the writer Jeanette Winterson has observed, and this has proven true for me. In opening my vault and shining some light on the times when I'd felt most vulnerable or out of control, I ended up discovering more community than I'd ever known. Yes, I was already "well-known" at that point, but this was different. The broader strokes of my story had been told plenty of times—by me and by others—and yet with the space and energy to write a book and for the first time in decades being unharnessed from the political world my husband inhabited, I found myself putting in the left-out parts, the feelings and experiences that were more personal, less likely to show up on a Wikipedia page or in a magazine profile. With the book, I showed myself from the inside out, less guarded than I'd ever been, and I was surprised to find how quickly others dropped their guards in response.

Almost none of what readers were excited to talk with me about had to do with the color of our skin or which political party we belonged to. Our common ground seemed to stretch past those things—to dwarf them, almost—and it wasn't especially exalted or glamorous territory we were exploring, either. Nobody came up to me at book events desperate to talk about the time they'd worn a ball gown or interacted with a senator or done a White House tour. Nobody much cared about my professional life or achievements, either.

Instead, we connected over things like how many of us had insisted on a nearly all-peanut-butter diet as kids, or had struggled to find the right career as adults, or needed two tries to pass a licensing exam, or who had a dog that couldn't be house-trained, or a spouse who was aggravatingly never on time. It was the mundane grind of being human, I found, that built the platforms between us, putting what made us the same ahead of all that made us different. I can't even begin to describe the frequency with which I was approached in cities all around the country by women who would grip my hands tightly, look into my eyes, and say, "You know when you talk about eating a Chipotle bowl in your car at the strip mall during your lunch break and that's what counted as your 'me-time'? I know that feeling *exactly*. That's my life, too."

For each little point of connection between us, I also felt the possibilities for a kind of understanding that went beyond the things we shared. Because the truth is, for whatever we have in common, there is plenty we do not. We are different. The same way you can't truly know the innermost contours of my life or feelings, I can't know yours. I won't ever fully understand what it's like to be from Tucson, or Vietnam, or Syria. I can't know exactly what it feels like to be awaiting a military deployment, or farm sorghum in Iowa, or pilot an airplane, or struggle with addiction. I have my experiences of being Black and female, but that doesn't mean I can know what anyone else's Black and female body has been through.

All I can do is try to draw closer to your uniqueness, to feel linked by the small overlaps between us. This is how empathy works. It's how differentness starts to weave itself into togeth-erness. Empathy fills the gaps between us, but never closes them entirely. We get pulled into the lives of others by virtue of what they feel safe and able to show us, and the generosity with which we are able to meet them. Piece by piece, person by person, we begin to apprehend the world in more fullness.

I think the most we can ever do, really, is to walk partway across the bridge toward another person and feel humbled that we get to be there at all. I used to think about this as I lay next to Sasha and Malia at bedtime in the evenings. I'd watch them drift off to sleep, their lips parted, the arcs of their little chests rising and falling beneath the sheets, and feel struck by the realization that no matter how much I tried, I'd never know even half their thoughts. We're alone, each one of us. That's the ache of being human.

What we owe one another is the chance to build whatever platforms we can between us, even if they're made of peanut butter and Chipotle bowls and they still only get us halfway. This isn't an argument for brazenly spilling all your secrets. It doesn't mean you need to do something big and public like publish a book or go on a podcast, either. There's no requirement to disclose every piece of private anguish you carry or every opinion in your head. Maybe, for a while, you just listen. Maybe you become a safe vessel for the stories of others, practicing what it feels like to receive another person's truth with kindness, remembering to protect the dignity of those who are bold enough to share in an honest way. Be trustworthy and tender with your acquaintances and their stories. Keep confidences, resist gossip. Read books by people whose perspective is different from yours, listen to voices you haven't heard before, look for narratives that are new to you. In them and with them, you might end up finding more room for yourself.

There's no way to eliminate the ache of being human, but I

do think we can diminish it. This starts when we challenge ourselves to become less afraid to share, more ready to listen— when the wholeness of your story adds to the wholeness of mine. *I see a little of you. You see a little of me.* We can't know all of it, but we're better off as familiars.

Any time we grip hands with another soul and recognize some piece of the story they're trying to tell, we are acknowledging and affirming two truths at once: We're lonely and yet we're not alone.

The 2008 Democratic National Convention in Denver.

CHAPTER NINE

THE ARMOR WE WEAR

A NY TIME I give a major speech, I try to learn all the words by heart long before I get to the stage. I rehearse and prepare for weeks in advance, leaving as little to chance as I possibly can. The first time I ever spoke live on television in front of a huge national audience happened to be in 2008, when I gave a prime-time address at the Democratic National Convention, speaking at Denver's Pepsi Center. This was just a few months ahead of the election, when Barack and I were still in the process of introducing ourselves to the public, and it involved a mini disaster.

My brother, Craig, had been chosen as my warm-up act that evening. He gave a charming introduction, ending it by asking everyone to help him welcome to the stage "my little sister and our nation's next First Lady, Michelle Obama!"

The crowd burst into applause as I walked out from the wings. I met Craig midway to the podium and gave him a hug, feeling my nerves fluttering, but knowing that my brother was there to steady me with a last supportive message. As Craig wrapped his arms around me, I felt him pull me extra close, putting his lips to my ear so that I'd be able to hear him over peppy music and a roaring crowd of more than twenty thousand people. I waited for him to pump me up with a "You got this!" or "I'm proud of you, sis!," but instead he leaned down and said, "Left prompter is *OUT*."

As we released our embrace, Craig and I gave each other exaggerated *it's-all-good, we're-on-live-television* smiles before parting ways. My mind, meanwhile, was racing, still trying to process his words. I made my way toward the rostrum, waving at the crowd, feeling like I was barely inside my own body, all the while thinking, *What did he just say?*

I took my place in front of the mic and worked to compose myself, using the extended applause as a chance to get my bearings. I glanced to the left, solving the mystery in real time.

One of the two teleprompters had gone dead, thanks to some technical glitch. What this meant was that any time I looked toward the left side of the arena, I wouldn't be able to see the text of my speech projected on the glass screen of a teleprompter, which had been put there specifically to help me keep my rhythm and stay on cue. The screen was blank. I was standing there on live television, knowing I was supposed to speak for sixteen minutes straight. There was no pausing the show or calling for help. For a second, I felt wildly alone—and also wildly exposed.

I kept smiling. I kept waving. I kept buying a little time, trying to settle my nerves. The crowd was on its feet now, continuing to whoop its encouragement. I quickly looked in the other direction to confirm that the right-side teleprompter was at least still working. *Okay,* I thought, *there's that.*

I also remembered that I had one other tool to rely on, something known as the "confidence monitor," which was a giant digital screen set up in the center of the arena, positioned slightly above the crowd and just below the bank of network news cameras that were capturing every second of the proceedings. Like the teleprompter, the confidence monitor would scroll the words of my speech in oversized letters, enabling me to look directly into the cameras while keeping track of my lines. We'd done a run-through earlier in the day in the cavernous, empty stadium, and everything had functioned perfectly.

Knowing it was time to speak, I looked out, seeking the reassurance of the confidence monitor's presence in the middle of the venue.

That's when I realized we had another issue.

Ahead of my appearance, the Democratic Party had printed and distributed thousands of pretty blue-and-white signs that said MICHELLE. It seemed as if every third person in the crowd was now waving one energetically overhead. Perhaps to prevent anyone from getting whacked inside all the waving, the signs had been designed vertically rather than horizontally. Each one was slender and several feet tall, a narrow slat-like rectangle with a long handle attached.

What nobody seemed to have anticipated, however, was that once people got out of their seats and held their signs up to show their support, all those slats formed an enormous, swaying fence, one that was so tall and dense that it all but blocked the words being displayed on my confidence monitor. I could hardly see anything at all.

ONE OF THE greatest lessons life has taught me is that adaptability and preparedness are paradoxically linked. For me, preparedness is part of the armor I wear. I plan, rehearse, and do my homework ahead of anything that feels even remotely like a test. This helps me to operate with more calm under stressful circumstances, knowing I will most often, regardless of what happens, find some pathway through. Being organized and prepared helps keep the floor feeling more solid beneath my feet.

As I wrote about in *Becoming,* Craig used to put our family through rigorous and regularly scheduled fire drills, making sure that the four of us knew every possible exit from our small apartment, that we'd rehearsed opening various windows, locating the fire extinguishers, and that, if needed, we could carry our dad's weakened body down the stairs. It all seemed a little dramatic at the time, but I now understand why it mattered. Craig, as I've mentioned, was a worrier by nature, and this was his way of converting his worries into something more concrete and actionable. He was making us more agile as a family, showing us every escape route, every possible means of surviving something tough. He wanted us to know all our options, and beyond that to have practiced using every tool at our disposal so that we'd have a full range of them if disaster ever struck. This lesson has stayed with me. Preparedness becomes a hedge against panic. And panic is what will lead you into disaster.

That night in Denver, I leaned on the one thing I was absolutely certain I could count on—something I'd lean on many times in the eight years to follow—and that was my own readiness. Through weeks of careful and slightly anxious preparation, I had managed to armor myself against panic. I had memorized and rehearsed every word of that speech. I knew it inside and out. I'd spent many hours writing it, practicing it, and running through the words until one line flowed readily into the next, until every cadence felt natural and easy—a true reflection of my feelings. In that vulnerable and exposed moment, I had one last form of protection: I'd done the fire drill. I could stop fretting about everything that was broken and blocked and rely on what was in my head and also in my heart. I had what I needed, it turned out, even with my nerves going haywire and tens of thousands of people watching, even with a malfunctioning teleprompter and a confidence monitor obscured by a sea of waving signs. I spoke for the next sixteen minutes, not missing a single word.

FROM AN EARLY age, I liked the feeling of achievement, of powering through challenges and pep-talking myself through fear. I wanted to live a big life, even if I had no idea what a big life exactly was, or how a kid from the South Side of Chicago went about getting it. I just knew that I wanted to aim myself high. I wanted to be excellent.

Like a lot of children, I was fascinated by stories of pioneers, explorers, hurdle leapers, and envelope pushers—anyone who tested the limits or moved the margins on what seemed possible. I checked out library books that told the stories of Amelia Earhart, Wilma Rudolph, and Rosa Parks. I worshipped Pippi Longstocking, the fictional red-headed Swedish girl who sailed the seven seas with her pet monkey and a suitcase full of gold.

I fell asleep at night with some of those journeys alive in my head. I wanted to be a boundary pusher and a margin mover myself, but I was also not naïve. Even young, I was aware of the counternarrative that existed for kids like me. Already, I could feel the press of low expectations, this pervading sense that as a Black girl from a working-class community, I wasn't expected to amount to much or go very far.

This feeling lived not just in my school, but in my city and my country beyond it. It's odd but real and also, I believe, incredibly common—to know as a kid that you are smart and capable of all sorts of excellence, but to simultaneously recognize that much of the world maintains an entirely different view of you. It's a tough starting place. It can breed a certain desperation and demands a level of vigilance. As early as the first grade, my school was putting students into "learning tracks," plucking out a slim handful of overachievers for higher-level learning and leaving the other students behind, investing less in them, assigning them to a lower place inside the larger system. We may have been too young to articulate what was happening around us, but I think many of us sensed it. You were aware that if you made one mistake, or had one stumble, or there was one distracting crisis at home, you could be immediately and often permanently relegated to the group that got less.

When you're a child in this sort of environment, you can

palpably sense the fact that your opportunities are few and that they disappear quickly. Success is like a lifeboat that must be leapt after. Striving for excellence is an attempt not to drown.

The good news is that when you're young, ambition can be tantalizingly pure, a pulsing conviction that despite it all, you are unstoppable, that you've got what it takes. This combination of dream and drive is something that sits inside you, lit like a flame. It's what Tiffany, the teenager I wrote about earlier, was expressing when she declared, "I want to take over like Beyoncé, *but bigger.*"

At some point, however, life will inevitably complicate any dream, whether it's breaking into a certain professional field, performing on a big stage, or making meaningful social change. The limits come pretty quickly into view. Obstacles crop up. Naysayers emerge. Unfairness clutters the road. Practical concerns will often assert themselves. Money gets tight. Time grows short. The trade-offs become numerous, and they are often plainly necessary to make. Ask anyone who's gotten themselves even partway to where they want to be. Getting to where you want to go, at some point, will almost by necessity start to feel like a fight.

This is when agility starts to really matter. You have to begin playing both offense and defense at the same time, pushing yourself forward while also doubling back to guard your resources, advancing toward your goals without fully draining your strength. It can get complicated quickly. You will need to armor up as well. If you want to break barriers and knock down walls, I've found, you'll need to find and protect your own boundaries, watching over your time, your energy, your health, and your spirit as you go. The world turns out to be full of lines and limits, some of them difficult to cross, some of them necessary to cross, and some of them better off exploded altogether. Many of us spend full lifetimes trying to discern which we cross and which we don't.

The point is that nobody survives a hero's journey undefended. The challenge in leading a big life becomes trying to find ways to protect your dreams and your drive, to remain tough without being overly guarded, to stay nimble and open to growth, allowing others to see you for who you are. It's about learning how to shelter your flame without hiding its light.

A COUPLE OF years ago, I met a bright and voluble young woman named Tyne. She worked in book publishing and had come with a group of her colleagues to visit our offices in Washington to discuss my ideas for this new book.

During that conversation, Tyne brought up something that had especially stuck with her after reading *Becoming*. It was a brief anecdote in which I described how, during my first visit to England as First Lady, while attending a reception at Buckingham Palace and feeling a moment of warm connection inside of a conversation, I'd instinctively reached out and laid a hand affectionately on the shoulder of the Queen of England. Her Majesty, who was eighty-two years old at the time, hadn't seemed bothered in the least. She'd responded, in fact, by slipping her arm around my back. And yet, our exchange had been caught on camera and promptly sent shockwaves through the British press, generating headlines around the globe. "Michelle

Obama Dares to Hug the Queen!" I was accused of being disrespectful, an audacious violator of the royal norms, an up-
ender of the established order. The suggestion behind it was
not so subtle: I was a trespasser, unworthy of the company I
was keeping.

I'd had no idea you weren't supposed to touch the Queen of
England. All I'd been trying to do, in that strange first year as
First Lady, and in that strange palace environment, was be my-
self.

This story takes up barely a page in my memoir, but it had
stayed on Tyne's mind. Why? Because she could read between
the lines. As a woman of color, she recognized a certain feeling, something we both shared, which is the ongoing challenge of trying to feel comfortable in places in which you are
a minority.

For her, having a job in book publishing—a field that had
been traditionally led by white people and duly shaped by their
concerns—was symbolically not all that different from having
been invited to a reception at Buckingham Palace. We both
knew the discomfort. The lines were everywhere. These places
were laden with quiet protocols and deep traditions, giving
newcomers a steep, if not impossible, learning curve to traverse
and no map to operate with. There were plenty of subtle cues
to remind us that we just barely belonged, that our presence
was experimental, almost—conditional on our adhering to
someone else's idea of good behavior. Nobody needed to say
any of it out loud, because the history tracked so deep: For a
long time prior, people like us would normally have been
stopped at the gates.

What I've learned is that you don't easily lose your sense of being an outsider, even when you make it inside. There's a tension that stays with you, clinging like a fog. You can't help but wonder sometimes: *When will this get less hard?*

Many of us "code-switch" in order to get by, changing our behavior, appearance, or manner of speaking in order to better fit into the culture of our workplace. I discovered the necessity of code-switching pretty early in life, as many kids do, using it as a tool to get around. My parents drilled into us the importance of what they'd been taught to think of as "proper" diction, instructing us, for example, to say "aren't" rather than "ain't." But when I took that diction out into my neighborhood, I'd quickly get dressed down by other kids, accused of being "uppity" or "talking like a white girl." Not wanting to be excluded, I'd adjust a little bit, presenting myself more like those kids. Later, showing up at places like Princeton and Harvard, I leaned hard on my so-called uppity diction to get by, presenting myself more like the students around me, hoping to avoid being stereotyped.

Over time, I grew more and more adept at reading the environments I was in, picking up on little cues around me. I figured out almost unconsciously how to switch up my behavior in order to suit the existing vibe and context, whether it was a South Side community meeting attended by mostly blue-collar African American women during my time working for the City of Chicago, or a corporate board meeting full of wealthy white men, or eventually an audience with the Queen of England. I became versatile, fluid in how I communicated, feeling that it helped me be able to connect with more people, extending myself over lines of race, gender, and class. I didn't overthink it because for most of my life, I felt as if I had little choice but to make those adjustments.

In this respect, code-switching has been a survival skill for many BIPOC for a long time now. As much as it's often a response to negative stereotyping, it can also serve as a kind of passport: I used it a means to get myself further, across more boundaries and into spaces where I otherwise wouldn't likely have fit at all.

And yet, there are downsides to normalizing this type of practice, or viewing it as a sustainable path toward equity. Many folks react not just to the strain of having to continually make adjustments, but to the basic unfairness of the premise, especially when those adjustments involve hiding or minimizing one's racial, ethnic, or gender identity in order to advance professionally or to make those who aren't marginalized more comfortable. What are we sacrificing? Who does it serve? Are we compromising too much or denying our authentic selves in order to be accepted? This raises an important and overarching question about inclusivity: Why should individual people have to try to change themselves when, really and truly, it's their workplace that needs to change?

The problem is that these are thick questions and complicated societal issues, a lot to take on, especially when most of us are really just trying to get through our workday. Code-switching can be draining, but so too is challenging systemic bias, even with something as purportedly simple as dressing in clothes you feel comfortable in or wearing your natural hairstyle to work. The choices can be costly either way.

That day in D.C., Tyne mentioned that even years into her

career and after several promotions, she still struggled sometimes with feeling like a foreigner at work, trying to parse a
culture that didn't always seem like hers. She was often assessing the boundaries, she said, sensing that her acceptance somehow hinged on her ability to conform to the norms of others—to
perhaps present as less "other" herself. She said she'd been
consciously trying to limit her code-switching at work, hoping
to drop some of her self-consciousness about being a Black
woman in a white space. She hoped it might actually help her
professionally if she spent less time worrying about violating
some unspoken code and instead tried to feel more like herself.
She was weighing the risks, though, knowing that for someone
like her, a casual reach could more readily get judged as an
overreach.

"Pretty much every day at work," she told me, with a touch
of weariness and a touch of humor, "I feel like I'm deciding
whether or not to hug the Queen."

I'VE THOUGHT A lot about Tyne's comment since then, struck
by the potency of the metaphor. What she described was familiar, a feeling I've wrestled with for much of my professional
life. It was similar to the tension many of my friends reported
feeling inside their own work environments, the challenges that
come with trying to navigate a set of invisible lines and to figure out the difference between reach and overreach.

Like Tyne, they found themselves weighing the risks and
rewards of dropping some of their armor in order to be more
fully seen and heard as themselves. *Whose rules am I playing*

by? How guarded should I be? How assertive? How real? In many instances, they were trying to figure out whether they could last in their jobs—whether or not they'd find enough bandwidth to advance and thrive, or whether too much hiding or worrying would ultimately lead them to feel demoralized and burned-out.

Years ago, when I started my career in corporate law, I got to know a few of the women who were above me in rank at the office, those who had made partner at the large international firm where we worked, often against some stiff odds. They'd spent years climbing the hierarchical ladder, navigating a power structure that had been built, maintained, and protected pretty much exclusively by men, dating all the way back to the firm's founding by two Civil War veterans back in 1866. These women were always welcoming and supportive of me personally, genuinely invested in my success. I couldn't help but note, though, that they carried themselves with the rugged bearing of pioneers.

Most of them were tough as nails, pressed for time, and running an emphatically tight ship at the office. It was rare to hear any of them talking about their families. As I recall, nobody ever rushed off to a Little League game or a pediatrician's appointment. The boundaries were solidly intact. Their armor was on, their personal lives almost miraculously hidden away. There was little room for the warm and fuzzy. If anything, there was almost an edge to their excellence. Starting the job, I'd been aware that a couple of my female higher-ups seemed to be eyeballing me with some caution, wondering basically: *Can she grind?* They were quietly assessing whether my legal skills and level of commitment would measure up to theirs, whether I could keep pace and thereby not damage the standing of women more generally inside the firm. This, of course, was another unfortunate aspect of being among the "onlies" in a castle not built for us. We all got lumped together, which tended to add to the pressure on everyone. Our fates felt linked. *If you screw up, we're all seen as screwing up.* Everyone knew the stakes.

What these female partners were communicating—what they *had* to communicate, really—was that their standards were far higher than anyone else's at the firm. They'd earned their way past the gates and into the club, but still, it was as if their acceptance was forever conditional, like they'd never stop having to prove they belonged.

As a young female lawyer, I remember reading in *The New York Times* about a survey that documented how generally fatigued and dissatisfied lawyers were in their jobs, most especially the women. It raised a set of vexing questions for me as I thought about everything I'd put into my relatively young career at that point, all the tuition loans I'd taken out, all the hours I'd already logged. I had to consider what I wanted my future to look like, how much misery I was willing to accept or endure. What responsibility did I have to model perfection and strive for overachievement simply to justify occupying a spot that otherwise would be filled by a man? What sort of power did I have to change a culture that operated on these norms? And how much energy could I summon for that particular fight in that particular sphere?

The women who had trailblazed a path inside the world of corporate law were, by and large, leading lives that I did not envy, making sacrifices I wasn't sure I was ready or able to make myself. But the fact that I got to see any of it, to be there at all, and that I felt some freedom to choose how I wanted to proceed with my own life, was largely due to the work they'd put in, the armor they'd donned. These women had borne the brunt of pushing through a set of previously locked gates, paving the way for a new generation to more readily assess, lobby for change, or retreat as we saw fit. They'd built the platform I was now standing on.

It's easy to be critical of one's forebears and their choices, to judge them for their compromises or hold them responsible for changes they were unable to make. The amount of armor being worn by an older generation will often appear rigid and outmoded to younger people, but it's important to consider the context. The fact that more and more Black women these days feel free to bring their full aesthetic into their professional lives, to wear their hair braided or in dreads to work, or that young people can sport body modifications or dyed hair without feeling othered, or that women have protected breastfeeding spaces at work, has more than a little to do with the work put in by people like those female partners at my law firm. They had to prove their way forward, so that the rest of us might eventually have to prove at least a little bit less.

Ultimately, I drew a line that worked for me. I took a risk and moved away from practicing law and went on to specifically seek out workplaces with a different sort of governing code, jobs that would allow me to at least occasionally duck out for dance recitals and pediatrician's visits. I left the legal profession, knowing I'd be more passionate and more effective working elsewhere. But the mentorship I received in that law firm, particularly from the senior women, gave me something I ended up needing to carry into the White House as well. They helped me learn to think carefully about how I wanted to pick my battles and manage my own resources. They taught me that in order to even begin to change a paradigm, you have to be able to maintain a thick skin and double down on the professional discipline and hard work.

None of it was ideal, but it was the reality of that moment. It was also, in some respects, a furthering of my education about life on any sort of frontier, confirmation of what I'd picked up at Princeton and after that at Harvard Law School— not through the book-learning parts but through the experience of being a double minority, of being an outsider in those most insidery places. You had to remain both armored and agile. You had to stay tough in order to get through.

NEARLY EVERYONE, I believe, wears at least a little armor to work. And appropriately so. In some ways, it's one of the tenets of being a professional: You're tasked with bringing a tougher, stronger version of your regular self to your job. You keep your vulnerabilities in check, your messes largely at home. You maintain boundaries and rely on your colleagues and bosses to do the same. You're there to do a job, after all, not necessarily to build lifelong friendships or get your personal issues worked out, or to work out the personal issues of others. Whether it's educating middle-schoolers, operating a health clinic, making pizza, or running a tech company, you're meant to contribute to the larger endeavor, to exercise discipline, keeping your feelings for the most part stowed elsewhere. The work becomes your focus, your obligation. It's the reason you're being paid.

And yet, no human enterprise is ever quite this tidy. No lines remain that clean. Helpfully in some instances and unhelpfully in others, the pandemic further kicked down a lot of walls, exposing more disparities and more truths between us. As we have attempted videoconferences with toddlers squirming on our laps against the backdrop of our half-cleaned kitchens, as many of us continue to try to conduct business despite yapping dogs and roommates on nearby screens, we've seen the boundaries diminishing and the clutter grow more prominent, all of it possibly underscoring what's always been true: We are whole and uncontainable people with whole and uncontainable lives. Our messes sometimes travel with us to work. Our vulnerabilities surface, our worries spill over. Our personalities, not to mention those of others around us, aren't so easily tamped into a mold.

Do I fit in my job? Does my job fit me? What adjustments can I make? What adjustments can I reasonably expect the people around me to make? How human or not are any of us allowed to be? Where are the lines? Whom do I connect with? How do I cope? These seemed to be some of the questions Tyne was considering that day.

I know from experience that our armor can often serve us— some of it will always likely be necessary—but I also believe that in many instances, it can be defeating. Or at least exhausting. Walk around wearing too much of it, being too defensive, too prepared for combat, and it'll slow you down, interfering with how you move, interfering with your fluidity, your ability to make progress on the job. When you're hiding behind a mask, it's possible to become alienated even from yourself. When you're trying to stay tough and invulnerable, you may miss out on building authentic professional relationships that will help you grow, advance, and use your full set of skills. Presume the worst of the people around you and they'll be more likely to presume the worst about you. There are costs associated with each choice we make. The bottom line is that when we spend a lot of time worrying about how we fit and whether we belong—if we must continuously contort, adjust, hide, and guard ourselves at work—we risk losing opportunities to be seen as our best and truest selves, as expressive, fruitful, and full of ideas.

This is the challenge and the drain of feeling othered. Many of us are left spending precious time and energy pondering those royal boundaries, the hard-to-parse difference between reach and overreach. We are required to think hard about our resources and how we spend them. Am I safe to express my opinion in a meeting? Is it okay to present a point of view or possible solution to a problem that's informed by my differentness? Will my creativity be seen as insubordinate? Will my perspective be judged as disrespectful, an unwelcome challenge to the norms?

WHEN I MOVED to Washington in 2009, I didn't know a whole lot about how life in the White House worked. But I did know a fair amount about what it's like to start a new job.

I'd done it a number of times at that point, and I'd also supervised a lot of new hires in the various management roles I'd held. Having worked in law, city government, the nonprofit sector, and healthcare, I understood that you don't just go barreling into a new position and expect the role to suit you perfectly. You have to do your research, sit back a little, and think strategically as you learn and adapt to the new job. You have to toe the line, in other words, before you can even begin to think about trying to redraw it.

I've written before about how being First Lady of the United States is a strange and strangely powerful sort of non-job. It comes with no salary, no supervisor, and no employee handbook. As a lifelong box checker, I was determined to make sure I got it right. I was going to go in prepared. After Barack was elected president, I immediately set about trying to learn what would be expected of me and how I could do the best possible job while also trying to bring my own energy and creativity to it. And I thought maybe, if I did it well enough, I could change some of the paradigms surrounding how people saw the role.

One of the first things I did was to ask my new chief of staff to go day by day and week by week through Laura Bush's official schedule, compiling a list of appearances she'd made and events she'd organized. My plan was to spend the first year pointedly doing everything Laura had done, while also developing my own set of priorities and plans to launch initiatives. In the meantime, I would not be caught taking any shortcuts. This was a form of insurance policy, another tool. As the first Black woman in the role, I was aware of the tightrope I'd be walking. I was clear on the fact that I'd have to earn my way into acceptance. Which meant I'd need to put an edge on my excellence. I wanted to make absolutely certain that people understood I was capable of executing every last duty I'd inherited, so that I couldn't be accused of being lazy or disrespectful of the role.

Many of the First Lady's responsibilities, it turned out, had been accrued through tradition, often hundreds of years of it. None of it was written down anywhere; the expectations were all just baked into the role. I was supposed to host an array of events, from state dinners to the annual Easter Egg Roll. I was expected to have tea with the spouses of visiting dignitaries and provide vision for the holiday decorating each year. Otherwise, I could choose causes I wanted to support and issues I was interested in addressing.

What I hadn't quite anticipated were some of the more subtle, less-spoken-about expectations that seemed to come with the territory. As we got ready for Barack's swearing-in, I'd been informed, for instance, that the four First Ladies immediately preceding me had carried fancy handbags made by the same New York designer on Inauguration Day. I learned that another iconic designer, Oscar de la Renta, liked to talk about how he'd dressed every First Lady since Betty Ford, which suggested he'd presume the same about me. Nobody was insisting that I make any of these same choices, exactly, but the assumptions did seem to float in the air.

There was a sense, as Barack and I moved into a historic home and into these historic roles, that things had always been done a certain way, that even some of the small traditions existed as a form of honor, a genteel style of continuity passed from one era to the next. Any choice not to hew to them seemed to carry with it a whiff of insolence. And if you grew up Black in our country, you know the dangers associated with being labeled as insolent.

I DID NOT end up carrying the prescribed brand of handbag on Inauguration Day, and I waited six years to wear anything by Oscar de la Renta, opting instead to use my platform to help showcase the talent of underrepresented designers. These were judgment calls I felt safe making, lines I was happy to draw, in part because they were about my own appearance, what I put on my own body. But still, I remained careful with my image, my words, my plans, and my projects. I was careful with every one of my choices, aware of the dangers of the perceived over-reach. That we'd made it to the White House at all felt radical to some people, an upending of the established order. We knew that if we wanted to make progress, we'd need to be prudent about how we earned and spent our credibility.

Barack's inheritance happened to include two messy foreign wars and a burgeoning economic recession that was growing more dire by the week. The West Wing communications team made it crystal clear that his success was tied at least in part to mine. (*If you screw up, we're all seen as screwing up.*) Any gaffe from me—any flub, any statement or professional move that garnered a critique—could potentially dent Barack's approval rating with the public, which in turn could lessen his sway with legislators and derail his efforts to get important bills passed in Congress, which could then of course translate to losing his chance for reelection, which would in turn cost a lot of people in the administration their jobs. Not only that, but I was aware that if the first non-white president failed or otherwise flamed out, it could conceivably shut and lock the door for future candidates of color.

I walked around with those warnings clanging in my head. They were there any time I spoke with a reporter and each time I launched a new initiative as First Lady. They were with me whenever I stepped out in front of an audience and glimpsed the ocean of lofted cellphone cameras, all those hundreds of little false mirrors being held up, all those individual impressions being made.

And yet I knew that if I worried too much about such things, I'd never manage to be myself. I had to establish a boundary between other people's worries and my own. I had to trust my instincts, remember my own center, and avoid getting too rigid with self-consciousness, too armored-up by anxiety or defensiveness. What I tried to do was to keep myself agile, tacking back and forth between the familiar shores of caution and boldness. I lived by the code I'd learned growing up on Euclid Avenue, the one that always put preparedness and adaptability way ahead of fear.

All the while, though, I was contending with another label, an even more insidious one that I couldn't seem to shake.

Spending time with children is the best antidote I've found
to the challenges of facing injustice, fear, or grief.

CHAPTER TEN

GOING HIGH

WHEN BARACK RAN for president, I received a quick and wounding lesson in how stereotypes get reconstituted as some form of "truth." The more I campaigned for him in public, and the more influential I became, the more I started to see my gestures manipulated and misinterpreted, my words twisted, and my facial expressions turned into cartoons. My passionate faith in my husband's candidacy, the idea that he had something to offer our country, was more than once depicted as an unbecoming type of fury.

If you were to believe some of the imagery and right-wing chatter, I was a full-on, fire-breathing monster. I walked around with a furrowed brow, perpetually seething with rage. This unfortunately fit with a larger, more entrenched perception that researchers have documented recently in workplace studies: If a Black woman expresses anything resembling anger, people are more likely to view it as a general personality trait rather than as being connected to any type of inciting circumstance, which of course makes her easier to marginalize, and easier to write off. Anything you do—any action you take—can be seen as stepping over a line. In fact, you can be dismissed as someone who simply lives on the wrong side of the line. All context gets erased when that label gets affixed: *Angry Black Woman! That's just who you are!*

This is not all that different from how the word "ghetto" gets put on a neighborhood. It's a quick and efficient dismissal, a coded piece of bias that warns others to stay away, to retreat in fear and take their investments elsewhere. It overlooks your riches, your vibrancy, your uniqueness and potential, and instead banishes you to the fringes. And what happens if being stuck on those margins makes you angry? What happens if living in an uninvested-in neighborhood causes you to behave in the manner of someone who is, in fact, boxed in and desperate? Well, then, your behavior now only confirms and compounds the stereotype, further boxing you in, further delegitimizing what you might have to say about any of it. You can find yourself voiceless and unheard, living out the failures someone else has prescribed for you.

It's a terrible feeling. And it's one I understand.

No matter how calm I stayed and how diligently I worked as First Lady, the impression of me as aggressive and angry and therefore unworthy of respect felt, at times, almost impossible to undo. When, in 2010, I began speaking publicly about the childhood obesity epidemic in our country and advocating for relatively simple changes we could make in order to offer more healthy food choices at school, a group of prominent conservative commentators seized on the old stereotype and used it to attack. They painted me as an overreaching, fist-waving destroyer, bent on wrecking the happiness of children and sticking my nose in places I didn't belong. I was going to put people in jail, they suggested, for eating French fries. I was pushing a government-enforced diet. The conspiracies handily spiraled outward from there. "If the government is allowed to dictate our diet, what's next?" ranted one Fox News commentator. "Do they start deciding who we'll marry, where we'll work?"

None of it, of course, was true. But when lies are built on top of deeply rooted stereotypes, they become far easier to perpetuate. And undoing stereotypes is difficult and tedious labor. I quickly realized that there were traps laid everywhere. If I tried to address the stereotype head-on, discussing it in a friendly, upbeat interview (in this case with Gayle King on *CBS This Morning* in 2012), here's an example of what came back:

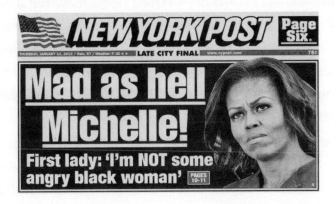

Could I get pissed off about being seen as forever pissed off? I surely could, but who would that serve? How powerful would I ever become then?

Instead, I had to go high.

OF ALL THE questions I get asked, there's one that comes up more often and more predictably than any other. Nearly every time I talk to an interviewer or sit down with a new group of people, I can basically count on someone raising it, while others lean in to listen.

What does it really mean to *go high*?

It seems possible that I might spend years answering this question. So let me try here.

I first publicly uttered the words "When they go low, we go high" while speaking at the 2016 Democratic National Convention in Philadelphia. Hillary Clinton was running for president, as was Donald Trump. My job was to rally Democratic voters, reminding everyone to stay involved and do the work it would take to get their candidate elected, including voting on Election Day. As I often do, I talked about how the issues of the day mattered to me as a parent to my two daughters, how the choices Barack and I made were always guided by the principles we wanted our kids to recognize as valuable.

Truthfully, I had no idea that the phrase "we go high" would attach itself to me for years to come, becoming almost synonymous with my name. All I was doing, really, was sharing a simple motto that my family tried to live by, a convenient bit of shorthand Barack and I used to remind ourselves to hang on to our integrity when we saw others losing theirs. "Going high" was a way to describe a choice we were trying to make to always try harder and think more. It was a simplification of our ideals, a soup pot full of ingredients, everything we'd gleaned from our upbringings that had been simmered into us over time: *Tell the truth, do your best by others, keep perspective, stay tough.* That's basically been our recipe for getting by.

Privately, Barack and I have committed and recommitted to the idea of going high many times, especially as we have gone through hard-hitting campaigns and political battles, trying to navigate life in the public eye. We invoke it any time we feel like we are being tested, as a reminder to steady ourselves when confronted by a moral challenge. What do you do when others are at their worst? How does one respond when feeling attacked? Sometimes it's very easy to know, the answers feel entirely clear, and other times it can be more difficult, the circumstances more ambiguous, the right way through taking more thought.

Going high is like drawing a line in the sand, a boundary we can make visible and then take a moment to consider. Which side of this do I want to be on? It's a reminder to pause and be thoughtful, a call to respond with both your heart and your head. Going high is *always* a test, as I see it. Which is why I felt compelled to raise the idea at the 2016 convention in front of all those people: As a nation, we were being tested. We were facing a moral challenge. We were being called upon to respond. It wasn't the first time, certainly, and it surely wouldn't be the last.

And yet the problem with any simple motto, I suppose, is that it can be easier to remember and repeat (or to emblazon on a coffee mug or T-shirt, tote bag, baseball cap, set of No. 2 pencils, stainless-steel water bottle, pair of athleisure leggings, pendant necklace, or wall tapestry, all of which can be found for sale on the internet) than to put into active daily practice.

Don't sweat the small stuff? Keep calm and carry on?

Sure, yes, amen to all of it. But now tell me *how*.

These days, when people ask me to explain what it means to go high, I sometimes sense a slightly less polite question riding on its back side, tinged by a natural skepticism, a feeling brewed by weariness and arriving when our efforts seem fruitless and our tests don't end:

But wait, have you seen the world lately? How much worse can things get? Where is the energy to fight?

After George Floyd died with a police officer's knee on his neck on a Minneapolis street corner in May 2020, people wrote me, asking whether going high was really the correct response. After the Capitol building was marauded, after Republican officials continued to support false and undermining claims about our elections, they wondered something similar. The provocations are endless. We've seen more than a million Americans die in a pandemic that highlights every disparity in our culture. We've seen Russian troops slaughtering civilians in Ukraine. The Taliban has banned girls going to school in Afghanistan. In the United States, our own leaders have moved to criminalize abortion while communities are routinely devastated by gun violence and hate crime. Trans rights, gay rights, voting rights, women's rights—all remain under attack. Any time there's another injustice, another round of brutality, another incident of failed leadership, corruption, or violation of rights, I get letters and emails that pose some form of this same question.

Are we still supposed to be going high?

Okay, what about now?

My answer is yes. Still yes. We need to keep trying to go

high. We must commit and recommit ourselves to the idea. Operating with integrity matters. It will matter forever. It is a tool.

At the same time, though, I want to be clear: Going high is something you do rather than merely feel. It's not some call to be complacent and wait around for change, or to sit on the sidelines as others struggle. It is not about accepting the conditions of oppression or letting cruelty and power go unchallenged. The notion of going high shouldn't raise any questions about *whether* we are obligated to fight for more fairness, decency, and justice in this world; rather, it's about *how* we fight, *how* we go about trying to solve the problems we encounter, and *how* we sustain ourselves long enough to be effective rather than burn out. There are some who see this as an unfair and ineffective compromise, an extension of respectability politics, in which we conform to rather than challenge the rules in order to get by. *Why,* people rightly wonder, *do we need to try to be so reasonable all the time?*

I can see how some think that reason leaves no room for rage. I understand the perception that going high means that you somehow remove yourself and remain unbothered by all that might otherwise gall and provoke you.

But it's not that at all.

When I first said those words on the convention stage in Philadelphia in 2016, I was neither removed nor unbothered. In fact, I was pretty agitated. At that point, I had been thoroughly provoked by the bile coming out of the mouths of Republican officials on a regular basis. I was tired after nearly eight years of seeing my husband's work undermined and his character denigrated, including through bigoted attempts to call his citizenship into question. (There was that refrain again: *I don't see you as being entitled to what you have.*) And I was angry that the chief instigator of that bigotry was now out campaigning to be president.

But where was my actual power? I knew that it didn't reside in my hurt and rage, at least as they existed in raw or unfiltered forms. My power lay in whatever I could manage to do with that hurt and rage, where I could take it, what sort of destination I chose for it. It hinged on whether or not I could elevate those rawer feelings into something that would become harder for others to write off, which was a clear message, a call to action, and a result I was willing to work for.

That's what going high is for me. It's about taking an abstract and usually upsetting feeling and working to convert it into some sort of actionable plan, to move through the raw stuff and in the direction of a larger solution.

I want to be clear that this is a process, and not always a quick one. It can take time and patience. It's okay to sit and stew for a while, to live inside the agitation caused by injustice or fear or grief, or to express your pain. It's okay to grant yourself the space you need to recover or heal. For me, going high usually involves taking a pause before I react. It is a form of self-control, a line laid between our best and worst impulses. Going high is about resisting the temptation to participate in shallow fury and corrosive contempt and instead figuring out how to respond with a clear voice to whatever is shallow and corrosive around you. It's what happens when you take a reaction and mature it into a response.

Because here's the thing: Emotions are not plans. They don't solve problems or right any wrongs. You can feel them—

you *will* feel them, inevitably—but be careful about letting them guide you. Rage can be a dirty windshield. Hurt is like a broken steering wheel. Disappointment will only ride, sulking and unhelpful, in the back seat. If you don't do something constructive with them, they'll take you straight into a ditch.

My power has always hinged on my ability to keep myself out of the ditch.

WHEN PEOPLE ASK me about going high, I explain that for me, it's about doing what it takes to make your work count and your voice heard, despite the despites. It helps if you're able to stay agile and adapt to change as it comes. And all of that becomes more possible, I've found, when you are ready and practiced with a full range of tools. Going high is not just about what happens on a single day or month or inside one election cycle, either. It happens over the course of a lifetime, the course of a generation. Going high is demonstrative, a commitment to showing your children, your friends, your colleagues, and your community what it looks like to live with love and operate with decency. Because in the end, at least in my experience, what you put out for others—whether it's hope or hatred—will only create more of the same.

But make no mistake: Going high is work—often hard, often tedious, often inconvenient, and often bruising. You will need to disregard the haters and the doubters. You will need to build some walls between yourself and those who would prefer to see you fail. And you will need to keep working when others around you may have grown tired or cynical and given up. The late civil rights leader John Lewis tried to remind us of this. "Freedom is not a state; it is an act," he once wrote. "It is not some enchanted garden perched high on a distant plateau where we can finally sit down and rest."

We live in a time where reacting has become almost too easy, too convenient. Rage spreads easily, along with hurt, disappointment, and panic. Information and misinformation seem to flow at the same rate. Our thumbs get us into trouble, becoming easy vectors for our fury. We can type up a few angry words and launch them like rockets into the digital stratosphere, never knowing precisely where or how or who those words will hit. And yes, our rage is often warranted, along with our despair. But the question is: What are we doing with it? Can we yoke it to discipline in order to make something more lasting than noise? Complacency these days often wears the mask of convenience: We might click on "like" or hit a re-post button and then applaud ourselves for being active, or regard ourselves as an activist, after three seconds of effort. We've become adept at making noise and congratulating one another for it, but sometimes we forget to do the work. With a three-second investment, you may be creating an impression, but you are not creating change.

Are we reacting or are we responding? It's worth thinking about sometimes. It's a question I ask myself before I post anything on social media or make any sort of public comment. Am I being impulsive, just trying to make myself feel better? Have I tied my feelings to something concrete and actionable, or am I just being driven by them? Am I ready to put in the actual work involved in making change?

For me, the process of writing can be an incredibly helpful

tool when it comes to going high. It's a means through which I am able to move through my emotions, filtering them into useful form. During Barack's campaign and throughout my years in the White House, I was lucky enough to work with talented speechwriters who would sit down with me and let me verbally dump my brain into theirs, taking notes as I worked through my most visceral feelings, helping me to make sense of my thoughts and begin to shape them.

Saying things out loud to a trusted listener has always pushed me to test my ideas in the bright light of day. It allows me to unpack my ire and my worries and to start seeking a broader reasoning. I'm able to sort out what's productive and what's not, landing upon a higher set of truths for myself. I've learned that my initial thoughts are rarely all that valuable; they're just the starting point from which we move forward. Seeing everything on the page, I then continue to refine, revise, and rethink, finding my way toward something with a real purpose. My writing process has become one of my life's most powerful tools.

If that first convention speech in Denver in 2008 marked a kind of beginning for me, the on-ramp leading to my life as First Lady, then the one I gave in 2016 felt a bit like an off-ramp, the beginning of the end.

I had my words, my message, my core set of feelings. It was all memorized and well-practiced, locked in my head. Once again, though, things went slightly awry. This time it wasn't a broken teleprompter, but rather an epic summer-season thunderstorm that happened to park itself over Philadelphia just as my plane was beginning to approach.

I was traveling with a handful of staffers and due to start

my convention speech in about an hour when suddenly the air grew bumpy, juddering us in our seats. Our Air Force pilot's voice came over the intercom, telling everyone to buckle up. He mentioned something about possibly needing to divert our landing to Delaware due to the weather ahead. This immediately set off a round of panicky chatter among members of my team about how to deal with the delay: I was the keynote speaker that night at the convention, the anchor around which the prime-time agenda had been built.

The juddering, it turned out, was only an appetizer, since a minute or so later the plane heaved violently to one side, as if it were being flicked out of the way by some enormous night-monster floating somewhere out there in the lashing rain. For a couple of seconds, it seemed like we might be plummeting, sideways and down, as if we were fully out of control. Around me, I heard people starting to scream and sob as lightning flared outside our windows and the plane jackhammered through the clouds. I could make out the dim lights of a city below. I wasn't thinking about dying. I just wanted to give that speech.

At this point, I was nearly eight years into my existence as First Lady. I'd sat at the bedsides of military service members who were trying to heal from devastating war injuries. I'd cried with a mother whose fifteen-year-old daughter had been fatally shot in a Chicago park on her way home from school. I'd stood inside the tiny prison cell where Nelson Mandela had spent the better part of twenty-seven years in solitude and yet had found the fortitude to carry on. We'd celebrated the passage of the Affordable Care Act, the Supreme Court's affirmation of marriage equality, and dozens of other triumphs, small and large.

And I'd gone to the Oval Office and put my arms around Barack, both of us wordless and broken on the day a gunman in Connecticut shot twenty elementary school students dead.

Again and again, I'd been confounded, humbled, and shaken by the world we lived in, brought low by the job and then high again. I'd been exposed to what felt like every angle of the human condition, pummeled by alternating waves of joy and anguish, reminded constantly that little was predictable and that for every couple of steps we took forward, there would inevitably be something that tore open old wounds and set us all back.

Hardly a day passed when I didn't think of my father and the disease that had slowly robbed him of his strength and mobility, the patience and grace he'd shown when dealing with the emotional and physical hurdles it brought—the way he'd continued to show up for his family, renewing his sense of hope and possibility more or less daily in order to move forward. He had given me the road map for what "going high" looked like. I understood what we as a nation were up against in 2016, the contest of another election and a choice that felt starker than anything I'd known. Sitting on that airplane, I was stirred up. I was worried. And I was also armored. I knew that if anything was ever going to toss me off course at this point, it would have to be a whole lot bigger than a layer of unstable air over Philadelphia.

We made it to the ground. We made it to the convention center. In short order, I made it into my dress and heels and lipstick and onto that stage. I summoned my calm, checked the teleprompters and the confidence monitor, smiled and waved at the crowd, and then started to speak.

It's strange to say that after you've done it once or twice, you can start to feel actually comfortable performing in front of a stadium-sized crowd, but it's true. Or maybe more accurately, you just grow more accustomed to the discomfort of performing. You become comfortably afraid. The nerve-racking zing of adrenaline, all the uncertainties that come with facing a live and worked-up audience, they start to impact you less than they once did. The overall sensation begins to feel more like fuel than fear. Especially when you have something you really want to communicate.

The speech I gave that night in Philadelphia was no less heartfelt than the first one I'd given in Denver all those years earlier. What was different was that we would soon be leaving. Regardless of what happened at that convention, or at the election to follow, regardless of who became president, my family would be walking out of the White House in about six months' time and going on a vacation. One way or another, we'd be dusting our hands of the whole presidential endeavor.

I was full of feelings that evening. But I was trying to channel all of them into a plan. I reminded people that no conclusion was foregone. I said that we couldn't afford to be tired or frustrated or cynical about the approaching election. We had to make the choice to go high. And we'd have to earn the victory, knocking on doors and getting out every vote. I ended my speech by saying, "So let's get to work."

Then I went back to the airport and got back on that plane, lifting off into the still-unsettled air.

WHAT I SAID that evening may have helped to lodge the phrase "When they go low, we go high" into the broader zeitgeist, but in the end, the rest didn't translate. For whoever heard the call, too many of us forgot to do the work. More than ninety million eligible voters stayed home on Election Day in 2016. And with that, we took ourselves right into the ditch. We lived with those results for four years. We are living with them still.

How do we right ourselves inside a storm that shows no sign of abating? How do we find stability when the air around us remains unsettled and the ground seems to shift constantly beneath our feet? I think it begins, in part, when we are able to find a sense of agency and purpose inside of ongoing flux, when we remember that small power can be meaningful power. Casting a vote matters. Helping a neighbor matters. Lending your time and energy to a cause you believe in matters. Speaking up when you see a person or group of people being denigrated or dehumanized matters. Showing your gladness for another soul, be it your child, or a coworker, or even someone you pass on the street, matters. Your small actions become an instrument for your own visibility, your own steadiness and sense of connection. They can help remind you that you, too, matter.

The problems around us are only compounding. We will need to rediscover our trust in other people, to restore some of our lost faith—all that's been shaken out of us in recent years. None of it gets done alone. Little of it will happen if we isolate inside our pockets of sameness, communing only with others who share our exact views, talking more than we listen.

A few days before I gave that speech in Philadelphia, the online magazine *Slate* ran a story with the headline "Is 2016 the Worst Year in History?," citing everything from Trump's apparent popularity to police shootings, the Zika virus, and Brexit as potential evidence. But see, what's interesting is that we hadn't yet met 2017, which became, according to news coverage of a Gallup global survey on emotional health, "The World's Worst Year in at Least a Decade."

This was followed, of course, by a new year and then a new year after that, each one marked by new crises and new catastrophes. *Time* magazine declared 2020 "The Worst Year Ever," though many would argue that 2021 ended up being no better. The point is, uncertainty is a constant; we will continue to struggle, to contend with fear, to search for some sense of control. We won't ever necessarily have our bearings inside the historical moment we occupy, either. Are things trending toward the better or the worse? For whom? And how do we even measure? What might be a good day for you could be a terrible day for your neighbor. One nation might thrive while another suffers. Joy and pain often live in close proximity; they intermingle. Most of us exist in the in-between, following that most innate of human impulses, which is to hang on to hope. *Don't give up,* we tell one another. *Keep working.*

This matters, too.

WHEN I BECAME a parent and started asking my own mother questions about how to parent well, one of the things she told me was, "Don't ever pretend that you have all the answers. It's okay to say 'I don't know.'"

I began this book by describing some of the questions I get

asked by others. I will end it by reminding you that I don't actually have all that many answers to give. I believe that real answers come from longer, deeper dialogues—a conversation we all try to have together.

We can't know for sure what the future holds, but I do think it's important to remember that we are also not helpless in the face of our worries. We are capable of creating change by design, change that's a response to flux rather than a reaction to it. We can operate from hope rather than fear, pairing reason with rage. But we'll need to renew our sense of possibility many times over. I think of my father's silent credo any time his cane failed him and he crashed to the floor: *You fall, you get up, you carry on.*

A motto like "We go high" does nothing if we only just hear it and repeat it. We can't coast on words alone. We can't declare ourselves sad or angry or committed or hopeful and then just sit down and rest. It's the kind of lesson we'll only continue to learn. As we saw in the 2016 election, it can be presumptuous to assume everything will work out in your favor, and dangerous to leave your fate entirely in the hands of others when it comes to choosing your leaders. We have to make hopeful choices, to commit and recommit to the work involved. Freedom is no enchanted garden, as John Lewis said. It's a barbell we keep hoisting overhead.

Sometimes going high might mean that you have to make a choice to operate inside of certain margins, even if the margins themselves are a provocation. You may need to climb partway up a grand staircase so that you can be better seen and heard when addressing the ballroom crowd.

While we were in the White House, I knew I had to stay

armored and also accept some of the trade-offs, understanding that I represented more than just myself. I needed to stick with my work, my plans, my hopes—to focus on action rather than reaction. Getting defensive would only backfire. I had to go about building my legitimacy and credibility somewhat slowly, detouring as best I could around the traps, keeping myself out of the ditch. Did this involve strategy and compromise? Yes, it did. Sometimes you have to clear the path in order to be able to walk on it yourself, as well as to ready it for others. As I've said, it's often tedious, inconvenient, and bruising work. But in my experience, this is what it takes if you're trying to enter a new frontier.

There's a type of question I get often from young people who are feeling both motivated and impatient, fed up with the way things are. It's a question that gets at the nature of activism, resistance, and change more generally: How much do we abide by and how much do we reject? Do we tear down our systems or try to stay patient and reform them from the inside? Are we more effective agitating for change at the margins or inside the mainstream? What does true boldness look like? When does civility become an excuse for inaction?

These are not new questions. It's not a new debate. Each generation rediscovers it on its own. And the answers aren't straightforward. Which is why the debate stays fresh, the questions remain open, and, if you're lucky, why your own kids and grandkids will come to you someday, burning with passion, frustrated and impatient and ready to challenge, pondering the very margins you tried to widen for them, asking these same questions all over again.

I was barely a year old when John Lewis and about six hundred other civil rights advocates marched across the Edmund Pettus Bridge in Selma, Alabama, enduring violent attacks by segregationist sheriff's deputies and state troopers while trying to draw attention to the need for voting rights to be protected by federal law. I was too young to remember the day Dr. Martin Luther King Jr. stood on the steps of the state capitol in Montgomery, addressing not just the 25,000 or so people who'd ultimately joined Lewis and the others on the march, but also a country that was finally paying attention to the struggle. What Dr. King said that day, among other things, was that the struggle was far from over, the destination far from reached. "I know you are asking today," he said to the crowd, " 'How long will it take?' "

The answer he gave, while calling for Americans to commit to nonviolence and keep working toward justice, while exhorting everyone to continue practicing both faith and vigor, was "Not long."

I sometimes think that when we have our debates about the nature of change and progress, what we are largely debating is the meaning of the phrase *Not long*. Does it take years, or decades, or generations to arrive in the vicinity of fairness and peace? Do we get there in steps or strides or leaps? What strategies are required? What compromises become necessary? Which sacrifices get made? How long is *Not long*?

When Barack's parents got married in Hawaii in 1961, interracial marriage was considered illegal in nearly half the country, barred in twenty-two states. It wasn't until I was ten years old that American women were given the legal right to apply for a credit card without their husband's permission. My grandfather grew up in the South during a time when Black people got shot for just trying to show up and vote. I thought about this any time I stood on the Truman Balcony of the White House, watching my two dark-skinned girls as they played on the lawn.

As a Black First Lady, I was an "only." It meant that I needed to help the world adapt and adjust to me at the same time I myself was adapting and adjusting to the role. Barack was doing much the same as president. We were different, yes, but also not really. We had to show this to people again and again, enduring the challenges to our integrity. We had to stay agile and keep our feet out of the traps. Plenty of people I know are given this same task in their own personal and professional spheres—being challenged to educate, explain, and represent all at once—even if they don't want or relish the added work. It requires patience, deftness, and often some extra armor.

As much as the White House looked and felt like a palace, I was still me inside it. I grew more comfortable in that space, showing more of myself over time. If I liked to dance, I could dance. If I liked to crack jokes, I could do that, too. As I learned the job, I started to test the boundaries more, giving myself more permission to be expressive and creative, connecting my work as First Lady more fully to my personality. This meant that I showed up on TV and had fun dancing with Jimmy Fallon or doing push-ups with Ellen DeGeneres to promote my children's health initiative, Let's Move! I could jump rope and play soccer with kids on the White House lawn. I could rap with a *Saturday Night Live* star to remind young people why it's important to try to get a college degree. My goal was always to do serious work in a joyful way, to show people what's possible if we keep choosing to go high.

The best means to fight an ugly stereotype, I figured, was to be myself, to keep demonstrating how wrong it was, even if it took years, even if some people would never do anything but buy into it. At the same time, I tried to remain persistent about working to change the systems that had created the stereotype in the first place. I had to grow my power judiciously and use my voice thoughtfully, in a way that I hoped would only widen the margins for whoever came next. I knew I'd have a better shot at success if my efforts went directly into achieving the goals I'd set for myself as First Lady, and if I could avoid getting diverted or distracted by those who would much rather see me fail. I saw it as a challenge, a kind of moral test. As always, I was budgeting my energy carefully, counting the steps.

Supreme Court justice Ketanji Brown Jackson tells a meaningful story about her experience as an undergraduate student at Harvard. She had come to campus in 1988, arriving from south Florida, eager to study government. She loved theater and was excited to audition for plays. She joined the Black Students Association as well.

When a white student hung a Confederate flag in a dorm-room window that prominently faced one of the campus quads, the BSA quickly organized a series of protests. Jackson was among a group of mostly Black students who dropped everything and started circulating petitions, passing out flyers, and helping plan rallies, which successfully put pressure on the college's administration and resulted in significant media coverage across the United States. Their pushback was effective, but the future Supreme Court justice was already wise enough to recognize a certain trap.

"While we were busy doing all of those very noble things, we were not in the library studying," she later recounted. There was a cost to doing that work, to being put on the defensive. It stole their energy and kept them out of play rehearsals, study halls, and social events. It kept them from being seen in other realms, as creative and fruitful and full of interesting ideas. "I remember thinking how unfair it was to us," she said.

It dawned on her then that this was, in fact, part of bigotry's larger mechanism, a way of keeping the outsiders from getting too far inside, to get them off the staircase and kicked out of the ballroom. It was, she said, "exactly what the student who had hung the flag really wanted: For us to be so distracted that we failed our classes and thereby reinforced the stereotype that we couldn't cut it at a place like Harvard."

BEING ON THE outside is difficult. Fighting for equity and justice from a place on the outside is harder still. Which is why I believe you need to choose your fights, be careful with your feelings, and think about your long-term goals. The most effective among us learn that this, in itself, is important—a vital part of going high.

I speak often with young people who are wrestling with how to best spend their energy, time, and resources. They are frequently feeling pressure, caught between worlds, struggling with a sort of survivor's guilt, having left a family or a community behind in order to pursue new dreams. When you start to get yourself somewhere, people who never saw you as different might now start to see you as different, or changed. They assume that since you made it through the gates, you must now live in the palace. This becomes another complexity to carry. It gives you more to navigate. More to negotiate. You may get a college scholarship and quickly become the pride of your household or your neighborhood, but that doesn't mean you now have the means to pay your uncle's electric bill or come home every weekend to care for your grandmother or baby siblings. Success involves making many difficult choices and drawing the lines that go with them, trusting that your progress will pay dividends over time, if only you can keep yourself on track. You just need to keep telling yourself: *Not long.*

Justice Jackson has said that the greatest gift her parents gave her as a child was a form of toughness, a headstrong type of confidence. Raised with a distinctive African name, often an "only" at school and later working in law, she learned to build a mental wall between herself and the judgments of others, remaining doggedly focused on her larger goals, refusing to get knocked off course by unfairness or aggression. She's credited her success to three things—hard work, big breaks, and having a thick skin. The thick-skin part means learning what to do with your rage and your hurt, where to put it, how to convert it into actual power. It means picking a destination and understanding it will take some time to get there. "The best thing that you can do for yourself and your community," Jackson said, speaking to a Black student group in 2020, "is to stay focused."

Going high is about learning to keep the poison out and the power in. It means that you have to be judicious with your energy and clear in your convictions. You push ahead in some instances and pull back in others, giving yourself opportunities to rest and restore. It helps to recognize that you are operating on a budget, as all of us are. When it comes to our attention, our time, our credibility, our goodwill toward and from others, we work with a limited but renewable set of resources. We fill and empty our pockets repeatedly throughout life. We earn, save, and spend.

"Are we rich?" my brother asked my dad once when we were little kids.

My father just laughed and said, "No." But the next time he got a paycheck, he went to the bank and instead of depositing it, he cashed it in, coming home with a fat pile of bills, which he then spread out on the foot of his bed so that Craig and I could see every dollar. To me, it seemed like there were loads of them.

For a few minutes, it even looked like we were rich.

My dad next went and found the stack of bills that arrived each month, and one by one, he opened the envelopes and explained to us how much we owed for which things—this much for electricity, that much for the car payment, more for the gas that cooked our food and the groceries that filled our fridge. He started sliding the approximate amount of money that was due into the various envelopes, talking about the other things we paid for—gas in the car, for example, the rent that went to Aunt Robbie each month, new clothes for school, our annual summertime week at a family resort in Michigan, some savings for the future.

Bill by bill, he drew down the mountain of cash until finally there was just a single twenty left lying on the bed, meant to signify the money we had left over for treats like ice cream and drive-in movies.

We weren't rich, my dad was telling us, but we were wise. We were careful. We were aware. We could see the edge, but that didn't mean we'd ever slip over it. If we were smart about our spending, he was trying to show us, we'd always be okay. We'd have ice cream. We'd have movies. We'd get to college someday. Our prudence was what allowed us to reach.

I took this approach into my work as First Lady, staying mindful of my resources—how much I had to give and what I still had to earn. I tried to remain strategic in my efforts, to stick with actionable plans and leave the thoughtless raging to others. I wore the healthiest armor I could find. I kept myself physically fit. I ate well and prioritized sleep. I fed my happiness and sense of stability through time spent with friends and family, drawing on the strength of my Kitchen Table. When my fearful mind revved up, I talked back to it, quieting it down. When I felt my feelings getting strong—when something made me angry, when I felt frustrated and ready to boil over—I took some time to process those feelings privately, often using my mom and my friends as sounding boards, trying to come up with better plans.

I knew my story. I knew myself. And I also knew that I couldn't be all things to all people. This helped to steady me against harsh criticisms and misinterpretations. I understood my priorities and had many years of practice at maintaining boundaries, which helped me to say "no" clearly but graciously to many of the requests that came in. I embraced the power of small by narrowing my focus, choosing to work on a few key issues that were meaningful to me as I stayed dedicated to my family. And I tried to be kind to myself, to both protect and share my light while drawing from the boundless light offered by others, the many people I encountered along the way, all over this beautiful and broken world.

Any time I felt my stress level rising or my cynicism beginning to stir, I made a point of visiting a school or inviting a group of children to the White House, which immediately restored any lost perspective and helped clarify my purpose all over again. Kids, for me, are always a reminder that we are all born loving and open-minded, free of hate. They are the reason the rest of us maintain a thick skin and keep trying to clear the path. Watching a child grow into an adult, you understand both how mundane and profound the process can be, how it happens slowly and quickly all at once, in steps and also in strides. You start to see the meaning of *Not long*.

MY DAUGHTERS LOVE to look back at our old family photos and giggle about what they see—not just in the pictures of themselves as cute babies or having little-kid birthday parties but in the older ones, too. They might find an image of me at seventeen, sporting an Afro and dressed head to toe in 1980s denim, or one of Barack as a round-faced boy splashing in shallow waves in Hawaii, and laugh. Or they'll marvel at a photo of my mom, looking youthful and elegant in a sepia-toned portrait from the late 1950s. They'll say we look exactly like ourselves, finding it to be almost a kind of miracle, this consistency across time.

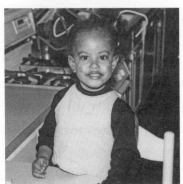

And the funny thing is, it's both true and not true. We do look like ourselves—there's that same ageless curve of my mother's cheek, there's that recognizable exuberance in Barack's boyish smile—but of course we are also different than we once were. Our clothes, our hair, the smoothness of our skin, the quality of the photograph itself—all of it speaks to the years that have passed, the journeys undertaken, the losses and gains, the endless cycling of one era into the next. This is what makes old photos so entertaining, so fun to stare at: They show us our own consistency. And they show us how much we change.

Someday we will look back at this time we're now in. We will view it from a different historical perch, a set of future circumstances that we can hardly imagine now. I wonder what we will make of this time, what will feel recognizable and what will feel ancient. Which stories will get told? What changes will we have managed to make? What will we have forgotten and what will we have enshrined?

It can be difficult to talk about hopeful ideas—things like repair, restoration, and reinvention—in part because next to everything that has made us fearful and sad in recent years, all the tangible and concrete ways we have suffered, these can feel like comparatively abstract concepts. But progress requires creativity and imagination. It always has. Ingenuity is born of boldness. We have to be able to envision what's possible, summoning it from the unknown—whatever does not yet exist, the sort of world we hope to live in—in order to even begin to actualize a plan to get there.

Every latent dream awakens only when someone is glad for it. When a teacher says, *I am glad that you came to school today.* Or a colleague says, *I am glad you are expressing your thoughts.* Or a life partner says, *I am glad that after all this time, you still wake up next to me in the morning.* We can remember to give these messages first, to put them up front. *I am glad that we work side by side. I'm glad for who you are. And I'm glad for myself, too.* This is the light we carry, and the light we are capable of sharing.

SO WHAT ABOUT going high? Can we still? Should we still? In the face of all that's grim and unrelenting and anguished and infuriating about the world we live in, does it even work? Where does integrity get us in hard times?

I hear all the raw feelings these questions come wrapped in—the anger and disappointment, the hurt and panic that so many of us understandably feel. But keep in mind how quickly they can take us into the ditch.

What I want to say, what I will always want to remind you of, is this: Going high is a commitment, and not a particularly glamorous one, to keep moving forward. It only works when we do the work.

A motto stays hollow if we only repeat it and put it on products we can sell on Etsy. We need to embody it, pour ourselves into it—pour our frustration and hurt into it, even. When we lift the barbell, we get our results.

What I want to say, then, is stay vigorous and faithful, humble and empathetic. Tell the truth, do your best by others, keep perspective, understand history and context. Stay prudent, stay tough, and stay outraged.

But more than anything, don't forget to do the work.

I'll keep opening your letters. I'll continue answering the question. And I'll stick with my same answer about whether going high matters.

It's yes, always yes.

ACKNOWLEDGMENTS

I'VE BEEN LUCKY to have the support of many wonderful people as this book has come together. What I want to say to each, from my heart, is: *I am glad for you.*

To Sara Corbett, thank you for being a true partner and friend to me over the years. Thank you for your passion, your commitment, and your unwavering belief in this book. Thank you for fearlessly diving in to this work with such grace, traveling with me all over the country, and listening to me share my thoughts and ideas. You willingly inhabited both my brain and my life with a discerning and compassionate ear—and I could not imagine doing this work with anyone else. You are truly a gift to me.

At Crown, Gillian Blake steered our process deftly every step of the way: She is a wise, tireless, and fantastically talented editor who poured herself into making this a better book. Maya Millett loaned her big heart and keen literary intellect to editing these pages as well, offering all sorts of key suggestions and encouragement. Together, they helped sharpen my thoughts and organize my ideas, and were a wonderful, steadying presence over the course of some hectic months. I am deeply grateful to you both, as well as to Daniel Crewe, who provided helpful editorial notes from the UK.

Part of the fun of publishing two books in four years is that you get to work with many of the same people for a second time, and it only gets better: David Drake has played a vital role in shepherding my last two books into the world. He's unflaggingly generous with his wisdom, refreshingly open to outside-the-box thinking, and works overtime to ensure the excellence of everything. He's become a friend to everyone on my team. Madison Jacobs, likewise, has been a bright and indefatigable source of support for us all, involved in every aspect of publication and someone we have genuinely come to love.

I'm once again grateful to Chris Brand for his beautiful cover design and creative direction, and to Dan Zitt for producing the audiobook. Gillian Brassil returned to provide research assistance and expert fact-checking. She is a dream to work with—rigorous and curious, as buoyant as she is efficient. Miller Mobley, my favorite photographer on the planet, has shot the images on my last two book covers. He and his team work with great energy and professionalism and always put me at ease. I respect and appreciate you all.

I continue to benefit from the considerable talents of stylist Meredith Koop, who has a perfect eye and a wonderful spirit. Yene Damtew and Carl Ray have been by my side for every step of this journey, bringing artistry and warmth and adding to my confidence. Katina Hoyles has supported us all in innumerable ways. These people mean so much more to me than what their titles connote. They occupy important seats at my Kitchen Table and are like family to me.

Through our D.C. office, I am supported by an incredible team of brilliant women, who share their light with me on a daily basis and whose diligence, hard work, and optimism are the fuel for everything I do. Thank you to Crystal Carson, Chynna Clayton, Merone Hailemeskel, and Alex May-Sealey. And, of course, to Melissa Winter: Nothing is possible without your even keel and stellar leadership. I am so very glad for each one of you.

At Penguin Random House, I remain humbled by the steadfast partnership of Markus Dohle, whose enduring enthusiasm and commitment to quality publishing is remarkable to behold. Madeline McIntosh, Nihar Malaviya, and Gina Centrello have guided this project expertly and admirably, operating with consistent grace and the highest of standards. Thank you for everything you do.

I'm indebted to the hardworking production team at Crown—Sally Franklin, Linnea Knollmueller, Elizabeth Rendfleisch, and Mark Birkey—as well as to Denise Cronin for helping this book find its audience abroad. Michelle Daniel, Janet Renard, Lorie Young, Liz Carbonell, and Tricia Wygal provided top-notch copyediting and proofreading; Scott Cresswell co-produced the audiobook; Jenny Pouech helped with photo research; Michelle Yenchochic and her team at Diversified Reporting provided transcription; and North Market Street Graphics assisted with page composition. I'm glad for you, one and all. Further thanks to the broader collection of talented people at Penguin Random House: Isabela Alcantara, Todd Berman, Kirk Bleemer, Julie Cepler, Daniel Christensen, Amanda D'Acierno, Annette Danek, Michael DeFazio, Camille Dewing-Vallejo, Benjamin Dreyer, Sue Driskill, Skip Dye, Lisa Feuer, Lance Fitzgerald, Lisa Gonzalez, Carisa Hays, Nicole Hersey, Brianna Kusilek, Cynthia Lasky, Sarah Lehman, Amy Li, Carole Lowenstein, Sue Malone-Barber, Matthew Martin, Lulu Martinez, Annette Melvin, Caitlin Meuser, Seth Morris, Grant Neumann, Ty Nowicki, Donna Passannante, Leslie Prives, Aparna Rishi, Kaitlyn Robinson, Linda Schmidt, Matt Schwartz, Susan Seeman, Damian Shand, Stephen Shodin, Penny Simon, Holly Smith, Pat Stango, Anke Steinecke, Kesley Tiffey, Tiana Tolbert, Megan Tripp, Sarah Turbin, Jaci Updike, Valerie Van Delft, Claire von Schilling, Gina Wachtel, Chantelle Walker, Erin Warner, Jessica Wells, and Stacey Witcraft.

This book's subject matter was born out of a series of roundtable conversations I've had with various groups over the past several years, both virtually and in person—including gatherings with young women in Chicago, Dallas, Hawaii, and London; a memorable discussion with students from twenty-two different colleges across the country; as well as countless interactions with book clubs and community groups during the *Becoming* book tour. These were profound and stimulating experiences, always a valuable reminder of what's truly precious in this world. Thank you to each and every person who shared their thoughts, worries, and hopes with me along the way, trusting me enough to show me their full selves. Your light matters to me, more than you know.

To Tyne Hunter, Ebony LaDelle, Madhulika Sikka, and Jamia Wilson: I'm especially grateful to you for lending your insight, candor, and deep thoughts early on in this process. Our dialogue helped me to land on some of this book's core ideas.

Lastly, to my family and to the rest of my Kitchen Table: Your love and sturdiness are immeasurable and have kept me grounded and hopeful during these strange and uncertain times. Thank you for always getting me through.

RESOURCES

MENTAL HEALTH HELPLINES AND RESOURCE REFERRALS

Samaritans
A helpline for anyone in times of need
Call 116 123 or email jo@samaritans.org
www.samaritans.org

Switchboard LGBT + Helpline
A helpline, information and referral service for lesbians,
gay men and bisexual and trans people
Call 0300 330 0630, email chris@switchboard.lgbt
or use their webchat service
www.switchboard.lgbt

Mindline Trans+
A helpline and information service for anyone identifying as
transgender, non-binary or genderfluid
Call 0300 330 5468
www.mindlinetrans.org.uk

Mind Infoline
An information service for anyone affected by
mental health problems
Call 0300 123 3393 or email info@mind.org.uk
www.mind.org.uk

Pandas Foundation
A helpline and information service for every parent or
network affected by perinatal mental illness
Call 0808 1961 776, text 'PANDAS' to 85258 or
email info@pandasfoundation.org.uk
www.pandasfoundation.org.uk

Rethink Mental Illness
An advice service for adults affected by mental illness
Call 0808 801 0525 or email advice@rethink.org
www.rethink.org

FINDING AND PAYING FOR THERAPY

Black, African and Asian Therapy Network
For services that offer free counselling to serve the BME community
www.baatn.org.uk/free-services

Black Minds Matter UK
Connecting Black individuals and families with
free mental health services
www.blackmindsmatteruk.com

Psychology Today
Therapist directory including filters for insurance and
sliding scale payment
www.psychologytoday.com

NOTES

ix   *"If someone in your family"* Alberto Ríos, *Not Go Away Is My Name* (Port Townsend, Wash.: Copper Canyon Press, 2020), 95.

INTRODUCTION

19   *Young adults are reporting* Barbara Teater, Jill M. Chonody, and Katrina Hannan, "Meeting Social Needs and Loneliness in a Time of Social Distancing Under COVID-19: A Comparison Among Young, Middle, and Older Adults," *Journal of Human Behavior in the Social Environment* 31, no. 1–4 (2021): 43–59, doi.org/10.1080/10911359.2020.1835777; Nicole Racine et al., "Global Prevalence of Depressive and Anxiety Symptoms in Children and Adults During COVID-19: A Meta-Analysis," *JAMA Pediatrics* 175, no. 11 (2021): 1142–50, doi.org/10.1001/jamapediatrics.2021.2482.

19   *more than 7.9 million children* Imperial College London, COVID-19 Orphanhood Calculator, 2021, imperialcollege

london.github.io/orphanhood_calculator/; Susan D. Hillis et al., "COVID-19–Associated Orphanhood and Caregiver Death in the United States," *Pediatrics* 148, no. 6 (2021): doi .org/10.1542/peds.2021-053760.

PART ONE

21 *"Nothing can dim"* Maya Angelou, *Rainbow in the Cloud: The Wisdom and Spirit of Maya Angelou* (New York: Random House, 2014), 69.

44 *those who are happier in life* Kostadin Kushlev et al., "Do Happy People Care About Society's Problems?," *Journal of Positive Psychology* 15, no. 4 (2020): 467–77, doi.org/10.1080 /17439760.2019.1639797.

54 *Fox News was running chyrons* Brian Stelter and Oliver Darcy, *Reliable Sources,* January 18, 2022, web.archive.org /web/20220119060200/https://view.newsletters.cnn.com /messages/1642563898451efea85dd752b/raw.

70 *a type of "rocket fuel"* CBS Sunday Morning, "Lin-Manuel Miranda Talks Nerves Onstage," December 2, 2018, www .youtube.com/watch?v=G_LzZiVuw0U.

72 *he was looking for the exit signs* The Tonight Show Starring Jimmy Fallon, "Lin-Manuel Miranda Recalls His Nerve-Wracking Hamilton Performance for the Obamas," June 24, 2020, www.youtube.com/watch?v=wWk5U9cKkg8.

72 *"I'm really nervous"* "Lin-Manuel Miranda Daydreams, and His Dad Gets Things Done," *Taken for Granted,* June 29, 2021, www.ted.com/podcasts/taken-for-granted-lin-manuel -miranda-daydreams-and-his-dad-gets-things-done-transcript.

80 *"When a kid walks"* The Oprah Winfrey Show, "Oprah's

Book Club: Toni Morrison," April 27, 2000, re-aired August 10, 2019, www.facebook.com/ownTV/videos/the-oprah-winfrey-show-toni-morrison-special/2099095963727069/.

82   *when teachers take the time* Clayton R. Cook et al., "Positive Greetings at the Door: Evaluation of a Low-Cost, High-Yield Proactive Classroom Management Strategy," *Journal of Positive Behavior Interventions* 20, no. 3 (2018): 149–59, doi.org/10.1177/1098300717753831.

102   *More than three-quarters* "Toughest Admissions Ever," *Princeton Alumni Weekly,* April 20, 1981, 9, books.google.com/books?id=AxNbAAAAYAAJ&pg=RA16-PA9; "Slight Rise in Admissions," *Princeton Alumni Weekly,* May 3, 1982, 24, books.google.com/books?id=IhNbAAAAYAAJ&pg=RA18-PA24.

103   *one in eight in my class* "Toughest Admissions Ever."

106   *"It is a peculiar sensation"* W.E.B. Du Bois, *The Souls of Black Folk* (New York: Penguin, 1989), 5.

112   *The Mellon Foundation* Monument Lab, *National Monument Audit,* 2021, monumentlab.com/audit.

114   *Stacey Abrams, the voting-rights activist* Stacey Abrams, "3 Questions to Ask Yourself About Everything You Do," November 2018, www.ted.com/talks/stacey_abrams_3_questions_to_ask_yourself_about_everything_you_do/transcript; Jim Galloway, "The Jolt: That Day When Stacey Abrams Was Invited to Zell Miller's House," *The Atlanta Journal-Constitution,* November 10, 2017, www.ajc.com/blog/politics/the-jolt-that-day-when-stacey-abrams-was-invited-zell-miller-house/mBxHu03q5Wxd4uRmRklGQP/.

115   *"I don't remember meeting"* Sarah Lyall and Richard Fausset, "Stacey Abrams, a Daughter of the South, Asks Georgia to

Change," *The New York Times,* October 26, 2018, www.ny
times.com/2018/10/26/us/politics/stacey-abrams-georgia
-governor.html.

117 *"I've spent my life"* "Stacey Abrams: How Can Your Response to a Setback Influence Your Future?," *TED Radio
Hour,* October 2, 2020, www.npr.org/transcripts/919110472.

PART TWO

119 *"We are each other's"* Gwendolyn Brooks, *Blacks* (Third
World Press, 1991), 496.

127 *a 2021 survey* Daniel A. Cox, "The State of American Friendship: Change, Challenges, and Loss," June 8, 2021, Survey
Center on American Life, www.americansurveycenter.org
/research/the-state-of-american-friendship-change-challenges
-and-loss/.

127 *"Men, women, children"* Vivek H. Murthy, *Together: The
Healing Power of Human Connection in a Sometimes Lonely
World* (New York: HarperCollins, 2020), xviii.

128 *people tend to feel embarrassed* Ibid., xvii.

134 *A lonely brain becomes hyper-tuned* Munirah Bangee et al.,
"Loneliness and Attention to Social Threat in Young Adults:
Findings from an Eye Tracker Study," *Personality and Individual Differences* 63 (2014): 16–23, doi.org/10.1016/j.paid
.2014.01.039.

135 *Disconnection from others* Damaris Graeupner and Alin
Coman, "The Dark Side of Meaning-Making: How Social Ex-
clusion Leads to Superstitious Thinking," *Journal of Experimental Social Psychology* 69 (2017): 218–22, doi.org/10.1016
/j.jesp.2016.10.003.

136 *"She has similar hair"* Tracee Ellis Ross, Facebook post, De-

cember 27, 2019, facebook.com/TraceeEllisRossOfficial/posts /10158020718132193.

139 *you are likely to live longer* Julianne Holt-Lunstad, Timothy B. Smith, and J. Bradley Layton, "Social Relationships and Mortality Risk: A Meta-Analytic Review," *PLOS Medicine* 7, no. 7 (2010): doi.org/10.1371/journal.pmed.1000316; Faith Ozbay et al., "Social Support and Resilience to Stress," *Psychiatry* 4, no. 5 (2007): 35–40, www.ncbi.nlm.nih.gov/pmc /articles/PMC2921311/.

139 *Scientists have linked* Geneviève Gariépy, Helena Honkani-emi, and Amélie Quesnel-Vallée, "Social Support and Protection from Depression: Systemic Review of Current Findings in Western Countries," *British Journal of Psychiatry* 209 (2016): 284–93, doi.org/10.1192/bjp.bp.115.169094; Ziggi Ivan Santini et al., "Social Disconnectedness, Perceived Isolation, and Symptoms of Depression and Anxiety Among Older Americans (NSHAP): A Longitudinal Mediation Analysis," *Lancet Public Health* 5, no. 1 (2020): doi.org/10.1016/S2468-2667 (19)30230-0; Nicole K. Valtorta et al., "Loneliness and Social Isolation As Risk Factors for Coronary Heart Disease and Stroke: Systematic Review and Meta-Analysis of Longitudinal Observational Studies," *Heart* 102, no. 13 (2016): 1009–16, dx.doi.org/10.1136/heartjnl-2015-308790.

139 *Even small social interactions* Gillian M. Sandstrom and Elizabeth W. Dunn, "Social Interactions and Well-Being: The Surprising Power of Weak Links," *Personality and Social Psychology Bulletin* 40, no. 7 (2014): 910–22, doi.org/10 .1177/0146167214529799.

140 *"society's default emotion"* Edelman Trust Barometer, "The Trust 10," 2022, www.edelman.com/sites/g/files/aatuss191 /files/2022-01/Trust%2022_Top10.pdf.

141 *Jonathan Haidt has pointed out* Jonathan Haidt, "Why the

Past 10 Years of American Life Have Been Uniquely Stupid," *The Atlantic,* April 11, 2022, www.theatlantic.com/magazine /archive/2022/05/social-media-democracy-trust-babel /629369/.

145   *"She is a friend"* Toni Morrison, *Beloved* (New York: Knopf, 1987), 272–73.

148   *Researchers at the University of Virginia* Simone Schnall et al., "Social Support and the Perception of Geographical Slant," *Journal of Experimental Social Psychology* 44, no. 5 (2008): 1246–55, doi.org/10.1016/j.jesp.2008.04.011.

189   *"If somebody's going to be"* Scott Helman, "Holding Down the Obama Family Fort, 'Grandma' Makes the Race Possible," *The Boston Globe,* March 30, 2008.

194   *which can consume about 20 percent* Matt Schulz, "U.S. Workers Spend Up to 29% of Their Income, on Average, on Child Care for Kids Younger Than 5," LendingTree, March 15, 2022, www.lendingtree.com/debt-consolidation /child-care-costs-study/.

PART THREE

215   *"What we don't see"* *Octavia E. Butler: Telling My Stories,* gallery guide, Huntington Library, Art Collections, and Botanical Gardens, 2017, media.huntington.org/uploadedfiles /Files/PDFs/Octavia_E_Butler_Gallery-Guide.pdf.

226   *Government statistics show* David Murphey and P. Mae Cooper, *Parents Behind Bars: What Happens to Their Children?,* Child Trends, October 2015, www.childtrends.org/wp -content/uploads/2015/10/2015-42ParentsBehindBars.pdf.

232   *"For a long time, I looked"* " 'Unity with Purpose': Amanda Gorman and Michelle Obama Discuss Art, Identity, and Op-

timism," *Time,* February 4, 2021, time.com/5933596/amanda -gorman-michelle-obama-interview/.

234 *"You just shift your perspective"* Ariel Levy, "Ali Wong's Radical Raunch," *The New Yorker,* September 26, 2016, www.newyorker.com/magazine/2016/10/03/ali-wongs-radical -raunch.

238 *"For a long time, I was"* Hadley Freeman, "Mindy Kaling: 'I Was So Embarrassed About Being a Diversity Hire,'" *The Guardian,* May 31, 2019, www.theguardian.com/film/2019 /may/31/mindy-kaling-i-was-so-embarrassed-about-being-a -diversity-hire.

238 *She likened the feeling* Antonia Blyth, "Mindy Kaling on How 'Late Night' Was Inspired by Her Own 'Diversity Hire' Experience & the Importance of Holding the Door Open for Others," *Deadline,* May 18, 2019, deadline.com/2019/05/mindy-kaling -late-night-the-office-disruptors-interview-news-1202610283/.

239 *"It took me a while"* Freeman, "Mindy Kaling."

240 *"Language is a finding place"* Jeanette Winterson, "Shafts of Sunlight," *The Guardian,* November 14, 2008, www.the guardian.com/books/2008/nov/15/ts-eliot-festival-donmar -jeanette-winterson.

269 *researchers have documented recently* Daphna Motro et al., "Race and Reactions to Women's Expressions of Anger at Work: Examining the Effects of the 'Angry Black Woman' Stereotype," *Journal of Applied Psychology* 107, no. 1 (2021): 142–52, doi.org/10.1037/apl0000884.

271 *"If the government is allowed"* John Stossel, "Michelle Obama and the Food Police," *Fox Business,* September 14, 2010, web.archive.org/web/20101116141323/http://stossel .blogs.foxbusiness.com/2010/09/14/michelle-obama-and-the -food-police/.

271 *Mad as hell Michelle! [image] New York Post,* January 12, 2012, nypost.com/cover/post-covers-on-january-12th-2012/.

278 *"Freedom is not a state"* John Lewis, *Across That Bridge: Life Lessons and a Vision for Change* (New York: Hyperion, 2012), 8.

283 **Slate** *ran a story* Rebecca Onion, "Is 2016 the Worst Year in History?," *Slate,* July 22, 2016, www.slate.com/articles/news_and_politics/history/2016/07/is_2016_the_worst_year_in_history.html.

284 *according to news coverage* Jamie Ducharme, "Gallup: 2017 Was the World's Worst Year in at Least a Decade," *Time,* September 12, 2018, time.com/5393646/2017-gallup-global-emotions/.

284 *"The Worst Year Ever" Time,* December 14, 2020, cover, time.com/5917394/2020-in-review/.

287 *"I know you are asking"* Martin Luther King Jr., "Our God Is Marching On!" (speech, Montgomery, Ala., March 25, 1965), American RadioWorks, americanradioworks.publicradio.org/features/prestapes/mlk_speech.html.

290 *"While we were busy"* Ketanji Brown Jackson, "Three Qualities for Success in Law and Life: James E. Parsons Award Dinner Remarks" (speech, Chicago, Ill., February 24, 2020), www.judiciary.senate.gov/imo/media/doc/Jackson%20SJQ%20Attachments%20Final.pdf.

291 *"The best thing that you can do"* Ibid.

PHOTOGRAPH CREDITS

PAGE 2: Courtesy of the Obama-Robinson Family Archive

PAGE 11: Photos by Isaac Palmisano

PAGE 22: Photo by Merone Hailemeskel

PAGE 50: Photos by Pete Souza, courtesy Barack Obama Presidential Library

PAGE 76, TOP: Photo by Chuck Kennedy, courtesy Barack Obama Presidential Library

PAGE 76, MIDDLE-LEFT: Photo by Amanda Lucidon, courtesy Barack Obama Presidential Library

PAGE 76, MIDDLE-RIGHT: Photo by Chuck Kennedy, courtesy Barack Obama Presidential Library

PAGE 76, BOTTOM: Photo by Samantha Appleton, courtesy Barack Obama Presidential Library

PAGE 88: Courtesy of the Obama-Robinson Family Archive

PAGE 120, TOP: Photo by Lawrence Jackson

PAGE 120, BOTTOM: Photo by Jill Vedder

PAGE 150: Courtesy of the Obama-Robinson Family Archive

PAGE 186: Courtesy of the Obama-Robinson Family Archive

PAGE 216: © DOD Photo/Alamy

PAGE 244: © Gary Caskey/UPI/Alamy

PAGE 268, TOP: Photo by Sonya N. Herbert, courtesy Barack Obama Presidential Library

PAGE 268, MIDDLE: Photo by Lawrence Jackson, courtesy Barack Obama Presidential Library

PAGE 268, BOTTOM: Photo by Samantha Appleton, courtesy Barack Obama Presidential Library

PAGE 295, ALL: Courtesy of the Obama-Robinson Family Archive

ABOUT THE AUTHOR

MICHELLE OBAMA served as First Lady of the United States from 2009 to 2017. A graduate of Princeton University and Harvard Law School, Mrs. Obama started her career as an attorney at the Chicago law firm Sidley & Austin, where she met her future husband, Barack Obama. She later worked in the Chicago mayor's office, at the University of Chicago, and at the University of Chicago Medical Center. Mrs. Obama also founded the Chicago chapter of Public Allies, an organization that prepares young people for careers in public service. She is the author of the #1 global bestseller *Becoming* and the #1 national bestseller *American Grown*. The Obamas currently live in Washington, D.C., and have two daughters, Malia and Sasha.

ABOUT THE TYPE

This book was set in Sabon, a typeface designed by the well-known German typographer Jan Tschichold (1902–74). Sabon's design is based upon the original letterforms of sixteenth-century French type designer Claude Garamond and was created specifically to be used for three sources: foundry type for hand composition, Linotype, and Monotype. Tschichold named his typeface for the famous Frankfurt typefounder Jacques Sabon (c. 1520–80).